Research Perspectives in Language and Education

Linguistic Insights

Studies in Language and Communication

Edited by Maurizio Gotti,
University of Bergamo

Volume 289

PETER LANG
Bern · Berlin · Bruxelles · New York · Oxford

David Hirsh (ed.)

Research Perspectives in Language and Education

PETER LANG
Bern · Berlin · Bruxelles · New York · Oxford

Bibliographic information published by die Deutsche Nationalbibliothek
Die Deutsche Nationalbibliothek lists this publication in the Deutsche Nationalbibliografie; detailed bibliographic data is available on the Internet at ‹http://dnb.d-nb.de›.

Library of Congress Cataloging-in-Publication Data
A CIP catalog record for this book has been applied for at the Library of Congress.

ISSN 1424-8689
ISBN 978-3-0343-4219-3 (Print)
E-ISBN 978-3-0343-4473-9 (E-PDF)
E-ISBN 978-3-0343-4474-6 (EPUB)
DOI 10.3726/b19346

bern@peterlang.com, www.peterlang.com

Contents

DAVID HIRSH
Introduction 7

Section 1
Studies of Vocabulary

XUAN WANG
The Relationship between Vocabulary Size and Reading Ability:
Measuring Vocabulary Size both Receptively and Productively 11

YAN LI
The Role of Vocabulary Knowledge in Second Language Writing .. 37

APISAK SUKYING
A Taxonomy of English Affix Acquisition in EFL Learners 49

Section 2
Studies of Language and Education

MAKOTO TAKENOYA
Pronunciation Instructions in Japanese
Elementary School English Textbooks 85

RAHMA FITRIANA / DAVID HIRSH
EFL Learner Perceptions on Translanguaging 119

MARIANA SÁEZ
Use of Language Learning Strategies in Textbooks:
A Comparative Study 149

WENJUN BU / DAVID HIRSH
To Speak or Not To Speak: Chinese International Students' Considerations of Oral Participation and Quietness in Australian Tutorials 167

QIAN YANG / DAVID HIRSH
Academic Adaptation of International Students in Higher Education 209

Notes on Contributors 251

DAVID HIRSH

Introduction

This volume brings together studies in vocabulary, language and education, reflecting learning and education in Australia, Chile, China, Indonesia, Japan and Thailand. Each study arrives at an enhanced understanding of important constructs affecting students at various levels of the education system.

In the volume's first chapter, Xuan Wang examines the relationship between vocabulary size and reading ability in her quantitative study of high school students in China. Exploring vocabulary knowledge in the receptive and productive dimensions, the study offers theoretical insights into the predictive strength of measures of vocabulary size on subsequent reading comprehension.

Following this, Yan Li discusses the theoretical nature of vocabulary knowledge and its role in second language writing, looking in fine detail at current understandings in this under-researched area of study. This theoretical paper presents current understandings of the relationship between measures of receptive and productive vocabulary knowledge, expert ratings of writing quality, and expert ratings of the vocabulary component in writing.

In his empirical chapter, Apisak Sukying constructs a detailed representation of affix acquisition in English through a study of high school students in Thailand, arriving at a suggested five-stage order of affix acquisition for his participant group. This leads to a discussion of the effect of affix knowledge on vocabulary acquisition, with pedagogical implications for the language classroom.

Adopting a text analysis approach, Makoto Takenoya analyses pronunciation features appearing in 14 textbooks used in second language learning programs in elementary schools in Japan. Exploring both segmental and suprasegmental aspects of pronunciation, the study suggests ways in which EFL textbooks could more effectively attend to pronunciation to reflect current understandings of the role of pronunciation in language learning and language use.

In their co-authored paper, Rahma Fitriana and David Hirsh shed light on student perceptions towards translanguaging practices among bilingual university students in Indonesia in a language classroom setting. The study presents a multifaceted model of student perceptions of translanguaging, with suggestions that a translanguaging approach to language use in the classroom can be facilitative of learning in various dimensions.

Mariana Sáez examines language learning strategy activities appearing in textbooks at three levels of the education system (Grades 5, 7 and 9) in language classrooms in Chile. Exploring memory, cognitive and metacognitive strategies, the study displays patterns of strategy use in the textbooks in a general sense, and also across the three grade levels reflective of students at different stages of language learning.

Wenjun Bu and David Hirsh explore Chinese students' considerations of oral participation and quietness during tutorials in a postgraduate coursework program in an Australian university. The findings shed light on the underlying considerations of Chinese international students' choice to speak or not to speak in Australian tutorials, and their perceptions towards quietness in tutorials.

In the final chapter of the volume, Qian Yang and David Hirsh investigate the adaptation experiences of international students in a postgraduate coursework program in an Australian university. The study offers a series of suggestions for improving international student experiences and performance in higher education, particularly for students from East Asia studying in Anglo-Western universities.

This volume presents a range of research methodologies and, in this regard, there are insights offered for future research students. Suggestions for further research are provided to guide research students seeking to embark on their own studies of language and education, as well as implications for language teachers, EFL textbook developers, and providers of international education.

Section 1
Studies of Vocabulary

XUAN WANG

The Relationship between Vocabulary Size and Reading Ability: Measuring Vocabulary Size both Receptively and Productively

Introduction

Even though a lot has been written about how second language (L2) reading is related to vocabulary knowledge, there has been continuous interest in exploring their impacts on each other (Cheng/Matthews 2018; Laufer / Aviad-Levitzky 2017; Lawrence *et al.* 2019). Previous research has suggested that L2 reading is a promising approach to expanding L2 learners' vocabulary knowledge and enhancing their acquisition progress (Nakanishi 2015; Suk 2017; Vidal 2011). The contribution of vocabulary knowledge to reading ability, meanwhile, has been indicated in studies on lexical coverage, suggesting that sufficient vocabulary is required in the comprehension of written discourses (Laufer 2013; Schmitt *et al.* 2011; Webb/Macalister 2013).

Although notable correlations between vocabulary knowledge and reading ability have been found (Cervetti *et al.* 2016; Stæhr 2008), one issue still in need of consideration is whether the full nature of vocabulary knowledge has been explored when explaining its role in L2 reading comprehension. For instance, whilst many studies in the literature have explored the relationship between reading ability and receptive vocabulary size, few studies could be identified that explore its relationship to productive vocabulary size. However, receptive and productive vocabulary knowledge relates to the different forms of word knowledge possessed by a language learner (Nation 2001; Webb 2009), and receptive vocabulary size does not fully explain the nature of vocabulary size. The current study aims to investigate the relationship between vocabulary size and L2 reading ability by measuring vocabulary size both receptively and productively. Exploring this relationship assists in enriching the measurements for vocabulary size, establishing a more comprehensive link between reading ability and vocabulary knowledge, and understanding the form-meaning interaction between receptive and productive vocabulary knowledge.

Literature Review

Receptive and productive vocabulary knowledge relates to the different forms of word knowledge

Vocabulary size can be measured scholarly through a number of approaches, particularly with the help of the constructs of receptive and productive vocabulary knowledge. A positive and significant correlation (r = 0.78) between receptive and productive vocabulary size has been found in the literature (Laufer 1998), and language learners' receptive vocabulary size is larger than their productive vocabulary size (Fan 2000; Laufer 1998; Webb 2008). This is because receptive and productive vocabulary relate to the different forms of word knowledge possessed by a language learner, and productive learning is more difficult than receptive learning. In the receptive process, learners develop an understanding of the form of a word and begin to learn its meaning, but they may not necessarily use this word. Productive knowledge, on the other hand, is gained through a learner implementing their productive skills, such as speaking and writing. In addition, in formal language learning conditions, learners receive more practice in receptive rather than productive learning conditions, which may be a significant factor in accounting for differences in the amount of vocabulary acquired through receptive or productive learning.

The relationship between receptive and productive vocabulary size varies from study to study due to learners' varied language proficiency (Fan 2000), where researchers use measures that include full as well as partial knowledge (Webb 2008) and different modes of vocabulary instruction (Moskovsky *et al.* 2015). However, receptive and productive learning processes are not mutually exclusive, as there are productive features of receptive learning and vice versa. There are complex interactions between receptive and productive knowledge in language acquisition. For example, when listening or reading, learners not only receive knowledge of new words but also produce meaning. In a study by Webb (2009), receptive learning contributed more to receptive knowledge of meaning than productive learning, while productive learning resulted in higher achievement in multi-aspect vocabulary knowledge both receptively and productively. These findings indicated that solely employing productive learning of word pairs may be more effective than employing receptive learning of word pairs alone. As Zhong (2018) demonstrated, productive word use in prompted sentence writing was primarily related to receptive knowledge of form and meaning. Webb (2009) and Zhong's (2018) studies both indicated the importance of productive learning in acquiring vocabulary, yet the interaction between receptive learning and productive vocabulary knowledge still requires further exploration. Accordingly, the breadth of productive vocabulary knowledge is a focus of the current study, and its interaction with receptive learning is also considered.

Divergent attitudes towards whether receptive vocabulary knowledge is the most important factor in influencing reading comprehension

Vocabulary size has been broadly employed when measuring L2 learners' vocabulary knowledge because statistical analysis has demonstrated the notable contribution of vocabulary size to a learner's ability to perform in a foreign language (Milton 2013). In a study by Stæhr (2008), English as a foreign language (EFL) learners' vocabulary size – when measured receptively – correlated more strongly with their reading ability (0.83) than with their writing and listening (0.73 and 0.69) abilities. Stæhr (2008) investigated the contribution of receptive vocabulary size to these language abilities within groups of learners with a score above average in each individual skill: receptive vocabulary size was found to account for 72% of the variance in reading ability, 52% of the variance in writing ability, and 39% of the variance in listening ability. Studies focusing on lexical coverage also provide further academic evidence that acquiring sufficient vocabulary is essential to improving language learners' reading ability, and vocabulary size assists with the degree to which they can comprehend reading materials (Laufer / Ravenhorst-Kalovski 2010; Nation 2006). Although the notable relationship between receptive vocabulary size and reading ability has been reported in the literature, divergent findings on this relationship have also emerged. Alavi and Akbarian (2012) stated that participants' scores at low and middle levels in their study did not indicate significant correlations between five categories of the TOEFL reading test and receptive vocabulary knowledge. They suggested that learners' proficiency levels and learning context may influence the relationship between their reading performance and vocabulary knowledge, and that this relationship is more complicated than previously thought.

Other factors, including syntactic knowledge (Shiotsu/Weir 2007), grammatical knowledge (Zhang 2012) and morphological awareness (Zhang 2017), have been explored to highlight a higher predictability than vocabulary size. All these knowledge types that demonstrated higher predictabilities are related to the form-meaning framework. For example, morphological awareness is based more strongly on the recognition of forms than meaning, and this not only links to receptive vocabulary knowledge but also relates to productive vocabulary knowledge. This is because controlled productive vocabulary knowledge not only requires learners to recognise meaning, but also requires them to produce the right forms of these words. However, vocabulary size in the studies by Shiotsu and Weir (2007) and Zhang (2012) and Zhang (2017) was only measured receptively rather than both receptively and productively. Receptive and productive vocabulary knowledge focuses on different dimensions in this form-meaning framework, and receptive vocabulary size cannot represent productive vocabulary size, let alone vocabulary size as a whole. Reasons for why other factors demonstrate a higher predictability than vocabulary size should also be considered. This could be due to the importance of these knowledge types themselves, but it could also be the result of exclusive dimensions of vocabulary size. Therefore, this highlights the importance of enriching the measurements for vocabulary size and the necessity to measure vocabulary size both receptively and productively when exploring the relationship between receptive vocabulary size and reading ability.

Enriching the measurements for vocabulary size when exploring the relationship between reading ability and vocabulary knowledge

In order to avoid representing the wrong form of vocabulary knowledge, Milton, Wade and Hopkins (2010) enriched the measurements for vocabulary size by investigating vocabulary knowledge in two different formats: written and aural tests. X-Lex (Meara/Milton 2003) was used to measure written vocabulary size and A-Lex (Milton/Hopkins 2006) was employed to measure vocabulary size in an aural format. IELTS sub-scores from 30 English as a second language (ESL) intermediate- and advanced-level learners were used to represent their performance of four different learning skills. Milton *et al.* (2010) suggested that it was not necessary to measure vocabulary knowledge in both written and aural forms and that only one form is required. Although they deny the importance of aural forms when measuring the relationship between reading ability and vocabulary knowledge, their research has raised awareness of the need to enrich the measures used for vocabulary size.

Cheng and Matthews (2018) explored the predictive ability of receptive/orthographic vocabulary knowledge and productive/orthographic vocabulary knowledge for L2 reading. Scores from 250 tertiary-level Chinese EFL learners illustrated that productive/orthographic vocabulary knowledge explained 33% of the variance in the L2 reading scores, whilst receptive/orthographic vocabulary knowledge did not significantly contribute to this model. The format of controlled-production vocabulary levels test (Laufer/Nation 1999) was employed to measure productive/orthographic vocabulary knowledge. While this test is widely used to measure L2 productive vocabulary knowledge, it is context-dependent and relies on the receptive knowledge of participants who need to understand the meaning of sentences and then recall suitable words to fill the sentence gaps. Therefore, the measurement of productive/orthographic vocabulary knowledge in the study by Cheng and Matthews (2018) also depends on receptive vocabulary knowledge.

In summary, L2 learners require different dimensions of word knowledge to achieve sufficient receptive and productive vocabulary size; likewise, it is necessary to add the productive measures in order to fully assess the nature of vocabulary knowledge. While many studies in the literature have explored the relationship between reading ability and receptive vocabulary size, few studies could be identified that explore the relationship between reading ability and productive vocabulary size. This study endeavored to explore this link from three dimensions: the relationship between reading ability and receptive vocabulary size, the relationship between reading ability and controlled productive vocabulary size and, finally, the relationship between reading ability and free-productive vocabulary size.

Research Questions

The current study aims to explore the relationship between vocabulary size and reading ability by measuring vocabulary size both receptively and productively. In order to elaborate on the importance of measuring both receptive and productive vocabulary size, a dependent t-test was conducted to investigate whether receptive vocabulary size significantly differs from productive vocabulary size. Then, the second research question posed investigated the relationship between vocabulary size and reading ability by investigating to what extent three types of vocabulary size can predict the variance observed in L2 reading. Since learners' proficiency levels and learning context may influence the relationship between their reading performance and vocabulary knowledge (Alavi/Akbarian 2012), two sub-questions were designed to explore this relationship with different groups of participants. The

IELTS organisational website reports that Band 4 aligns to B1 in the CEFR (Common European Framework of Reference for Languages) when mapping IELTS tests to international standards, indicating that these learners have entered the stage of becoming independent users. Therefore, Band 4 (raw reading scores no lower than 15 out of 40) was used to distinguish higher-level participants from the sample. Accordingly, the specific research questions are as follows:

1. Does receptive vocabulary size significantly differ from productive vocabulary size?
2. To what extent can three types of vocabulary size predict the variance in L2 reading?

Materials and Methods

Participants

Participants in this study were recruited from Grade 11 in three high schools of different performance levels in a northern city of China. Two hundred and forty-six participants completed all vocabulary size tests that included two translation tests, the Lex30, and one IELTS reading practice test from the General Training Module. One hundred and thirty-nine of the participants were male, and 107 were female. One hundred and twenty-one participants were from the science stream and 125 were from the arts stream. Participants were aged 17 to 18 years old, received around five hours of English classroom instruction per week and were encouraged to spend an average of one to two hours on homework and practice on a daily basis. None of them had overseas study experience and English was a compulsory subject for all students regardless of which stream (science or arts) they were in.

Instruments

Three test booklets were designed for this research. The first booklet included two translation tests to measure participants' receptive and controlled productive vocabulary size. The English-Chinese Vocabulary Translation (ECVT) test was used to measure receptive vocabulary size, and the Chinese-English Vocabulary Translation (CEVT) test was used to measure controlled productive vocabulary size. The ECVT included 90 target English words in nine groups and asked participants to translate these words into Chinese. The CEVT included 90 target Chinese words in nine groups and asked participants to translate these words into English. One hundred and eighty words were selected in order to test participants' receptive and controlled productive vocabulary size. These words were divided into nine groups, with each group containing 20 words which represented one vocabulary size level of 1,000 words. These words were selected from the NGSL which lists words according to their rank of frequency in this corpus. Of the 9,000 words which are listed on the *New General Service List* (NGSL) (Browne *et al.* 2013) in descending order of frequency, every 99th and 100th word was selected as a target word in the two translation tests. Every 100th word was translated into Chinese as target words for the CEVT test. The first one or two letters of the English word were provided to assist participants and ensure they selected the correct English word when there was the possibility that more than one word was a suitable translation. The first letter was only provided for those English words containing less than 10 letters and the first two letters were provided for words containing 10 letters or more. The current study developed vocabulary translation tests as opposed to employing multiple choice questions, and, furthermore, sentence gap-filling was used to minimise the effect of guessing and context. The validity and reliability of the ECVT and CEVT tests were verified in the pilot study.

The second booklet was a reading proficiency test. This test comprised one reading test (General Training Module) selected from Cambridge IELTS 10 (2015) to investigate participants' reading proficiency. The reading test comprised three sections: two short factual texts based on social contexts, two short factual texts based on employment contexts and one long complex text. Section 1 comprised one text on smoke alarms and one text on Sydney Opera House tours; Section 2 included one text on sending marketing samples directly to customers via mail and one text on job specifications; and, finally, Section 3 was a long text explaining the history, advantages, and uses of Kauri gum from Kauri trees. The reading test contained 40 questions relating to these passages and participants were required to finish it within one hour. This study employed IELTS General Training Reading, which combines short factual texts with a long complex text that has a similar context to academic texts. Employing this reading test can improve research reliability and validity when measuring reading ability, as only using academic or general texts may not be sufficiently comprehensive for participants in this EFL context. China is both large in area and population and, as a result, there are substantial differences between teaching resources and education conditions among rural areas, inland cities and coastal cities (Wang/Chen 2012). Consequently, students' academic performance, particularly their English proficiency levels, tends to vary greatly. Thus, the test used in the current study included both general and academic reading, allowing for a more comprehensive exploration of the reading ability of participants.

The third booklet was the Lex30 test (Meara/Fitzpatrick 2000), which is an independent measure of productive vocabulary. Lex30 provides 30 stimulus frequent words and requires test participants to write at least four associated words for each stimulus word. These responses are then analysed to investigate participants' frequency levels. The test participant is then given a score with 120 being the maximum, and the higher the score is the larger productive vocabulary a learner has. However, one problem associated with Lex30 is that it only reflects the level of a test participant's productive vocabulary but does not indicate the specific size of their productive vocabulary. In the third booklet, Lex30 was with the following instruction: Please write at least four associated words for each stimulus word and avoid repetition. Furthermore, the 30 target words were: Attack, board, close, cloth, dig, dirty, disease, experience, fruit, furniture, habit, hold, hope, kick, map, obey, pot, potato, real, rest, rice, science, seat, spell, substance, stupid, television, tooth, trade, and window.

Procedure

As participants were recruited from different schools or majors, the research was conducted over separate time periods. In each time period, one group of participants from the same class took part in the study, and the duration of each time period was approximately three weeks. For example, the first group of participants in the main study contained 46 individuals from one high school. Research involving this group was carried out over three separate days, one week apart. On the first day of week one, participants were asked to complete the IELTS reading test within one hour; on the second day in week two, they were asked to complete the two translation tests in 50 minutes; and on the third day in week three, they were asked to take the Lex30 within 30 minutes. In the following time periods, students from other classes participating in the study were asked to complete the four abovementioned tests in the same order and format.

Marking tests

First, in terms of the reading tests, Cambridge IELTS 10 provided the accurate answers, and the researcher marked the tests according to these criteria. Raw reading scores rather than reading proficiency levels were employed in order to increase the reliability and validity of the results and have a suitable sized effect. This was done for the following reasons: First, the reading scores from the study can only reflect the potential reading ability of participants as opposed to their exact level of reading proficiency. Second, the distribution of recruited participants' reading scores on different levels of reading proficiency contained significant variance: 6 participants were in Band 6, 20 were in Band 5, 92 were in Band 4, and 128 were below Band 4. This being the case, sample sizing would be a main concern for this section because correlational research usually requires more than 30 participants, while Bands 5 and 6 in this study had less than 30 participants. Reporting a raw score for the reading test rather than strictly organising results using the IELTS band method could, therefore, decrease the effect sizes obtained for this study. Finally, researchers, teachers and trainers are not allowed to allocate a band level based on their own experience; only official IELTS organisations have the right to do so. Thus, with all such considerations, it was appropriate to use raw scores rather than band levels to represent participants' reading performance. Nevertheless, to distinguish higher-level participants, Band 4 (raw reading scores no lower than 15 out of 40) was chosen as an appropriate threshold due to its mapping to the CEFR.

In terms of the ECVT and CEVT tests, there were 90 lexical items for each test, and students' receptive and controlled productive vocabulary sizes were calculated based on the number of correct items. In the CEVT test, because at least one stimulus letter was given, only words without any spelling mistakes were accepted. Although, if the raw vocabulary scores on the VST, ECVT and CEVT tests were multiplied by 100, the calculation results could be used to simulate their vocabulary size. Furthermore, raw vocabulary scores remained in order to assess vocabulary size and were considered to be indicative of a participant's vocabulary size in the current study. This is because keeping raw scores allowed an order of magnitude to be kept so as to enhance precision, decrease statistical error and, finally, enhance the reliability of this study.

Lastly, in terms of the free-productive vocabulary test, Lex30, students' answers were entered into the online form of Lex30 to be calculated by its system. The spelling mistakes in these two tests were manually altered according to the following principles: This study accepted one missing letter, one wrong additional letter, or one incorrectly placed letter as correct; for example, with the word 'literature', various misspellings (e.g., *literture*, *literaturee*, and *litereture*) were accepted.

Results

Participants' lowest score on the ECVT test for receptive vocabulary size was 10 out of 90, while their highest score on the same test was 61 out of 90. Participants' lowest score on the CEVT test for controlled productive vocabulary size was 9 out of 90, while their highest score on the same test was 57 out of 90. Participants' lowest score on the Lex30 for free productive vocabulary size was 9 out of 120, while their highest score on the same test was 104 out of 120. Participants' lowest score on the IELTS General Reading practice test was 2 out of 40, while their highest score on the same test was 33 out of 40. Participants' mean score on the IELTS General Reading practice test was 14.4 out of 40, which was lower than the average number of marks required to achieve Band 4 based on a report from the IELTS organisational website (see Table 1).

	Minimum	Maximum	Range	Mean	Std. Deviation	Variance
ECVT	10.00	61.00	51.00	26.48	8.10	65.56
CEVT	9.00	57.00	48.00	24.90	6.79	46.15
Lex30	9.00	104.00	95.00	58.63	18.42	339.35
IELTS reading	2.00	33.00	31.00	14.41	6.39	40.89

Table 1. Descriptive Statistics of the ECVT, the CEVT, the Lex30, and the IELTS General Training Reading Practice Test ($N = 246$).

RQ1: Does receptive vocabulary size significantly differ from productive vocabulary size?

The Lex30 was chosen to investigate free productive vocabulary size, but it only reflects the breadth of productive vocabulary knowledge and not its specific size. Therefore, only ECVT and CEVT scores are analysed in this section. A paired-samples *t*-test was conducted to compare scores on the ECVT and CEVT tests. There was a significant difference in the score on the ECVT test ($M = 26.48$, $SD = 8.10$) and the score on the CEVT test ($M = 24.90$, $SD = 6.79$); $t(245) = 5.08$, $p < .001$ (see Table 2). Results indicated that scores did significantly differ between these two tests and the ECVT test had a higher average than the CEVT test. This also indicated that participants' receptive vocabulary size was significantly greater than their productive vocabulary size.

		Mean	Std. Deviation	Std. Error Mean	*t*	*df*	Sig.
Pair 1	ECVT	26.48	8.10	.52	5.08	245	.000
	CEVT	24.90	6.79	.43			

Table 2. Paired Samples Test of ECVT and CEVT Tests ($N = 246$).

RQ2: To what extent can three types of vocabulary size predict the variance in L2 reading?

A multiple regression was carried out to investigate whether receptive vocabulary size, controlled productive vocabulary size and free productive vocabulary size could significantly predict participants' reading ability. Tolerance levels, for each multiple regression analysis undertaken, were all above .20, meaning that multicollinearity was not an issue. Controlled productive vocabulary size ($B = .46, p < .05$), and free productive vocabulary size ($B = .07, p < .05$) significantly contributed to the model. However, receptive vocabulary size did not ($B = -.04, p = 0.56$). The results of the regression indicated that the model (controlled productive vocabulary size entered) explained 28.1% of the variance and that the model was a significant predictor of L2 reading scores, ($F(1, 244) = 95.35, p < .05$). Adding free productive vocabulary size in step two provided an additional 3.0% of unique explanatory power, resulting in a model that could explain 31.1% of the variance in L2 reading scores, ($F(2, 243) = 54.75, p < .05$) (see Table 3).

For 118 participants with a reading band no lower than Band 4, controlled productive vocabulary size ($B = .30, p < .05$) significantly contributed to the model in predicting participants' reading ability. However, receptive vocabulary size ($B = -.01, p = .89$) and free productive vocabulary size ($B = .01, p = .83$) did not. The results of the regression indicated that the model (controlled productive vocabulary size entered) explained 20.4% of the variance and that the model was a significant predictor of L2 reading scores, ($F(1, 116) = 29.67, p < .05$) (see Table 4).

Model		*df*	Mean Square	*F*	Sig.	*R*	*R* Square	Adjusted *R* Square
1	Regression	1	1040.568	95.345	.000	.530	.281	.278
	Residual	244	28.494					
	Total	245						
2	Regression	2	1555.918	54.752	.000	.557	.311	.305
	Residual	243	28.418					
	Total	245						

Table 3. Multiple Regression on the Relationship between Vocabulary Size and L2 Reading Ability for the Entire Group of Participants ($N = 246$).

Model		*df*	Mean Square	*F*	Sig.	*R*	*R* Square	Adjusted *R* Square
1	Regression	1	510.746	29.660	.000	.451	.204	.197
	Residual	116	17.220					
	Total	117						

Table 4. Multiple Regression on the Relationship between Vocabulary Size and L2 Reading Ability for Participants with Scores No Lower than Band 4 (n = 118).

Discussion

Does receptive vocabulary size significantly differ from productive vocabulary size?

Results from a paired-samples t-test conducted on participants' ECVT test scores and CEVT test scores demonstrated that the mean ECVT test score was higher than that of the CEVT test, and that the scores of each test did significantly differ. The results found in the current study supported the finding in the literature that receptive vocabulary size is significantly larger than their productive vocabulary size (Fan 2000; Laufer 1998; Webb 2008). This means that measuring receptive vocabulary size alone does not fully account for the nature of vocabulary size, and, furthermore, the inclusion of productive vocabulary size may enable the establishment of a more comprehensive model when exploring the relationship between vocabulary size and other variables.

To what extent can three types of vocabulary size predict the variance in L2 reading?

The current study explored the relationship between reading ability and three types of vocabulary size (receptive, controlled and free-productive). For all participants, the controlled and free-productive vocabulary size significantly contributed to the model, explaining 31.1% of the variance in L2 reading scores. Receptive vocabulary size, however, did not significantly contribute to this model. For participants with no lower than a Band 4, controlled productive vocabulary size still contributed significantly to the model in predicting reading ability, while neither receptive vocabulary size nor free productive vocabulary size significantly contributed to the model. This study found that controlled productive vocabulary size, compared to receptive vocabulary size, contributed more significantly to the model of predicting reading ability.

Findings associated with the relationship between reading ability and the three types of vocabulary size converge with the latest findings in the existing literature. In the study by Cheng and Matthews (2018) on the relationship between vocabulary knowledge and L2 reading, productive/orthographic vocabulary knowledge accounted for 32.8% of the variance in L2 reading, while receptive/orthographic vocabulary knowledge did not provide a statistically significant, unique contribution to the predictive power of the model. Furthermore, results obtained by Alavi and Akbarian (2012) on the relationship between five categories of a TOEFL reading test and receptive vocabulary knowledge demonstrated that the correlation among participants whose scores were at low-to-medium levels was not significant. Given this, the predictability of receptive vocabulary size based on reading ability among lower-level EFL learners may not be as significant as for more advanced learners. These findings suggest that productive vocabulary knowledge can explain variance in reading ability more so than receptive vocabulary size.

On the other hand, these findings are inconsistent with findings in the literature with regard to the high variance of receptive vocabulary size in L2 reading ability. In research conducted by Qian (2002), the scores of intermediate- and upper-level ESL learners on the Vocabulary Levels Test (VLT) represented 54% of the variance in their scores on the TOEFL reading sub-test. Furthermore, Stæhr (2008) found that vocabulary scores on the VLT explained up to 72% of the variance in the reading ability of learners with an above-average score. Although the statistically significant relationship between vocabulary size and reading ability has been noted in the current study and in the existing literature, findings with regard to whether receptive vocabulary size contributes significantly to reading ability have not been consistent. These divergent findings have close connections to issues discussed in the literature, particularly with respect to participants' levels of language proficiency, the complexity inherent in L2 reading, form-meaning connections and text characteristics.

Participants in the current study, and in the studies by Alavi and Akbarian (2012), and Cheng and Matthews (2018), were learners at a relatively lower level compared with participants in the studies by Qian (2002) and Stæhr (2008). However, studies reporting a strong variance in receptive vocabulary size in L2 reading ability recruited higher-level learners. Results from the current study suggest that, although this predictability also exists in lower-level EFL learners, other factors more comprehensively explained the notably higher variance in reading scores. Therefore, the current study demonstrates that receptive vocabulary size does not significantly contribute to the model in predicting reading ability, possibly due to participants' levels of English language proficiency. The predictability of vocabulary size based on reading ability among lower-level EFL learners may not be as significant as for more advanced learners.

Reading comprehension may be a more complicated process than traditionally thought, and other factors are likely to play a significant role in the reading process. For example, vocabulary size has shown a lower predictability compared with syntactic knowledge among tertiary ESL and EFL students (Shiotsu/Weir 2007), grammatical knowledge among advanced EFL learners (Zhang 2012), morphological awareness among ESL students (Zhang 2017), and L2 listening performance among EFL university students (Yamashita/Shiotsu 2017). Besides vocabulary knowledge, the other factors that have been identified in the literature support the finding in the current study that receptive vocabulary size explains a notable, but limited, variance in reading performance.

The relationship between form and meaning is also very complicated. The proposition that both receptive and productive vocabulary size can impact reading ability can be related to the study by Zhang (2017) on the effect of morphological awareness on reading comprehension. His results demonstrated that morphological awareness contributes significantly to reading comprehension and accounts for a higher predictive ability than the breadth of vocabulary knowledge. However, his study only measured the breadth of vocabulary knowledge as receptive vocabulary size. Morphological awareness is thought to be connected more to the recognition of forms than meaning and, therefore, is connected to controlled productive vocabulary knowledge, whereas receptive vocabulary knowledge is focused more on meaning. Without considering productive vocabulary size, the argument by Zhang (2017) that morphological awareness demonstrates a higher predictive power than does the breadth of receptive vocabulary knowledge does not fully explain the relationship between reading ability and vocabulary size. Results by Webb (2009) suggest that the type and amount of knowledge gained through learning can be significantly influenced by the direction of word pairs. Furthermore, receptive learning contributed more to the receptive knowledge of meaning than did productive learning, while productive learning resulted in higher achievements in both the receptive and productive knowledge of orthography, as well as in the productive knowledge of meaning, syntax and grammatical function (Webb 2009). Elgort *et al.* (2018) illustrated that form-focused elaboration not only improves form acquisition, but also enables meaning, even more so than elaboration that focuses specifically on acquiring meaning. This research suggests that the interaction between vocabulary knowledge of form and meaning is more complicated than what has been traditionally believed. However, investigations into receptive and productive knowledge have encompassed divergent aims. The finding that controlled productive vocabulary size accounts for a higher predictability than does receptive vocabulary size suggests a closer connection between forms of vocabulary knowledge and reading performance.

The fourth reason for the variance in the relevant research findings and literature overall may be due to the characteristics of the texts used in the reading test. The text in the IELTS General Training Reading practice employed in the current study included four short factual texts with regard to social and/or employment contexts and one long complex text. These texts differ from participants' textbooks and the topics of these texts are more complex than participants' textbooks. For example, job advertisements and magazine articles are not compulsory genres for secondary school students. Furthermore, the figures of the lexical profiles may have been influenced by the nature of the four short tests that were administered, each of which comprised approximately 360 words. Yet, Webb and Paribakht (2015) suggest that lexical profiles can vary significantly among diverse texts and that there is either no correlation or only a small correlation between lexical profiles and performance on the corresponding test items. Finally, 13 of the 40 questions required subjects to fill in the blanks for missing words. However, all missing words had appeared in the original text. Participants did not need to remember the exact form of each word when they completed these gaps. Producing the exact form of words for gap-filling questions was related to controlled productive vocabulary knowledge. Therefore, the inclusion of the format of gap-filling exercises in reading tests may have contributed to the closer relationship between reading performance and controlled productive vocabulary size, but its effect was limited.

Pedagogical insights

The findings of this study can provide additional insights that will assist language learning and teaching among elementary and intermediate

EFL learners in the following ways: Firstly, systematic and separate vocabulary activities and assessments for productive vocabulary knowledge are necessary because precisely measuring controlled productive vocabulary knowledge assists in understanding students' reading ability. Secondly, reading English is a complicated process for learners, and while this form of vocabulary learning is compulsory, other factors should be considered in terms of this learning method. EFL and ESL learners' prior knowledge of reading materials might be limited or incompatible to teachers' expectations, and the unique characteristics of varying academic cultures may largely influence learners' reading comprehension. For example, the Chinese academic culture tends to have a 'writer' focused culture while English-speaking academic cultures tend to have a 'reader' focused culture (Pinkham 2000). For Chinese writers, the main purpose of writing is to present their opinions and emotion, and they assume that the responsibility to understand their work lies with the readers. English writers, on the other hand, tend to report facts and argue their positions in an easily understood logic, and it is partially the writers' responsibility to report their key points in a way that can be understood clearly. The unique characteristics of Chinese academic culture may influence learners' reading comprehension, and, particularly, their understanding of passages in the IELTS practice test. The last passage in this test, for example, is equivalent to an academic report or article and could present unacknowledged challenges because it originated in an English academic culture. Therefore, they might not understand the purposes of the reading materials, or they may lack experience in interacting with the writers' text culture or social group (Brandt 2011). Therefore, it is necessary for EFL teachers to conduct a needs analysis and diagnostic tests before reading and also provide consistent feedback during and after reading processes (Kuzborska 2015).

Limitations of the study

The different results on free productive vocabulary size among all participants and higher-level participants might be influenced by participants' levels and the nature of the Lex30. Lex30 only reflects the breadth of productive vocabulary knowledge and not its specific size. Few studies in the literature explored the relationship between reading ability and free productive vocabulary size due to the challenges of measuring productive vocabulary size. However, reasons for the different results regarding free productive vocabulary size among all participants and higher-level participants merit further exploration.

In terms of participants, this study did not recruit university students due to significant variations in curriculum design, cultural background, or even whether they have previously prepared for IELTS tests. Importantly, the differences in curriculum design and the cultural background of students undertaking different majors make it challenging to represent a normal distribution of student populations when using samples. Moreover, the streams or majors are more complex and diverse among different universities, which could influence the reliability and validity of results. Therefore, this study only recruited students from high schools due to their varying performance levels and the systematic and clear distribution of the stream of subjects – science and arts – making the recruitment process more feasible and the samples more reliable and valid.

This study used quantitative research methods and did not focus on the qualitative dimensions of data. Asking participants to verbalise and report their thoughts while completing a task is an effective method for measuring their use of lexical inferencing strategies (Hu/Nassaji 2014; Nassaji 2003). However, if this research project were to include this method, it would be necessary to measure participants' vocabulary size and their vocabulary strategies over an extended period of time in order to accurately understand their evolving learning process. Learners tend to use different strategies under different conditions and it is difficult to determine how the strategies they employ influence their future processes of acquiring vocabulary. Secondly, this study did not seek to measure the growth of vocabulary size in a dynamic context; attempting to capture participants' learning conditions over their potentially long exposure to English would be overly challenging and imprecise given the variability in learning contexts over the many years of exposure to language learning for each participant.

This study investigated three types of vocabulary size and its relationship to reading ability. Although this study attempted to involve as many potential variables as possible, some language skills, particularly listening ability, were not measured as a potential variable. Listening was not included in the total score of the Gaokao (the national college entrance examination in China) and, as a result, participants would tend to lack listening strategies and practice. In addition, facilities in schools varied significantly and sound systems were not ideal for some classrooms. Utilising a listening test component was not practical for this study, nor would it represent the reasonable language proficiency levels of participants.

Recommendations for future research

In light of the limitations of this study, further studies can explore the relationship between vocabulary size and additional language skills such as EFL learners' listening, speaking and writing abilities. In addition, research questions in relation to vocabulary learning processes – for example, the types of tasks or the learning strategies utilised to acquire vocabulary – could be explored when investigating factors that might influence the relationship between vocabulary knowledge and language abilities. As this study only recruited EFL high school students, it would also be valuable to look at a new group of participants from an ESL context, such as students at tertiary or advanced levels. Finally, further studies could explore vocabulary growth using a dynamic approach and involve more qualitative methods such as think-aloud or retrospective interviews to explore L2 lexical inferencing strategies when acquiring vocabulary knowledge.

Conclusion

This quantitative study investigated the relationship between vocabulary size and reading ability in an EFL context by adding measurements of productive vocabulary size. Among the three types of vocabulary size, controlled productive vocabulary size was found to significantly contribute to the model of predicting the reading ability for all participants as well as the group of higher-level participants. Free productive vocabulary size only significantly contributed to the model for the entire group of participants. Receptive vocabulary size, however, did not significantly contribute to either model of reading ability prediction. These findings hope to advance previous understanding of the way in which reading ability relates to receptive and productive vocabulary size and provide a more comprehensive link between them. Establishing this link provides further theoretical and pedagogical implications for second language reading and vocabulary acquisition.

References

Alavi, Seyyed Mohammad / Akbarian, Is'haaq 2012. The Role of Vocabulary Size in Predicting Performance on TOEFL Reading Item Types. *System*. 40/3, 376-385.

Brandt, Deborah 2011. *Literacy as Involvement: The Acts of Writers, Readers, and Texts*. Carbondale, IL: Southern Illinois University Press.

Browne, Charlie / Culligan, Brent / Phillips, Joseph 2013. The New General Service List: <www.newgeneralservicelist.org>.

Cambridge IELTS 10 2015. *Examination Papers from University of Cambridge ESOL Examinations: English for Speakers of Other Languages*. Cambridge: Cambridge University Press.

Cervetti, Gina / Wright, Tanya / Hwang, Hye Jin 2016. Conceptual Coherence, Comprehension, and Vocabulary Acquisition: A Knowledge Effect? *Reading and Writing*. 29/4, 761-779.

Cheng, Junyu / Matthews, Joshua 2018. The Relationship between Three Measures of L2 Vocabulary Knowledge and L2 Listening and Reading. *Language Testing*. 35/1, 3-25.

Elgort, Irina / Candry, Sarah / Boutorwick, Thomas / Eyckmans, June / Brysbaert, Marc 2018. Contextual Word Learning with Form-focused and Meaning-focused Elaboration. *Applied Linguistics*. 39/5, 646-667.

Fan, May 2000. How Big is the Gap and How to Narrow It? An Investigation into the Active and Passive Vocabulary Knowledge of L2 Learners. *RELC Journal*. 31/2, 105-119.

Hu, Hsueh-chao Marcella / Nassaji, Hossein 2014. Lexical Inferencing Strategies: The Case of Successful versus Less Successful Inferencers. *System*. 45, 27-38.

Kuzborska, Irena 2015. Perspective Taking in Second Language Academic Reading: A Longitudinal Study of International Students' reading Practices. *Journal of English for Academic Purposes*. 20, 149-161.

Laufer, Batia 1998. The Development of Passive and Active Vocabulary in a Second Language: Same or Different? *Applied Linguistics*. 19/2, 255-271.

Laufer, Batia 2013. Lexical Thresholds for Reading Comprehension: What They are and How They Can be Used for Teaching Purposes. *TESOL Quarterly*. 47/4, 867–872.

Laufer, Batia / Aviad–Levitzky, Tami 2017. What Type of Vocabulary Knowledge Predicts Reading Comprehension: Word Meaning Recall or Word Meaning Recognition? *The Modern Language Journal*. 101/4, 729-741.

Laufer, Batia / Nation, Paul 1999. A Vocabulary-size Test of Controlled Productive Ability. *Language Testing*. 16/1, 33–51.

Laufer, Batia / Ravenhorst-Kalovski, Geke C 2010. Lexical Threshold Revisited: Lexical Text Coverage, Learners' Vocabulary Size and Reading Comprehension. *Reading in a Foreign Language*. 22/1, 15-30.

Lawrence, Joshua Fahey / Hagen, Aste Mjelve / Hwang, Jin Kyoung / Lin, Grace/ Lervåg, Arne 2019. Academic Vocabulary and Reading Comprehension: Exploring the Relationships across Measures of Vocabulary Knowledge. *Reading and Writing*. 32/2, 285-306.

Meara, Paul / Fitzpatrick, Tess 2000. Lex30: An Improved Method of Assessing Productive Vocabulary in an L2. *System*. 28/1, 19-30.

Meara, Paul / Milton, James 2003. *X_Lex, The Swansea Levels Test*. Newbury: Express.

Milton, James 2013. Measuring the Contribution of Vocabulary Knowledge to Proficiency in the Four Skills. In Bardel, Camilla / Lindqvist, Christina / Laufer, Batia (eds) *L2 Vocabulary Acquisition, Knowledge and Use: New Perspectives on Assessment and Corpus Analysis*. The European Second Language Association, 57-58.

Milton, James / Hopkins, Nicola 2006. Comparing Phonological and Orthographic Vocabulary size: Do Vocabulary Tests Underestimate the Knowledge of Some Learners. *The Canadian Modern Language Review*. 63/1, 127-147.

Milton, James / Wade, Jo / Hopkins, Nicola 2010. Aural Word Recognition and Oral Competence in a Foreign Language. In Chacón-Beltrán, Rubén / Abello-Contesse, Christián / del Mar Torreblanca-López, María (eds) *Further Insights into Non-native Vocabulary Teaching and Learning*. Bristol: Multilingual Matters, 83-98.

Moskovsky, Christo / Jiang, Guowu / Libert, Alan / Fagan, Seamus 2015. Bottom-up or Top-down: English as a Foreign Language Vocabulary Instruction for Chinese University Students. *TESOL Quarterly*. 49/2, 256-277.

Nakanishi, Takayuki 2015. A Meta-analysis of Extensive Reading Research. *TESOL Quarterly*. 49/1, 6-37.

Nassaji, Hossein 2003. L2 Vocabulary Learning from Context: Strategies, Knowledge Sources, and Their Relationship with Success in L2 Lexical Inferencing. *TESOL Quarterly*. 37/4, 645- 670.

Nation, Paul 2001. *Learning Vocabulary in Another Language*. Cambridge: Cambridge University Press.

Nation, Paul 2006. How Large a Vocabulary is Needed for Reading and Listening? *Canadian Modern Language Review*. 63/1, 59-82.

Pinkham, Joan 2000. *The Translator's Guide to Chinglish*. Beijing: Foreign Language Teaching and Research Press.

Qian, David 2002. Investigating the Relationship between Vocabulary Knowledge and Academic Reading Performance: An Assessment Perspective. *Language Learning*. 52/3, 513-536.

Schmitt, Norbert / Jiang, Xiangying / Grabe, William 2011. The Percentage of Words Known in a Text and Reading Comprehension. *The Modern Language Journal*. 95/1, 26-43.

Shiotsu, Toshihiko / Weir, Cyril 2007. The Relative Significance of Syntactic Knowledge and Vocabulary Breadth in the Prediction of Reading Comprehension Test Performance. *Language Testing*. 24/1, 99-128.

Stæhr, Stenius Lars 2008. Vocabulary Size and the Skills of Listening, Reading and Writing. *Language Learning Journal*. 36/2, 139-152.

Suk, Namhee 2017. The Effects of Extensive Reading on Reading Comprehension, Reading Rate, and Vocabulary Acquisition. *Reading Research Quarterly*. 52/1, 73-89.

Vidal, Karina 2011. A Comparison of the Effects of Reading and Listening on Incidental Vocabulary Acquisition. *Language Learning*. 61/1, 219-258.

Webb, Stuart 2008. Receptive and Productive Vocabulary Sizes of L2 Learners. *Studies in Second Language Acquisition*. 30, 79-95.

Webb, Stuart 2009. The Effects of Receptive and Productive Learning of Word Pairs on Vocabulary Knowledge. *RELC Journal*. 40/3, 360-376.

Wang, Qiang / Chen, Zehang 2012. Twenty-first Century Senior High School English Curriculum Reform in China. In Ruan, Jiening / Leung, Cynthia (eds) *Perspectives on Teaching and Learning English Literacy in China*. Dordrecht, Netherlands: Springer Science & Business Media, 85-104.

Webb, Stuart / Macalister, John 2013. Is Text Written for Children Appropriate for L2 Extensive Reading? *TESOL Quarterly*. 47/2, 300-322.

Webb, Stuart / Paribakht, Sima 2015. What is the Relationship between the Lexical Profile of Test Items and Performance on a Standardized English Proficiency Test? *English for Specific Purposes*. 38, 34-43.

Yamashita, Junko / Shiotsu, Toshihiko 2017. Comprehension and Knowledge Components that Predict L2 Reading: A Latent-trait Approach. *Applied Linguistics*. 38/1, 43-67.

Zhang, Dongbo 2012. Vocabulary and Grammar Knowledge in Second Language Reading Comprehension: A Structural Equation Modeling Study. *The Modern Language Journal*. 96/4, 558-575.

Zhang, Dongbo 2017. Derivational Morphology in Reading Comprehension of Chinese-speaking Learners of English: A Longitudinal Structural Equation Modeling Study. *Applied Linguistics*. 38/6, 871-895.

Zhong, Hua Flora 2018. The Relationship between Receptive and Productive Vocabulary Knowledge: A Perspective from Vocabulary Use in Sentence Writing. *The Language Learning Journal*. 46/4, 357-370.

YAN LI

The Role of Vocabulary Knowledge in Second Language Writing

Introduction

Vocabulary knowledge is an essential component for second language (L2) writing. However, learners may experience difficulties in selecting an appropriate word to express the precise intended meaning and using the word correctly in writing (Coxhead 2011; Henriksen 2008). The accuracy of word use in writing involves understanding different aspects and degrees of vocabulary knowledge. One useful way of distinguishing its multifaceted nature is the size (or breadth) and depth (or quality) dimension: the total number of and the extent to which words are mastered by learners. This chapter will first introduce how the two dimensions are conceptualized and measured in recent literature. Then previous studies will be reviewed to provide an indication of the contribution of vocabulary knowledge to L2 writing.

Defining size and depth of vocabulary knowledge

Size (or breadth) of vocabulary knowledge refers to the number of words known (Anderson/Freebody 1981), and it is associated with the degrees of paired associations between form and meaning (e.g., recall of the most frequent meanings through written forms). Depth generally refers to the subtle distinctions between words (Anderson/Freebody 1981) or how well words are known (Read 1993). In the literature, depth is often viewed from two distinct perspectives: 'word-centred' and 'lexicon-based'. Word-centred conceptualization focuses on the extent to which an individual word is comprehended and produced, and it can be further elucidated from component approach and developmental approach (Schmitt 2010). Nation's framework (2001) provides the most comprehensive description so far adopting the component approach. He grouped the multifarious vocabulary knowledge as form (spoken, written, word parts), meaning (form and meaning, concept and referents, association) and use (grammatical functions, collocation, constraints on use), and broke down these types of word knowledge into two categories: receptive and productive knowledge. Receptive knowledge (or passive knowledge) can be defined as the skill to comprehend words in listening and reading; productive knowledge, on the other hand, is the language ability required when producing words in speaking and writing. From a psycholinguistic standpoint, the mastery of depth lies in the automaticity of word use, which is also called control (Bialystok 1994) or vocabulary accessibility (Laufer/Nation 2001; Meara 1996). Schmitt (2010) suggests that the fluency of lexical processing benefits language use as a whole as this may allow more cognitive resources to be applied to other processes (e.g., planning).

However, this component approach doesn't represent the hierarchal ordering (i.e., which the lexical components are typically learned, used before others or should be taught before others) (Schmitt 2019). The other way of viewing a single word item is from a developmental approach, which considers that word knowledge components develop on a continuum moving from mere recognition of the form throughout understanding different degrees of partial knowledge towards more extended and precise knowledge. Henriksen (1999) suggests that partial to precise knowledge is an essential indicator of lexical competence, and vocabulary mastery should be operationalized as distinct levels of word comprehension along this dimension. In particular, Read (2004) agrees with Anderson and Freebody's (1981) definition of depth as precision of meaning, while he states that defining the criterion level of precision for all lexical items is complicated as "words vary in the extent to which they lend themselves to exact definition" (Read 2004: 213).

Lexicon-based view sees depth as connections built between items within the learners' lexical system (Dóczi/Kormos 2016). Henriksen (1999) provided the first network knowledge definition of depth. She views the process of acquiring depth of knowledge as a *semantization process* of words, which encompasses not only mapping meaning onto form (extensional links between concept and referents) but also building network between words (intensional links with other semantically related words), such as paradigmatic relations (antonymy, synonymy, hyponymy, gradation), syntagmatic relations (collocation) as well as syntactic and morphological restrictions. Items are closely connected in the lexical organization so that learning one word can have effects on learning another (Schmitt 2014).

Conceptualizing depth of vocabulary knowledge is not easy, and the types of approaches are overlapped and interrelated with each other. Based on previous research and analysis, the depth dimension can be loosely grouped as the following types of knowledge:

- Comprehensive word knowledge (including both receptive and productive knowledge)
- Automaticity of word use
- Precision of knowledge (or precision of meaning)
- Semantic network knowledge

The following section describes some widely known tests of size and depth of vocabulary knowledge, in order to explain how the knowledge is understood and captured in recent literature.

Measuring size and depth of vocabulary knowledge

The most standard measurement types are selected-response items and constructed-response items, which are in alignment with recognition and recall of knowledge. Recognition of knowledge refers to understanding the word knowledge presented; recall of knowledge means eliciting target word knowledge from memory using the corresponding stimulus provided.

Matching and multiple-choice formats are classic selected-response items. For example, Nation's original Vocabulary Levels Test (VLT) (1983) with its other versions: Vocabulary Levels Test (revised version, Schmitt/Schmitt/Clapham 2001), New Vocabulary Levels Test (Mclean/Kramer 2015), Updated Vocabulary Levels Test (Webb/Sasao/Balance 2017), employ a matching format to assess learner's recognition knowledge of meaning at the most frequent word frequency levels (e.g., 3000, 4000, 5000). Vocabulary Size Test (VST) (Nation/Beglar 2007) was designed to measure learner's vocabulary size from 1000 to the 14th 1000 word families. The test adopts a multiple-choice format with a higher difficulty level than VLT, as the distractors are semantically related to the correct answer. The Computer Adaptive Test of Size and Strength test developed by Laufer, Elder, Hill and Congdon (2004) adopts both selected-response and constructed-response items. Two distinctions fit in the test:

- Supplying the form for a give concept vs. supplying the meaning for a given form
- Recall vs. recognition (of form or meaning)

The former distinction aims to elicit learners' knowledge of word form when a major concept is given and retrieve meaning when the form is presented. The latter distinction is related to the two test forms mentioned before. Therefore, four tests are involved in CATSS and indicate different degrees of strength: active (form) recall, passive (meaning) recall, active (form) recognition, passive (meaning) recognition. See the following example:

Type 1: Active recall
Turn into water m__________

Type 2: Passive recall
When something melts it turns into __________

Type 3: Active recognition
Turn into water
a. elect b. blame
c. melt d. threaten

Type 4: Passive recognition
Melt
a. choose b. accuse
b. make threats d. turn into water

The vocabulary is sampled from most frequent words from 2000, 3000, 5000, 10000 (from Vocabulary Levels Test: Nation 1983; Schmitt *et al.* 2001), Academic Word List (AWL) (Coxhead 2000) levels as well as less frequent words. Words are tested based on the hierarchy of strength of form and meaning knowledge (i.e., active recall, passive recall, active recognition and passive recognition) in its computer-adaptive version, meaning that once a learner gives the correct answer to a certain modality, the word would not be tested on the subsequent modalities.

In most previous studies, depth of vocabulary knowledge is measured using lexicon-based approach, which views vocabulary as connected items within mental lexicon. Word association knowledge has been assessed based on this conceptualization and used to reflect the complex lexical networks. The word association test generally involves a stimulus word, and test-takers need to supply or select the related words. The categorizations of associations have been perceived as paradigmatic, syntagmatic, and 'clang' responses (Entwisle, 1966). Paradigmatic associations refer to the words that are semantically related to the prompt words, including superordinate, subordinate, coordinate, synonym and antonym. Syntagmatic relationship means the two words from different word classes collocate together. Clang responses are phonologically similar to the prompt word. Read (1993; 1998) developed the two original versions of Word Associates Test (WAT), which are most widely used to assess depth of vocabulary knowledge. The tests adopt selected-response items; test-takers, therefore, are only required to identify the meaning-related words. The newest version of WAT (1998) restricts the stimulus words to adjectives with multiple meanings and uses as he believes that "it will be necessary to develop tests that focus on more homogeneous subsets of vocabulary items so that greater consistency can be achieved in the semantic relationship among the words and in the pattern of responses elicited" (Read 1993: 369). The test consists total 40 items. The words were chosen carefully from Barnard's Second and Third Thousand Word Lists, which cover more high frequency academic vocabulary, thus ensuring that the test-takers have at least partial knowledge of the target words. To reduce the potential of guessing, eight associations and distractors are grouped into two sets of four. The left set are four adjectives, and the associates among them have paradigmatic relationships with the target word; the right set of words are four nouns, the associates can form syntagmatic relationships with the stimulus word. Test-takers are informed that there are four correct associates among the eight words, but the four associates are not evenly distributed (i.e., 1-3, 2-2, and 3-1). See the following example:

sudden

beautiful quick surprising thirsty	change doctor noise school

Size and depth of vocabulary knowledge and L2 writing performance

Learners' vocabulary knowledge of size can be well reflected in L2 writing. Laufer and Nation (1995) found that L2 learners' productive vocabulary size shown in the Lexical Frequency Profile (LFP), which analyzes the word use in different frequency levels of the written texts, was highly correlated with the active version of Vocabulary Levels Test (Nation 1983). It was also found that the range of vocabulary used in written texts is associated with learners' language proficiency levels. More proficient students tend to use more sophisticated words, whereas less proficient students make more use of the first 1000 most frequent words. The range of vocabulary displayed in written discourses is also termed as 'lexical diversity'. Some studies have shown that lexical diversity interacts with the scoring of writings substantially. For example, Engber (1995) found that there is a significant correlation (.45) between the lexical diversity and holistic gradings of multilingual learners' writings. Daller and Phelan's (2007) study further showed a higher correlation between infrequent word use, or 'lexical sophistication' and overall score, and that lexical diversity only moderately correlates with teacher grading. The knowledge of vocabulary size can also be a direct indicator of L2 writing quality. Stæhr (2008) found a fairly high correlation (.73) between vocabulary size assessed with the receptive version of Vocabulary Levels Test (RVLT) and overall writing rating score of a letter with secondary school English learners; in addition, 52% of the variance in learners' ability to obtain an average or above-average writing score is explained by vocabulary size. Dabbagh and Enayat (2019) also found vocabulary size can account for 19% of the variance in descriptive writing tasks. Wu, Dixon, Sun and Zhang's (2019) study indicated that both receptive and productive vocabulary size predict overall writing performance in a pair.

However, there is less clarity on the contribution of depth of vocabulary knowledge to writing performance. In Dabbagh and Enayat's (2019) study, receptive depth knowledge measured by WAT was not a strong predictor of students' descriptive writing score although it was significantly correlated with the writing scores. The same result was also demonstrated in Baba's (2009) study which measured the impact of size and depth of knowledge on summary writing. Wu *et al.'s* (2019) investigation showed that adjective synonym is a predictor for 9th graders' timed writing performance but not for 8th graders. They noted that this is because the development order of depth knowledge is slower. This result is also partially in alignment with Li and Schmitt's (2009) study, which reported that appropriate use of lexical phrases in academic writing is improved with the acquisition process of explicit and implicit learning. Guo, Crossley and McNamara (2013) examined the degree to which linguistic features predict writing proficiency in the Test of English as a Foreign Language (TOEFL iBT) writing tasks. It was found that noun hypernymy value evaluated by Coh-Metrix is a significant predictor of human ratings of the independent essays, explained 4.8% of the variance in the scores.

Research which focuses on the role of both size and depth of vocabulary knowledge in writing quality is scarce, with only few exceptions (Baba 2009; Dabbagh/Enayat 2019; Wu *et al.* 2019). For example, Wu *et al.* (2019) studied the effects of size and depth knowledge on 267 Chinese 8th and 9th graders' writing performance. The vocabulary size of learners was measured by both receptive and productive translation subtests. WAT and morphological awareness test (Berninger 2007) were used for measuring receptive synonym and collocation knowledge as well as receptive word parts knowledge. Then students were given 10 minutes to finish a descriptive free writing task. Their writing abilities were scored according to the adapted Kent *et al.*'s (2014) 5-point rubric by two raters: focus and idea generation, organization, word choice, grammar, sentence fluency and length of writing samples.

The results showed that vocabulary size could significantly predict overall writing performance and word use of the two graders whereas depth of vocabulary knowledge (i.e., adjective synonyms) only has a small predictive role in 9th graders' writings. The study also found that the association between vocabulary size and depth increased with grade and language proficiency. This may lead to more frequent use of depth knowledge for higher graders, and partially account for its emerging impact on the writing quality. Dabbagh and Enayat's (2019) research mainly investigated the interaction between size and depth dimension and L2 descriptive writing task. 67 Iranian university students who were at the intermediate English level took part in the study. VLT was used to measure learners' receptive size of vocabulary knowledge; WAT assessed the depth knowledge. Learners were then tasked to write two 250 words descriptive essays with questions provided as prompts. An adapted five-category analytic assessment scale (Polio 2013) was used to assess the quality of the essays: content, organization, vocabulary, language use and mechanics.

The results showed that size and depth dimensions of lexical knowledge in pair were not a significant predictor in explaining variance in overall writing scores and vocabulary component of descriptive writings. However, it was found that vocabulary breadth has a stronger predictive power than depth on the overall assessment and vocabulary component scores. The researchers suggest that this result may be mediated by the vocabulary component of the scoring scale, in which emphasis is given on lexical diversity and sophistication rather than depth.

Implications

Previous research has provided evidence that both size and depth dimensions of vocabulary knowledge are correlated with L2 writing performance. In comparison to depth, vocabulary size seems to make a more substantial contribution to writing quality. However, it is noteworthy that the findings should be compared and generalized with caution, as different measurements, writing tasks and scoring rubrics are involved. Studies are still needed in order to gain a deeper understanding of the relationship among the types and strength of vocabulary knowledge, lexical features in L2 writing texts and human gradings, which may better inform future vocabulary and writing instruction.

References

Anderson, Richard / Freebody, Peter 1981. Vocabulary Knowledge. In Guthrie, John (ed.) *Comprehension and Teaching: Research Reviews*. 77-117.

Baba, Kyoko 2009. Aspects of Lexical Proficiency in Writing Summaries in a Foreign Language. *Journal of Second Language Writing*. 18/3, 191-208.

Berninger, Virginia 2007. *Process Assessment of the Learner-Second Edition: Diagnostics for Reading and Writing (PAL-II Reading and Writing)*. San Antonio, TX: Psychological Corporation.

Bialystok, Ellen 1994. Analysis and Control in the Development of Second Language Proficiency. *Studies in Second Language Acquisition*. 16/2, 157-168.
Coxhead, Averil 2000. A New Academic Word list. *TESOL Quarterly*. 34/2, 213-238.
Coxhead, Averil 2011. 'What is the exactly word in English?': Investigating Second Language Vocabulary Use in Writing. *English Australia Journal*. 27/1, 3-17.
Dabbagh, Ali / Janebi Enayat, Mostafa 2019. The Role of Vocabulary Breadth and Depth in Predicting Second Language Descriptive Writing Performance. *The Language Learning Journal*. 47/5, 575-590.
Daller, Helmut / Phelan, David 2007. What is in a Tteacher's Mind? Teacher Ratings of EFL Essays and Different aspects of Lexical Richness. In Daller, Helmut / Milton, James / Jeanine Treffers-Daller (eds) *Modelling and Assessing Vocabulary Knowledge*. Cambridge: Cambridge University Press, 234-244.
Dóczi, Brigitta / Kormos, Judit 2016. *Longitudinal Developments in Vocabulary Knowledge and Lexical Organization*. New York: Oxford University Press.
Engber, Cheryl 1995. The Relationship of Lexical Proficiency to the Quality of ESL compositions. *Journal of Second Language Writing*. 4/2, 139-155.
Entwisle, Doris 1966. Form Class and Children's Word Associations. *Journal of Verbal Learning and Verbal Behavior*. 5/6, 558-565.
Guo, Liang / Crossley, Scott / McNamara, Danielle 2013. Predicting Human Judgments of Essay Quality in Both Integrated and Independent Second Language Writing Samples: A Comparison Study. *Assessing Writing*. 18/3, 218-238.
Henriksen, Birgit 1999. Three Dimensions of Vocabulary Development. *Studies in Second Language Acquisition*. 21/2, 303-317.
Henriksen, Birgit 2008. Declarative Lexical Knowledge. In Albrechtsen, Dorte / Haastrup, Kirsten / Henriksen, Birgit (eds) *Vocabulary and Writing in a First and Second Language: Process and Development*. New York: Palgrave Macmillan, 22-26.
Kent, Shawn / Wanzek, Jeanne / Petscher, Yaacov / Al Otaiba, Stephanie / Kim, Young-Suk 2014. Writing Fluency and Quality in

Kindergarten and First Grade: The Role of Attention, Reading, Transcription, and Oral Language. *Reading and Writing*. 27/7, 1163-1188.

Laufer, Batia / Nation, Paul 1995. Vocabulary Size and Use: Lexical Richness in L2 Written Production. *Applied Linguistics*. 16/3, 307-322.

Laufer, Batia / Nation, Paul 2001. Passive Vocabulary Size and Speed of Meaning Recognition: Are they Related? *Eurosla Yearbook*. 1/1, 7-28.

Laufer, Batia / Elder, Cathie / Hill, Kathryn / Congdon, Peter 2004. Size and Strength: Do We Need Both to Measure Vocabulary Knowledge? *Language Testing*. 21/2, 202-226.

Li, Jie / Schmitt, Norbert 2009. The Acquisition of Lexical Phrases in Academic Writing: A Longitudinal Case Study. *Journal of Second Language Writing*. 18/2, 85-102.

McLean, Stuart / Kramer, Brandon 2015. The New Vocabulary Levels Test. *Shiken*. 19/2, 1-11

Meara, Paul 1996. The Vocabulary Knowledge Framework. *Vocabulary Acquisition Research Group Virtual Library*. 1-11.

Nation, Paul 1983. Testing and Teaching Vocabulary. *Guidelines*. 5/1, 12-25.

Nation, Paul 2001. *Learning Vocabulary in Another Language (1st ed.)*. Cambridge: Cambridge University Press.

Nation, Paul / Beglar, David 2007. A Vocabulary Size Test. *The Language Teacher*. 31/7, 9-13.

Polio, Charlene 2013. Revising a Writing Rubric Based on Raters' Comments: Does it Result in a More Reliable and Valid Assessment? *Midwest Association of Language Testers. Michigan State University.*

Read, John 1993. The Development of a New Measure of L2 Vocabulary Knowledge. *Language Testing*. 10/3, 355-371.

Read, John 1998. Validating a Test to Measure Depth of Vocabulary Knowledge. In Kunnan, Antony (ed.) *Validation in Language Assessment*. Mahwah, New Jersey: Lawrence Erlbaum Associates Publishers, 41-60.

Read, John 2004. Plumbing the Depths: How Should the Construct of Vocabulary Knowledge be Defined? In Boggards, Paul / Laufer,

Batia (eds) *Vocabulary in a Second Language: Selection, Acquisition, and Testing*. Amsterdam: John Benjamins Publishing Company, 209-227

Schmitt, Norbert 2010. *Researching Vocabulary: A Vocabulary Research Manual*. New York: Palgrave Macmillan.

Schmitt, Norbert 2014. Size and Depth of Vocabulary Knowledge: What the Research Shows. *Language Learning*. 64/4, 913-951.

Schmitt, Norbert 2019. Understanding Vocabulary Acquisition, Instruction, and Assessment: A Research Agenda. *Language Teaching*. 52/2, 261-274.

Schmitt, Norbert / Schmitt, Diane / Clapham, Caroline 2001. Developing and Exploring the Behaviour of Two New Versions of the Vocabulary Levels Test. *Language Testing*. 18/1, 55-88.

Stæhr, Lars 2008. Vocabulary Size and the Skills of Listening, Reading and Writing. *Language Learning Journal*. 36/2, 139-152.

Webb, Stuart / Sasao, Yosuke / Ballance, Oliver 2017. The Updated Vocabulary Levels Test: Developing and Validating Two New Forms of the VLT. *International Journal of Applied Linguistics*. 168/1, 34-70.

Wu, Shuang / L. Quentin, Dixon / Sun, Haitao / Zhang, Peng 2019. Breadth or Depth: The Role of Vocabulary in Chinese English-Language Beginning Writers' Development. *International Journal of Bilingual Education and Bilingualism*. 1-17.

APISAK SUKYING

A Taxonomy of English Affix Acquisition in EFL Learners

Introduction

Knowledge of affixes, including prefixes and suffixes, is the ability to identify and manipulate the internal structure of a morphologically complex word (Carlisle 2003; Claravall 2016; Kuo/Anderson 2006; Lieber 2010). This knowledge helps learners to interpret the meanings of unconscious words by parsing affixed words into smaller, more meaningful morphological segments in written and spoken forms. Affixes can therefore function as 'hints' to expedite learners' acquisition of new vocabulary by connecting affixed items to the meanings of the familiar word parts to which they are attached. Knowledge of English affixes can also allow learners to see the connection between word family members, where one or more word family members are already known. In addition, such knowledge helps learners extrapolate from a syntactic category of other words based on a derivational suffix or coin a novel suffixed word to meet the demand for language communication. For example, adding *-ion* to a verb will designate a noun (create-creation), while adding *-ive* to a verb makes it an adjective (create-creative).

Affix knowledge includes both inflectional and derivational affixes of the word. Inflectional affixes (morphemes) do not involve word formation, and they never adjust the syntactic category of the word to which they are added (Claravall 2016). Instead, inflectional affixes make small changes to words that have significant syntactic consequences, indicating, for example, person and number in verbs, tenses, and numbers and grammatical cases in nouns. Conversely, derivational affixes (bound morphemes) are applied to word formations in which bound morphemes play a role. For instance, *underdevelopment* is seen as a different form of the word *underdevelop* or *develop*, and the word is created simply by adding the suffix *-ment* to the free morpheme *develop* and attaching the prefix *under-* to it. Bound morphemes involved in derivational affixes may adjust the syntactic category to which the word is attached. Therefore, the addition of the derivative *-able* to the verb *read* yields the adjective *readable*, whereas the addition of the derivative *-ness* to the adjective *sad* assigns the noun *sadness*.

Knowledge of affixes includes both form and meaning (Manova/Aronoff 2010). The form of an affix involves syntactic properties, while the meaning of an affix conveys semantic information. Regarding affix form, morphological affix acquisition is based on morphological information, including selectional restriction. Selectional restriction, where an affix requires the addition of another affix, is an indication of morphological ordering, i.e., the nominal suffix *-isation* in English always selects the adjectival suffix *-al*. The additional morphological restriction is viewed as either encoded in the word base or as encoded in the affix attached. Syntactic affix acquisition is based on the underlying notion that derivational affixes reflect grammatical knowledge and, vice versa, that grammatical knowledge reflects derivational affixes (Baker 1985). This is also known as the 'Mirror Principle' (Baker 1985). Manova and Aronoff (2010) further explain that derivational affixes are morphosyntactic: syntax is encoded into derivatives. That is, morphologically derivational forms (affixes) convey form, meaning, and syntactic properties that, in turn, mirror derivational affixes. Following the mirror principle, it is logical that the different tenses, including past, present, and future, are associated with a syntactic structure (syntax) based on grammaticalization.

Concerning psycholinguistic characteristics, Hay (2002) indicated that affix ordering depends on the degree of parsability, which involves different factors, including phonology, productivity, regularity, semantic transparency and frequency. The parsability determines affix order; that is, a more parsable affix should occur outside a less parsable affix since this order is easier to process. For instance, a parsability hierarchy of suffixes ABCDE in which E is the most parsable and A is the least parsable given that the combinations of ACD or BDE occur in a language, whereas the combinations of CAD and EDB are impossible. This affix ordering can be described as parsability Complexity-Based Ordering because a parsable affix adds an affixed item to a base step by step, making the latter more morphologically complex. However, parsability works in common with selectional restrictions on affix order (Hay/Plag 2004; Zirkel 2010).

Construct of word family knowledge

The concept of the word is inextricably linked to the idea of word families. Word families were described by Bauer and Nation (1993) as central organising units for language processing. In essence, the hypothesis is that new morphologically complex words can be acquired by reference to a word base, with the addition of accepted inflected and transparent derived affix forms, without separately learning particular forms (Bauer/Nation 1993). Thus, the size of one's affix knowledge base is directly proportionate to the size of one's vocabulary knowledge base (or 'lexicon').

The connection between affix knowledge and vocabulary size in the context of word families is particularly important for English learners. Approximately 34.7% of the words that occur in English school texts include inflectional and derivational affixes (Nation 2013: 391-392). More precisely, 21.9% (about one-fifth) of words are inflectional affixes, and 12.8% (about one-eight) are derivational affixes. Researchers in the field of vocabulary acquisition and development have had difficulty defining 'a word' and using it as a counting unit (Gardner 2007; Schmitt 2010). On the one hand, it might be perplexing to count only unique spellings as, while this avoids the role of morphological affixation altogether, it loses a great deal of psychological validity. For example, it is unlikely that English learners would be unable to see the linguistic connection between *develop* and *developed*, or *book* and *books*.

The relative influence of linguistic and psycholinguistic features on word family acquisition among English learners is a central issue facing EFL practitioners and vocabulary researchers alike. The concept of word families focuses on the psycholinguistic features of an affix, rather than its linguistic features (Bauer/Nation 1993). Focusing on eight phonological and morphological behaviours, Bauer and Nation (1993) analysed the 1,000,000 token Lancaster-Oslo-Bergen (LOB) corpus and created a seven-level taxonomy of the word-family schema to use as a general guide for the teaching and learning of morphologically complex words. These seven levels of word family criteria are not discrete and absolute but represent a cumulative hierarchy based on four principal factors: frequency, productivity, regularity and predictability (Bauer/Nation 1993).

Vocabulary researchers hypothesise that affixes are acquired according to numerical order (Ford *et al.* 2010; Gardner 2007; Hayashi/Murphy 2011; Manova/Aronoff 2010; Reichle/Perfetti 2003). That is, the pattern of affix acquisition starts with Level 1 affixes and progresses ascendingly to Level 7 affixes. At Level 1, a different form is labelled as another word, so *create*, *created*, *creating*, and *creates* are different words ('tokens'). At Level 2, inflected forms added to the same base are considered members of the same word family, given that they retain the same word class. Therefore, in the case of the *create* word family, there is only one word family at Level 2, rather than four different words at Level 1. From Levels 3 to 6, new members of the word family are added by prefixes and suffixes regardless of the change of syntactic categories of the word. Level 7 comprises a single criterion of classical roots and affixes, for example, *photography* and *embolism*. The different word family levels of affixes are as follows:

Level 1: Every different form is a different word
Level 2: Inflections
Level 3: The most frequent and regular derivational affixes
Level 4: Frequent, orthographically regular affixes
Level 5: Regular but infrequent affixes
Level 6: Frequent but irregular affixes
Level 7: Classical roots and affixes

The seven levels of the word family related to teaching and learning the correct affix developed by Bauer and Nation (1993) are based on four criteria: frequency, productivity, regularity, and predictability. However, the respective order of importance of these criteria remains unknown.

The critical principle of word family theory is that knowledge of a base word, or even a single inflected or derived member thereof, means other members can be learned with little or no additional effort (Bauer/Nation 1993). The rule-based nature of inflections appears to facilitate mental acquisition better than the derivational forms. For instance, inflections (Level 2 of word family formation) are all inflectional suffixes, which take on strict formations to mark grammatical functions. Such affixes preserve the core meanings of a base word (stem) but add a syntactic overlay as seen in numbers for nouns, verbal tenses, and comparative/superlative adjectives/adverbs. For example, the *-s* ending on the word *use* may mark a third-party subject or may mark a plural noun.

Unlike inflections, derivations all involve syntactic classes. Word family theory classifies syntactic derivations as Level 3 to Level 7. Such prefixes and suffixes are more complex and are therefore acquired later (Bauer/Nation 1993; Hayashi/Murphy 2011; Schmitt/Meara 1997; Schmitt/Zimmerman 2002; Sukying 2017, 2018, 2020). These derivational affixes may carry semantic and syntactic information, as in *useful* and *useless* or *reuse* and *misuse*. As such, the meaning of a syntactic class and use of a new derivational form may be ambiguous for low vocabulary learners. This information processing burden may lead to lower productive abilities in low vocabulary EFL learners, who exhibit more disambiguation errors during the process of retrieval in context.

Using Bauer and Nation's (1993) seven levels of affixes to help remember new words is one of the key mechanisms underlying English vocabulary learning strategies. Research also shows the relationship between affix knowledge and vocabulary (Hayashi/Murphy 2011; Mochizuki/Aizawa 2000; Schmitt/Meara 1997; Schmitt/Zimmerman 2002; Sukying 2017, 2018, 2020). However, little effort has been made to examine English affix acquisition. Understanding the nature of affix acquisition would thus shed light on the significance of affixes for learning English vocabulary. Specifically, from a lexical acquisition viewpoint, affix knowledge could help practitioners, including English language teachers, to decide which affixes their students should know and to develop learning activities and assessments related to these affixes.

The current study

This study explored the patterns of affix knowledge acquisition at different education levels. It also aimed to understand how students develop their affix learning and expand their word knowledge acquisition. For the present study, the word family construct is operationalised such that it can be interchanged with the affix knowledge construct. Therefore, here, receptive affix knowledge is the ability to recognise the form-meaning link of the affix, whereas productive affix knowledge refers to the ability to recall the form and meaning of an affix and the ability to use the affixation in appropriate contexts as measured by the writing task. Based on the study objectives, the following research questions were established:

1. Is there a taxonomy of affix acquisition in Thai EFL learners at two education levels?
2. How do Thai EFL learners develop their affix knowledge?

Participants

A total of 486 high school students voluntarily participated in the study. Participants were 221 lower secondary school students (LSS; grades 8 and 9) and 265 upper secondary school (USS) students. All participants were given a vocabulary size test (VST) (Nation/Beglar 2007) and a productive vocabulary levels test (PVLT) (Laufer/Nation 1999). The combined VST and PVLT scores were converted into a percentage. The percentage of known words can be used as a proxy for participants' vocabulary size (Nation/Beglar 2007), where every 1% of vocabulary knowledge is equal to 50 words (a total of 5,000 words). Thus, up to 30% is equal to 1,500 words, 30.1%-40% is equal to 2,000 words, and more than 40% is equal to 2,500 words. Twelve participants were selected for the qualitative analysis. These participants were randomly selected using a computer algorithm that selected the thirty-fifth case from each vocabulary group (maximum of four per group).

All the participants were Thai native speakers and none had studied English in an English-speaking country. At the time of data collection, the participants received an average of four hours of English instruction per week, including four 50-minute English sessions with Thai EFL teachers and one 50-minute session with native English speakers. Consistent with the Office of the Basic Education Commission, The Ministry of Education in Thailand, participants had been enrolled in English as a foreign language (EFL) classes for a minimum of seven years as a mandatory subject.

Research instruments

The two measures used in this study were a receptive affix knowledge (RAK) test and the less-controlled productive affix knowledge (LPAK) task. The RAK test was based on Mitchell and Brady (2014) and was presented in a five-point multiple-choice format (see Sukying 2017, for further details). The selection of the target affixes used in the RAK was based on Bauer and Nation (1993).

The LPAK was developed based on Schmitt and Meara (1997). The test was first used in Sukying (2017) and was used to assess learners' affix knowledge in a less controlled context. The test comprises two parts (Xa and Xb). Part Xa presents the meaning of target affixes, followed by a blank space for writing the affixes that the participants assumed were acceptable (Xa). In Part Xb, participants were required to compose a sentence using affixes from Part Xa. Here is the example of the test:

Item	Meaning	Prefix (es)
1a)	'before'	*pre-, ante-, fore-*
1b)	Write a sentence using a word that has the same prefix(es) you provided in 1a) ______________________________	

For each target affix, participants were asked to write acceptable affixes and then compose a sentence. In Part Xa, participants were awarded one point for each allowable affix they provided. To minimise the likelihood of guessing among the allowable affixes, one point was subtracted from each unacceptable affix. Two experienced native speakers (both English EFL teachers in Thailand) judged the correctness of participants' written sentences. Words with correct affixes were given one point. Based on Paribakht and Wesche's (1997: 181) scoring criteria, an affix with the right word form was given two points. A word used with semantic appropriateness in a sentence was given three points and an affix with the right word form, semantic appropriateness, and grammatical correctness in a sentence received four points. Minor spelling errors were ignored, and no points were subtracted if the composed sentence was incorrect due to partial knowledge of those affixes. The interpretation of the LPAK scores is illustrated in Table 1.

Possible scores	**Interpretation of scores**
1	The word is not familiar, and the non-word is given
2	The word is familiar, and the word with correct spelling is given
3	The word is used with semantic appropriateness in a sentence
4	The word is used with semantic appropriateness and grammatical accuracy in a sentence

Table 1. The meaning of the LPAK scores (adapted from Paribakht/Wesche 1997: 181).

Syntactic categories	**Affixes**	**To-tal**
Inflections	*-s, -es, -ed, -ing, -er, -est*	6
Derivations		
Verbs	*-en, -ify, --ise (-ize), -ate*	4
Adjectives	*-able, -ish, -less, -ly, -th, -al, -ful, -ous, -ant, -ary, -atory, -ent,* *-ory, -ic, -ive, -ar, -ible, -some, -esque*	19
Adverbs	*-ly, -ally, -most, -ward, -ways, -wise*	6
Nouns	*-er, -or, -ness, -y, -al, -ation, -ess, -ful, -ism, -ist, -ity, -ment, -age, -an, -ance, -ant, -dom, -eer, -ence, -ent, -ery, -ese, -ette, -hood, -i, -ian, -ite, -let, -ling, -ship, -ee, -ion, -ition, -th, -ure*	35
Prefixes	*un-, non-, in-, im-, il-, ir-, pre-, ante-, fore-, anti-, counter-, bi, mid-, semi-, sub-, mis-, post-, inter-, hyper-, circum-, re-, dis-, ex-, trans-*	24
Total		**94**

Table 2. The inflections and derivations used in the current study.

The LPAK test was developed to capture productive affix knowledge, where learners could use particular affixes in free production. The task uses both inflectional and derivational affixes, including 24 prefixes and 70 suffixes in English, as shown in Table 2 (Bauer/Nation 1993).

Procedure

Ethical approval was obtained from the Ethics Committee of the University of Sydney (Project No.: 2015/923) prior to the study and permission from the secondary school was also obtained. Students from Grade Eight to Eleven where then invited to participate in the study during their English class. Informed consent was sought from guardians or parents of all participants under 18 to ensure participation was voluntary.

Experienced invigilators, rather than the students' teachers, were selected to administer the tests to ensure that the research was blind to test administrators and impartial. The LPAK test was given first to avoid the possibility that students might draw a relationship between the written affixes appearing on the productive measure. Illustrations of the tasks were also provided to participants in their native Thai language prior to testing.

Data analysis

The raw total test scores of receptive and productive affix knowledge tests were converted into percentages. A repeated-measures ANOVA was also conducted to detect any significant differences on syntactic classes of an affix. The qualitative data included the description and analysis of the 12 participants' (or cases') responses on productive affix knowledge task.

Results

Taxonomy of receptive affix knowledge acquisition

The results shown in Figure 1 show that, overall, USS students perform better in all syntactic classes than LSS students. However, a similar trend in performance was observed for both LSS students and USS students. LSS students performed best on inflections in the form of inflectional verbal suffixes (71.95%), followed by derivational forms; prefixes (48.99%), verbs (41.63%), nouns (37.86%), adjectives (30.03%), and, finally, adverbs (25.79%). Similarly, USS students performed best on inflections in the form of inflectional verbal suffixes (88.68%). This was followed by derivational forms; prefixes (63.84%), then verbs (58.26%), nouns (49.33%), adjectives (36.98%), and adverbs (36.35%).

A repeated-measures ANOVA with a Greenhouse-Geisser correction indicated that participants performed differently on the various syntactic classes ($F(3.019, 1461.071) = 440.329, p < .001$), with a large effect size ($\eta^2 = 0.476, p < .001$), but no significant difference was found between adjective and adverb performance. Furthermore, there was a significant overall effect of Education Level ($F(1, 484) = 109.380, p < .001$) with a large effect size ($\eta^2 = 0.184, p < .001$). A significant Education Level x Syntactic Class interaction was also found ($F(3.019, 1461.071) = 5.126, p < .01$), with a small effect size ($\eta^2 = 0.010, p < .01$).

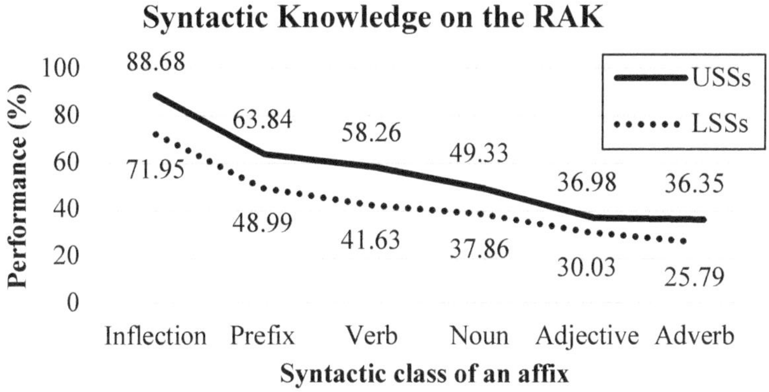

Note: N = 221 for LSS Students, N = 265 for USS Students
Figure 1. Correct responses to affix knowledge based on syntactic classes of the RAK.

Taxonomy of productive affix knowledge acquisition

As shown in Figure 2, Thai EFL participants (both LSS and USS students) performed best on inflectional verbal suffixes 37.48% and 38.34% for LLSs and USSs, respectively. As expected, performance on derivational suffixes dropped significantly for both education levels. LSS students obtained 13.48%, 0.52%, 2.46%, 3.44%, and 5.84% respectively for prefixes, verbs, nouns, adjectives and adverbs, while corresponding performances for USS students were 22.55%, 5.26%, 5.69%, 4.85%, and 7.66%. The participants' low performance on derivational suffixes illustrates the relative difficulty of processing syntactic information, which may require cognitive knowledge of grammatical function and metacognitive contextual transformation.

A repeated-measures ANOVA with a Greenhouse-Geisser correction showed that participants performed differently on the various syntactic classes in the LPAK test ($F(1.646, 796.462) = 469.524$, $p < 0.001$), with a large effect size ($\eta^2 = 0.492$, $p < 0.001$). There was also a significant difference in syntactic knowledge between LSS students and USS students ($F(1, 484) = 20.586$, $p < .001$), with a medium effect size ($\eta^2 = 0.041, p < 0.001$). Moreover, a significant Education Level x Syntactic Knowledge interaction was found ($F(1.646, 796.462) = 5.823, p < .01$), with a small effect size ($\eta^2 = 0.012, p < .01$).

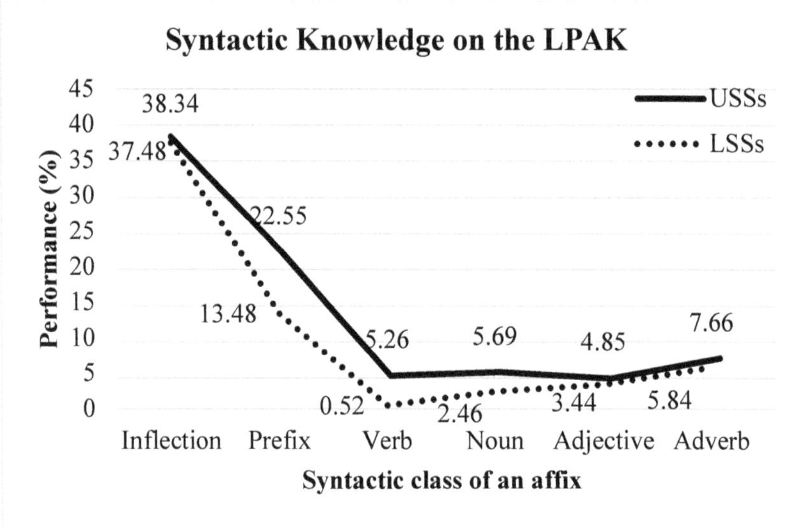

Note: N = 221 for LSS students, N = 265 for USS students

Figure 2. Syntactic knowledge of the affixes on the LPAK.

Taxonomy of the affixations in word family acquisition

This section provides deeper insights into the progressive nature of productive affix knowledge in the word family acquisition process. Here, the focus is the qualitative analysis of 12 participants' responses on the productive affix knowledge task. A participant's vocabulary size or lexicon is measured using the total number of known words on the vocabulary tests. As it is positively related to affix knowledge, vocabulary size can be viewed as a general measure of mastery of the affix acquisition process. Accordingly, three levels of vocabulary size (1500-word, 2000-word, and 2500-word levels) were selected for thematic comparison, considered to be small, medium and large vocabulary participants, respectively. There were four participants at each level.

The following sections show examples of sentences produced for each syntactic class on the writing task. These indicate the participants' abilities to use affixation in the context in accordance with their vocabulary size. Example sentences were broken down by vocabulary level to offer insight into the relationship between vocabulary size and productive affix use in context, where vocabulary level functioned as a proxy for vocabulary size. Syntactic classes of affixes are used as themes to compare participants' abilities to use affixations across vocabulary size levels.

Inflections

Participants at all vocabulary sizes had better mastery of inflections than derivations. Indeed, averaged across vocabulary level, the affix acquisition process was observed, whereby small vocabulary participants used less complex sentence patterns, and large vocabulary participants used more complex sentence patterns than medium vocabulary participants. For example, a small vocabulary participant wrote, "She is *writing* a homework." In comparison, a medium vocabulary participant wrote, "My home is *bigger* than Jim's home", and a large vocabulary student wrote, "This is the *biggest* house I have ever seen." The participants' written sentences suggest that the common English inflections are acquired and developed productively during secondary school years. The writing ability shown for each vocabulary size also suggests that participants' written sentences become more accurate and context-appropriate as their vocabulary size increased. Individual participants' written statements are shown in Table 3.

The analysis of individuals' written sentences suggests that the rule-based nature of inflections is a measure of their ability to apply known grammar rules to retrieve, in context, inflectional items among word family members. However, suitable contextual lexical use is challenging for participants, particularly for smaller vocabulary participants. In summary, the results indicate that the acquisition of inflections by EFL learners is an incremental process, which is largely a function of language exposure during secondary school years.

Partic-ipants	Inflections recalled	Sentences produced
S1	*-s, -ed, -er, -est*	I have four <u>chairs</u>. /She <u>stayed</u> at home last night. He is <u>shorter</u> than me. /She is the <u>tallest</u> in this group.
S2	*-er*	Roman is <u>taller</u> than Jack.
S3	*-ing, -er, -ed*	She is <u>writing</u> a homework. /He is <u>taller</u> than her. This is a <u>biggest</u> mango.
S4	*-ed, -est, -s, -es*	Yesterday, I <u>loved</u> her. /The test is <u>hardest</u>. I love <u>dogs</u>. /I eat <u>oranges</u>.
M1	*-s, -ed, -ing, -er, -est*	I have many <u>dogs</u>. /I <u>walked</u> to school. My mom is <u>cooking</u> in the kitchen.
M2	*-s, -es, -ed, -ing, -er, -est*	I've read two <u>books</u>. My mum is eating that two <u>mangoes</u>. Yesterday, I <u>walked</u> home with my brother. James's <u>talking</u> with his friends. I am <u>taller</u> than my sister. /I am <u>fattest</u> in my family.
M3	*-ed, -s, -ing, -er, -est*	I <u>walked</u> around the room. She <u>eats</u> breakfast with her friend. /I don't like <u>singing</u>. I am coming to school <u>earlier</u> my friend. I afraid to stay the <u>highest</u> of the building.
M4	*-s, -es, -ed, -er, -est*	I have 20 <u>cats</u>. /I will buy <u>boxes</u> tomorrow. I <u>watched</u> television yesterday. My home is <u>bigger</u> than Jim's home. My home is the <u>biggest</u> in the world.
L1	*-s, -es, -ed, -ing, -er, -est*	There are many <u>ducks</u> in Simon's farm. We have to prepare the <u>glasses</u> for the attendant tonight. He <u>loved</u> her. /<u>swimming.</u> /Teddy is <u>taller</u> than Smith. The <u>longest</u> river in the world is Nile river.
L2	*-s, -ed, -ing, -er, -est*	My favorite animal is <u>birds</u>. Yesterday, I <u>played</u> basketball with my boyfriend. I am <u>going</u> to Paris now. /I am <u>thinner</u> than Jenny. Bai-Yok build is the <u>highest</u> build.
L3	*-s, -es, -ed, -ing, -er, -est*	He always <u>presents</u> his <u>products</u>. That <u>painted</u> glass is beautiful. /<u>Loving</u> wins everything. An <u>injured</u> man was sent to hospital. He is <u>smaller</u> than me. This is the <u>biggest</u> house I have ever seen.
L4	*-s, -es, -ed, -er, -est*	She has many <u>neighborhoods</u>. You have about 50 <u>watches</u>. /Max <u>yelled</u> at me. Your room is <u>wider</u> than mine. This lipstick is the <u>cheapest</u> one I've ever bought.

Table 3. Inflections produced in the word family acquisition process.

Partici-pants	Prefixes recalled	Sentences produced
S1	*in-, pre-, re-*	The boy writes informal's letter. Today, I'm doing pretest exam. /I'm replay game.
S2	*un-, pre-, sub-*	I feel unhappy because I don't like test. Teacher has pretest for student. /I want submarine.
S3	*un-, in-, re-*	She is unhappy with English test. She is rewrite a novel.
S4	*un-, in-, im-, ir-, il-, dis-, re-, trans-*	I unfriend him. /I do prefix incorrect. He is immortal. /She is illure. /Internet is disable. /recycle/ Wood is transferred with a bus.
M1	*pre-, bi-, re-*	He previews goods. /My friend is bisexual. When play football, I restore energy with coke.
M2	*un-, pre-, sub-, re-*	Milk is uncountable noun. I have to do this pretest. This movie has Thai subtitle. You can retry this assignment.
M3	*un-, dis-, pre-, bi-, mid-, post-, re-*	My shoes disappear yesterday. People think wearing a seat belt isn't uncomfortable. I have a pretest in this morning. I searching about bipolar on Internet. I have just slept at midnight. I have a posttest in this morning too. Author rewrite his novel.
M4	*un-, im-, mis-, mid-, re-, pre-, anti-, bi-, sub-, post-, inter-, trans-*	The police was make over his face is unreal. The sun raise at 9am is the impossible story. The boss is misleading us. I will go to midyear sale at Robinson. I returned to my home. My friend is joining a pre-test in the room now. Antioxidant is important for human health. Many people are bisexual. I will go to Bang Krapi by subway train. My friends are joining a post-test in this room now. Internet. /He transforms his car.
L1	*un-, in-, dis-, mid-, re-, pre-, bi-, sub-, inter-*	She seemed unhappy in the party last night. This answer is incorrect. Cheat on test is dishonest in the test.

		Cinderella danced with Prince until midnight. Don't return. / I go to school by subway. Lilly have studied at Silver international School since 1999.
L2	*in-*, *bi-*, *re-*	Our answer are incorrect. /She's a bisexual. This house needs renovate so much.
L3	*un-*, *in-*, *re-*, *pre-*, *anti-*,	She is unhappy. /She is independent. He uses a reuse bottle.
L4	im-, *un-*, *il-*, *mis-*, *mid-*, *re-*, *pre-*, *anti-*, *bi-*, *sub-*, *post-*, inter-, *trans-*	Tyler is such an impatient guy. Tiana is really unfaithful. /What he did is illegal. Lauren misunderstood me. Midterm examination will be finished tomorrow. Ray just recreated that artwork. Jack took a pre-test yesterday. There're many antioxidants in lemons. Teala is bisexual. /I came home by subway yesterday. 1st of January is international New Year's Day. Andrea had his car transformed.

Table 4. Prefixal derivatives produced in the affix acquisition process.

Prefixes

As shown in Table 4, all participants could recall some affix forms and use them to write a sentence in context, although some sentences might appear unnatural to a native English speaker. For example, participant S1 wrote, "I'm *replay* game." In comparison, participant M2 noted, "You can *retry* this assignment." Participant L4 wrote, "Ray just *recreated* that artwork." Overall, the participants' written sentences show the developmental pattern of derivational prefix acquisition from smaller to larger vocabulary sizes. The data support the underlying notion of incremental affix learning, whereby examples with less complic ated affixations are acquired at earlier stages, and more complex and sophisticated affixations are acquired at later stages, using knowledge of previous word family forms.

Participants' ability to recall prefixes in context is directly related to their lexicon or vocabulary size. For example, *un-*, *pre-* and *re-* were recalled by participants at all vocabulary levels, although smaller vocabulary participants exhibited greater difficulty in the productive use of affixations in context. For example, participant S1's response was typical of all small vocabulary participants: "The boy writes *informal*'s letter." S1 could not recall *anti-*, *inter-* and *post-*. Conversely, *anti-*, *inter-* and *post-* were recalled and correctly used productively by medium and large vocabulary participants. For instance, participant M4 answered '*Antioxidant* is important for human health', and participant L4 wrote "There're many *antioxidants* in lemons."

Prefix recall improves in direct proportion to the vocabulary size of participants. For example, 11 out of 12 participants could recall *re-*, and ten of the 11 participants who recalled it could provide the correct prefixation (e.g., 'recreated'). However, only four participants could use the prefix productively in context; the others used incorrect grammar or semantic context; for example, S3 responded, "She is rewrite a novel." Another example is S4, who could recall six prefixes with similar senses (*un-*, *in-*, *im-*, *ir-*, *il-* and *dis-*), but was unable to use them grammatically. For instance, they stated "She is *illure*." and "I do prefix *incorrect*." In contrast, participant L4 retrieved three prefixed items (*im-*, *un-*, *il-*) and could use them productively; for example, "Tyler is such an *impatient* guy," "Tiana is really *unfaithful*", and "What he did is *illegal*." Consistent with Jiang's (2000) psycholinguistic model, these sentence patterns suggest that larger vocabulary participants are able to produce more complex prefixation in context-appropriate sentences because they have amassed significant exposure to syntactic knowledge used in the affix retrieval process.

Verbs

The analysis of qualitative data revealed that low vocabulary participants could not recall any forms of verbal suffixes, nor were they able to write them in a sentence. The results suggest that productive knowledge of verbal derivatives is poorer for low vocabulary EFL learners, which makes these forms harder to produce. A partial explanation may be that many base words are verbs, which cannot be transformed. Medium and large vocabulary participants were able to recall verbal affixes but were often unable to produce them in context. Participant M2 could remember *-ate*, but failed to produce any verbal affixation in context. M4 could recall *-ate*, *-ify*, and *-ize*, and two sentences were produced ("I *purify* my shirt" and "The teacher is *specialize* my research"). Participant L3 could recall *-en*, and *-ate* as verbal derivational suffixes, though was unable to provide any affixations and sentences in context. Similarly, participant L4 could recall *-ify* and *-ize*, as seen in '*verify*' and '*socialize*', and wrote, "You have to *verify* yourself to log into this website" and "There's no place to *socialize* here." The findings support the underling notion that learning is a cumulative process of acquiring affixes as a result of lexical exposure during school years.

Nouns

Participants' productive knowledge of noun derivatives indicates that this syntactic class is the last to be learned and incomplete mastery of noun-forming suffixes was often exhibited even by participants with a large vocabulary. For instance, participant S1 wrote, "*Exercising* is good idea" and participant S4 wrote, "I play with *neighbourhood*." In comparison, participant M1 wrote, "*Writer* is writing a book", and "*Artist* draws many pictures." Likewise, participant M4 produced, "*Walking* can help the earth to save CO2," "*Happiness* can make by yourself", and "Thai *community* is the best system in the world." Participant L1 wrote, "The English *teachers* at my school are kind", "The Chinese *tourists* are going to Hong Kong", and "*Sadness* isn't good for health." Participant L2 wrote, "The *culmination* in the world is Everest Mountain", and "E-bola *inflections* in Africa were died." Statements from each of the 12 case studies are detailed in Table 5.

Overall, the results indicate that the ability to recall affixes and use them in sentences develops with vocabulary size. Indeed, the participants' vocabulary size appeared to be positively related to their affix knowledge, and their productive affix knowledge of syntactic classes led to more complete mastery of productive use. For instance, if a learner realises the grammatical function and use of a noun, they may be able to produce the correct affixation in a meaningful grammatical context (e.g., "He is a trainer' or 'You need a reality check.") In contrast, the acquisition of knowledge of syntactic class may be problematic for those who have less exposure to grammatical use in context.

Participants	Nominal derivatives recalled	Sentences produced
S1	*-er*, *-ing*	I am a reader. Exercising is good idea.
S2	-	-
S3	*-er*	-
S4	*-hood*	I play with neigborhood.
M1	*-er*, *-ist*	A writer is writing a book. Artist draws many pictures
M2	*-tion*, *-ion*, *-ing*, *-ness*, *-ship*, *-hood*, *-y*, *-ment*	I'll break down my presentation into 3 parts. I have three missions in the game. Swimming is my favorite activity. Sadness makes me feel bad. I have a wonderful relationship with my sister. My childhood was amazing. Biology is a difficult subject. This is an easy assignment.
M3	-ion, *-ance*, *-ent*, *-er*, *-ant*, *-dom*	Everyone avoid about appearance of my sister. I'm not like to be dancer. /She is *different*. Rainforest is *abundant*. /I like about freedom.
M4	*-ing*, *-ness*, *-ity*	Walking can help the earth to save CO2. Happiness can make by yourself. Thai community is the best system in the world.
L1	*-er*, *-ist*, *-ness*	The English teachers at my school are kind. The Chinese tourists are going to Hong Kong. Sadness isn't good for health.
L2	*-ion*, *-er*, *-ist*, *-tion*	E-bola inflections in Africa were died. Researcher doing something in hospital. I wanna be *fashionist* in London. The culmination in the world is Everest Mountain.
L3	*-ion*, *-ee*, *-er*, *-ing*, *-ness*, *-ence*, -*ive*, *-or*	I have a tension. /He is a trainee. She is a trainer. /Loving can win everything. Happiness is around you. /I see no difference. He is not my relative. /She is an editor.
L4	*-ness*, *-ity*, *-ing*, *-ance*	I appreciate her kindness. /You need a reality check. Cleaning is a hard work. Many people admire her appearance.

Table 5. Nominal derivatives produced in the word family acquisition process.

Adjectives

The participants' appreciation of adjectival suffixes also follows a stage-wise development. Only one small vocabulary participant, S1, was able to recall the adjectival suffix *-ful* in a meaningful sentence, "She is the most *beautiful* in this group." In comparison, most medium vocabulary participants' written sentences showed contextually appropriate use of these suffixes. For example, participant M2 wrote "You're a *creative* person", "This is an *economic* business", and "Las Vegas is an *amazing* place." Participant M4 wrote "Thailand is the *helpful* country." However, there were exceptions. Participant M3 wrote, "I like *natural* face of woman", "She is *beautiful* girl", and "I am *hopeless* of my English skill." Likewise, participant M4 responded "This school is *careless* place."

Large vocabulary participants' ability to recall and produce adjectival affixes varied across the 15 adjectival suffixes. Participant L1 wrote, "This *talkative* girl is my friend", "Miss Thailand is sexy and *flawless* woman", and "She bought the *beautiful* pink dress yesterday." Similarly, participant L2 wrote, "My country is *peaceful*", "She's very *attractive*", and "I have to pay a price for being *careless*." Likewise, participant L3 produced, "The *painted* shirt is painted by me", "This is an *exclusive* moment", "She is *beautiful*", "He is a *careless* man", "This test is *different* from another", and "She is *amiable*." In a similar manner, participant L4 composed three sentences – "Fred gave a *beautiful* speech", "Violette is so *careless*", and "She looks *exotic*."

Together, these results indicate that EFL participants develop their syntactic affix knowledge along a continuum. Small to medium vocabulary participants have difficulty using adjectives, even when they can recall their form and meaning. For instance, M2 provided an adjectival *-ese* suffix but was unable to use the adjectival suffixation in context, as seen in "*Chinese* eats soup." In fact, '*Chinese*' in this context is a noun. Large vocabulary participants' productive knowledge of adjectives appeared to be more established and grammatically appropriate. To illustrate, participant L1 wrote, "She bought the *beautiful* pink dress yesterday", and participant L4 produced, "Fred gave a *beautiful* speech." These written sentences reveal that productive knowledge of affixation results from a continual learning process resulting from exposure to the target language in context.

Adverbs

Notably, the adverbial suffix *-ly* was recalled and used correctly by nine out of the twelve participants and by at least some participants at all vocabulary sizes. Among low vocabulary participants, two participants (S1 and S4) could recall an adverbial suffix *-ly*. Only participant S1 could write a sentence using the adverbial suffix *-ly* ("The turtles walk *slowly*"). This suggests that the recall and use of the *-ly* suffix can be problematic for low vocabulary EFL participants, given that they do not know its adverbial syntactic nature. For instance, participant S4 failed to use the adverbial suffix *-ly* in context ("She is *lovely*").

Sentence patterns show the progressive nature of adverbial suffix acquisition across vocabulary sizes. Participant M2 wrote, "She is singing *happily*", while participant M4 wrote, "Ticha walk *perfectly*." In comparison, three large vocabulary participants were able to recall and produce the adverbial suffix *-ly*. Participant L1 wrote, "I *rarely* read a book", while L3 produced, "I can see you *clearly*" and participant L4 composed the meaningful sentence, "This restaurant is *highly* recommended."

The participants' ability to recall and use an adverbial suffix was restricted to *-ly*, perhaps because it shows very high productivity and can be freely attached to any adjectives to create a new word of an adverbial class (e.g., popular–popularly, and final–finally). However, some participants, particularly smaller vocabulary participants, misconceived the adverbial *-ly* suffix (Level 3) due to the homograph of the adjectival *-ly* suffix (Level 5). For example, participant S4 wrote, "She is *lovely*", and participant M3 produced, "My pets are *lovely*." This suggests that the acquisition of syntactic functions and use of the adverbial suffix can be problematic for EFL learners with inadequate exposure to syntactic knowledge of affixes.

Discussion

The current study used the word family paradigm (Bauer/Nation 1993) to examine whether patterns of affix learning could form the basis for a taxonomy of affix acquisition. The results revealed a taxonomic hierarchy in Thai EFL participants' affix acquisition. Thai participants showed better awareness of affix knowledge on the RAK test compared to the LPAK task. Like the acquisition of vocabulary knowledge, this could be explained by the incremental continuum of the learning process (Nation 2013). More specifically, the LPAK task may have inflicted a much heavier processing demand on Thai EFL than the RAK test. It is also feasible that the productive use of affixes may not be established unless receptive knowledge is fully mastered. This taxonomic acquisition pattern implies that receptive affix knowledge enhances productive affix knowledge, which continues to grow gradually throughout the secondary school in Thai EFL participants.

The results reveal a strong pattern of affix knowledge acquisition at both education levels, but overall performance was significantly higher for USS students compared to LSS students. Specifically, it was shown that inflectional affixes are acquired before derivational affixes. Moreover, derivational affixes are acquired following a syntactic (i.e., linguistic) class order rather than the order predicted by a primarily psycholinguistic-determined word-family acquisition process (Bauer/Nation 1993). Derivational affix acquisition began with prefixes, then progressed to verbs, nouns, adverbs, and adjectives, as indicated by the combined average performance on the receptive and productive affix knowledge tasks. The qualitative results also confirm the syntactic pattern of affix acquisition; i.e., larger vocabulary participants generate more complex syntactic patterns of affixations and words than their smaller vocabulary peers. Therefore, the complexity of syntactic patterns reinforces the concept of cumulative acquisition.

Measures of receptive and productive affix knowledge used in the current study reveal varying degrees of affix knowledge. The receptive test reflects a learner's ability to recognise the form and meaning of an affix from the given alternatives. The productive task measures a learner's ability to draw on different types of knowledge, including cognitive knowledge and metacognitive strategies to relate meaning and form of the affix in unprompted contexts. The productive task also assesses a learner's ability to generate an affixation (word) and use it in a meaningful sentence. From a lexical perspective, the productive task is more difficult than the receptive task because producing semantic and syntactic affixation in spontaneous contexts generates greater processing demands than recognising the form and meaning of affixes. Indeed, receptive affix knowledge advances productive affix knowledge. Therefore, the productive use of an affix may not be established unless receptive affix knowledge is fully mastered. Spontaneous contexts also require additional consideration of grammatical functions and use (Nation 2013).

Productive use of an affix is built on receptive affix knowledge. The current study illustrates that knowledge of affixes on productive tasks requires a higher degree of mastery than receptive tasks. In fact, some receptive knowledge of affixes may plateau and fossilise before being mastered. Examples of affixes that may be fossilised in EFL contexts are *-i* (e.g., Israeli) and *-ite* (e.g., chalcopyrite), because these affixes are used in specific settings or disciplines. Indeed, several affixes were not mastered by Thai EFL participants during their secondary school year, and advanced learners may also fail to fully master some affixes.

The results also demonstrate that knowledge of the form and meaning of an affix is an essential element for the use of affixations. The Thai EFL participants showed a stronger recognition of form and meaning of the target affix than the ability to use affixations in genuine contexts, which is consistent with previous reports (Nation 2013). The current results suggest that productive use of an affix may not occur unless a particular affix is fully mastered, which is also consistent with previous studies showing that awareness of the form and meaning of the affix is a critical pathway to productive use (Laufer/Goldstein 2004).

The results support the growing acquisition of morphological patterns or structures, which lead to improved LPAK performance. The use of affixes to generate affixations or whole words in the context of sentence production is initially more advanced and complex for inflections. Additionally, prefixes are performed better initially, before a learner progresses to improved suffix performance. This developmental process of affix acquisition could be explained by linguistic and psycholinguistic characteristics of word family criteria (Bauer/Nation 1993). Derivational affixes, such as *-able*, *-ee*, *-ness*, are developed after inflectional affixes *-s*, *-ed*, *-ing*. That is, derivational affixes work across syntactic categories and indicate semantic and syntactic relations within the word. By contrast, inflectional affixes never adjust syntactic classes of the word, but rather indicate semantic and syntactic relations within a sentence.

Thai EFL participants demonstrate a stronger awareness of prefixes than suffixes, perhaps because processing prefixes involves orthographic and semantic transparency. Prefixes, in contrast to suffixes, have a peripheral position in the word form, which make them similar to inflectional affixes (Zirkel 2010) and easier to acquire. Furthermore, prefixes are typically word-class preserving (except, of course, a few prefixes such as *en-* as in encouragement and *ac-* as in accommodation). Nonetheless, suffixes involve both syntactic and semantic properties and therefore require awareness of their use within a sentence. Moreover, suffixes involve understanding functions; that is, knowledge of where and how new suffixation is located and used in a sentence. For example, *-ness* is added to an adjective like *sadness* and *happiness* but not a verb like *agreeness*.

The qualitative analysis of large and small vocabulary size participants resulted in a cross-sectional representation of the ongoing affix acquisition process in EFL participants. The productive task was the focus of this analysis. The results revealed a novel taxonomy of criteria for productive affix knowledge. Specifically, a continuum of affix learning was observed along the inflectional and derivational dimension.

One account for this pattern of development is that inflectional and derivational affixes require distinct processing demands. From a psycholinguistic perspective, inflectional affixes are attached to a base word as the whole word route (i.e., accessing the complex word as a whole). In contrast, derivational affixes are multi-affix additions to a base word, namely via a decomposition route (i.e., accessing the complex word via its morphological components). This affix combination depends on the Parsability Complexity-Based Ordering. That is, morphological complexity increases from the innermost to the outermost suffixes, and affix combinations typically occur step-by-step. Less parsable affixes cannot be added to more parsable affixes since this would lead to difficulty in processing. For instance, if the adverbial form of the base word 'create' is required, the learner must add an adjectival suffix *-ive* before producing the correct form of an adverb by attaching a suffix *-ly* to the adjectival base (create-creative-creatively). However, if the whole word route is used, the learner fails the task, producing an ungrammatical form such as *creately.*

Regarding linguistic characteristics, inflectional affixes never adjust the syntactic property of the word to which they are attached. Instead, the inflectional affixes affirm a close rule-based process, which allows the affix to be freely added to new lexical items to generate new forms of the word, irrespective of the change of a word class (i.e., *he uses a pencil,* or *he used a pencil*). Conversely, derivational affixes work across syntactic categories, generating new syntactic forms of the word; for example, *use-usable*, *develop-development*, *happy-happily.* This may require a heavier processing demand to cope with the use of knowledge of syntactic and semantic properties of the affix in sentence production.

The results also indicate a pattern of cumulative affix acquisition, whereby participants with a larger lexicon show more advanced patterns of affixation on productive tasks across the continuum of inflectional to derivational affixes. Beginning with inflectional affixes, for instance, the inflectional form *-est* resulted in the following responses: "*This is a biggest mango.*" → "*My house is the biggest in the world.*" → "*This is the biggest house I have ever seen.*" These sentence structures were produced by a small, a medium and a large vocabulary participant, respectively. While all three participants understood how to produce the affix *-est* in context, the level of productivity was proportionate to the participant's vocabulary size, as corroborated by the length of a sentence.

Similarly, in the context of derivational affixes, participants with a larger vocabulary size generate more productive sentences. The derivational prefix *re-* resulted in the following responses: "*She is rewrite a novel.*" → "*Author rewrite his novel.*" → "*Ray just recreated that artwork*," from a small, a medium and a large vocabulary participant, respectively. They show the advancing level of precision, as measured by the grammatically and semantically appropriate correctness of the response. With reference to suffixes, the development of a derivational affix occurs at a later stage, so that productivity is proportionate to the vocabulary size of a learner. Such progression can manifest within the derivational suffix *-er*: "*I am a reader*." → "*A writer is writing a book.*" → "*The English teachers at my school are kind.*" These structural patterns of productive use, which were observed in participants with small, medium and large vocabulary sizes, respectively, highlight the gradual acquisition of a derivational suffix throughout the language learning process.

There are three explanations for the observed order of derivational affixes or affix learning. The first is the concept of word family criteria (Bauer/Nation 1993), which argues that new forms of a morphologically complex word are acquired and possibly stored mentally, based on psycholinguistic criteria of the word family: frequency, regularity, predictability, and productivity. The current results demonstrate that regularity, including orthographic and semantic transparency, has a greater facilitative influence on affix acquisition, especially on derivational prefixes, than productivity, predictability, and frequency. However, the hierarchy of the acquisition of derivational suffixes based on psycholinguistic criteria of word family is ambiguous. This is perhaps because Bauer and Nation's (1993) list of affixes aims to provide the basis for the teaching and learning of affixes for learners with receptive knowledge, especially for reading. Consequently, the psycholinguistic characteristics of derivational suffixes in production are unclear. Thus, the influence of the word family criteria on the productive affix knowledge tasks remains tentative, and the pattern of results observed in the LPAK task provides only a partial picture of the possible effect of psycholinguistic factors. Further research into these affix knowledge aspects would afford greater insights into the role of psycholinguistic factors in affix learning in EFL learners.

A second explanation of the relationship between affix knowledge and vocabulary size is derived from linguistic characteristics. Bauer and Nation (1993) hypothesised that the size of one's affix knowledge base is directly proportionate to the size of one's lexicon. According to this view, participants with a large vocabulary size can see the relationship between a base word (form) and its derived forms from a morphologically complex word and, thus, can produce more grammatically correct affixations semantically appropriate in genuine contexts. According to this argument, vocabulary size is ostensibly feeding into the participant's ability to parse sentences into word parts, thereby increasing affix knowledge.

A third explanation is the concept of the cognitive load of lexical processing. The current results show that Thai EFL participants performed best on verbs, followed by nouns, adjectives, and adverbs. These findings are consistent with previous research, which generally indicates that verbs and nouns are easier to acquire than adjectives and adverbs (Schmitt/Zimmerman 2002), which may reflect the variability of syntactic characteristics of derivational suffixes. First, most base words (stems) are typically verbs; thus, EFL participants did not have to produce derived forms to supply grammatically appropriate verbs. Moreover, only one single processing is required to transform nouns into adjectives (*use-useful*), whereas dual processing (*use-useful-usefully*) is necessary for adverbs. In this regard, seeing the relationship between the base word 'use' and the suffix *-ful* as an adjective-forming derivative may not guarantee awareness of the use of the suffix *-ly* as an adverb-forming derivative. An alternative explanation is that the syntactic characteristics of verbs and nouns carry semantic information; i.e., verbs typically represent actions, while nouns often refer to names of people, places, and things.

The qualitative analyses performed in the current study revealed that affix task performance shows a particular developmental pattern of affix learning. Consistent with Bauer and Nation's (1993) concept of word family and previous studies (Hayashi/Murphy 2011; Schmitt/Zimmerman 2002; Sukying 2017, 2018), the participants' performance on both receptive and productive affix knowledge tasks indicated that inflectional affixes were acquired before derivational affixes, and prefixes were better known than suffixes. However, derivational suffixes showed different correctness rates according to their syntactic class. On the receptive affix knowledge task, verbal suffixes were performed better than nominal suffixes, adjectival suffixes, and adverbial suffix performance. Productive affix knowledge task performance showed the same pattern of learning with the order of adverbial and verbal suffixes interchanged.

Both the current data and the word family criteria support the claim that linguistic and psycholinguistic characteristics influence affix learning. However, psycholinguistic characteristics appear to influence the recognition of affixes rather than the production of affixes. With reference to Bauer and Nation's (1993) criteria of affix levels, regularity, including orthographic and semantic transparency, appears to have a more facilitative effect on the recognition of affixes than productivity, frequency, and predictability. Despite the psycholinguistic criteria of the word family rendering the pattern of affix learning on productive tasks unclear, the data show the syntactic classes that individual affixes carry have a facilitative effect of the production of affixations. Hence, participants may need to draw on different types and degrees of knowledge, including cognitive ability and metacognitive strategies, to merge or parse language to discern the relationship between base forms and their inflections and/or derivatives. Consequently, the access/retrieval process and contextual use of a new syntactic form require heavier cognitive and metacognitive demands in productive affix knowledge tasks, such that inadequate vocabulary size and education levels result in poorer performance.

Conclusion

This research examined whether a taxonomy of affix learning could be drawn from Thai EFL participants' affix task performance and explored the nature of the taxonomic criteria involved from linguistic and psycholinguistic perspectives. To achieve this, the participants' responses to affix knowledge tasks were analysed following Bauer and Nation's (1993) levels of affixes. The results indicated a five-stage taxonomy of affix acquisition, beginning with inflections and continuing to derivational affixes, starting with prefixes, then verbs, nouns, and, finally, adjectives and adverbs. In addition, both linguistic and psycholinguistic factors influenced Thai EFL participants' affix acquisition. Importantly, an affix is morphosyntactic and, thus, the nature of affix acquisition is lexically linguistic *per se*. Therefore, the syntactic characteristics of affixes associated with the formation of morphologically complex words influence the order of affix acquisition. Indeed, the results revealed that some syntactic categories of the affix are acquired and developed before others.

The results also show that receptive affix knowledge promotes productive affix knowledge and the five-stage taxonomy of affix acquisition is acquired at different speeds and varying levels throughout secondary school. This is consistent with the claims of previous studies that inflectional affixes are acquired and developed before derivational affixes (Anglin 1993; Hayashi/Murphy 2011; Mochizuki/Aizawa 2000; Nagy *et al.* 1993; Nation 2013; Schmitt/Meara 1997; Schmitt/Zimmerman 2002; Tyler/Nagy 1989; Sukying 2017, 2018, 2020; Zimmerman 2009; Zyzik 2009). This study also indicates that the notion of word family is crucial for teaching and learning morphologically complex words.

Overall, the discovery of a taxonomy of affix acquisition can form the foundation for revolutionary new pedagogical paradigms and research methodologies, as well as vocabulary assessment. Critically, the current study provides evidence that affix knowledge is a facilitative mechanism for vocabulary acquisition and growth.

The qualitative analysis demonstrated the mutual reinforcement of affix knowledge and vocabulary size and showed that Thai EFL participants' affix knowledge is directly proportional to their vocabulary size. Larger vocabulary participants produced more advanced and complex grammatical patterns of affixations than their smaller vocabulary peers. This result is also consistent with previous claims that understanding the syntactic behaviour of affixes contributes to a learner's vocabulary knowledge in context (Mochizuki/Aizawa 2000; Richards 1976; Webb 2005, 2008).

Nevertheless, it should be noted that, in the current study, the data were collected at a single point in time (a cross-sectional approach), meaning that the results only provide insights into participants' abilities on the day of testing, which may be affected by extraneous factors, such as fatigue, stress or motivation. Second, causal inferences cannot be made due to the absence of experimental manipulation of affix conditions within the current study. Finally, the measure of productive affix knowledge created and developed in the present study used the levels of word family formation suggested by Bauer and Nation (1993), and no other explanatory frameworks were used. In addition, the findings may not be generalizable beyond the Thai culture, and the education level was also restricted to secondary school.

To conclude, at present, there is a pressing need for longitudinal research to investigate the pattern of affix acquisition in EFL learners. It would also be useful to explore whether the current findings are replicated in different educational settings, such as at the university level. Future studies might use the current research design in different cultural and educational contexts to further increase our understanding of the affix learning process and its role in vocabulary development.

References

Anglin, Jeremy 1993. Vocabulary Development: A Morphological Analysis. *Monographs of the Society for Research in Child Development, Serial No. 238,* 58/10, 1-165.

Baker, Mark 1985. The Miror Principle and Morphosyntactic Explanation. *Linguistic Inquiry*, 16/3, 375-415.

Bauer, Laurie / Nation, Paul 1993. Word Families. *International Journal of Lexicography,* 6/4, 253-279.

Carlisle, Joanne F. 2000. Awareness of the Structure and Meaning of Morphologically Complex Words: Impact on Reading. *Reading and Writing,* 12/3, 169-190.

Carlisle, Joanne F. 2003. Morphology Matter in Learning to Read: A Commentary. *Reading and Writing,* 12/3, 169-190.

Carlisle, Joanne F. / Katz, Lauren 2006. Effects of Word and Morphemic Familiarity on Reading of Derived Words. *Reading Psychology,* 24/3, 291-322.

Claravall, Eric Blancaflor 2016. Integrating Morphological Knowledge in Literacy Instruction: Framework and Principles to Guide

Special Education Teachers. *Teaching Exceptional Children,* 48/4, 195-203.

Corson, David 1995. *Using English Words.* Dordrecht: Kluwer Academic Publishers.

Ford, Martin / Davis, Matthew H. / Marslen-Wilson, William 2010. Derivational Morphology and Base Morpheme Frequency. *Journal of Memory and Language*, 63/1, 117-130.

Gardner, Dee 2007. Validating the Construct of Word in Applied Corpus-based Vocabulary Research: A Critical Survey. *Applied Linguistics,* 28/2, 241-265.

Hay, Jennifer 2002. From Speech Perception to Morphology: Affix-ordering Revisited. *Language*, 78/3, 527-555.

Hay, Jennifer / Plag Ingo 2004. What Constrains Possible Suffix Combinations? on the Interaction of Grammatical and Processing Restrictions in Derivational Morphology. *Natural Language & Linguistic Theory*, 22/3, 565-596.

Hayashi, Yoko / Murphy, Victoria 2011. An Investigation of Morphological Awareness in Japanese Learners. *Language Learning,* 39/1, 105-120.

Henriksen, Birgit 1999. Three Dimensions of Vocabulary Development. *Studies in Second Language Acquisition,* 21/2, 303-317.

Kim, Cholo 2013. Vocabulary Acquisition with Affixation: Learning English Words based on Prefixes & Suffixes. *Second Language Studies,* 31/2, 43-80.

Kuo, Li-jen / Anderson, Richard C. 2006. Morphological Awareness and Learning to Read: A Cross-language Perspective. *Educational Psychologist*, 41/3, 161-180

Laufer, Batia 2017. From Word Parts to Full Texts: Searching for Effective Methods of Vocabulary Learning. *Language Teaching Research,* 21/1, 5-11.

Laufer, Batia / Goldstein, Zahava 2004. Testing Vocabulary Knowledge: Size, Strength, and Computer Adaptiveness. *Language Learning,* 54/3, 399-436.

Laufer, Batia / Nation, Paul 1999. A Vocabulary-size Test of Controlled Productive Ability. *Language Testing,* 16/1, 33-51.

Lieber, Rochelle 2010. *Introducing Morphology.* Cambridge: Cambridge University Press.

Manova, Stela / Aronoff, Mark 2012. Modeling Affix Order. *Morphology*, 20/1, 109-131.
McBride-Chang, Catherine / Wagner, Richard K. / Muse, Andrea / Chow, Bonnie W-Y / Shu, Hua 2005. The Role of Morphological Awareness in Children's Vocabulary Acquisition in English. *Applied Psycholinguistics,* 26/3, 415-435.
Mitchell, Alison / Brady, Susan 2014. Assessing Affix Knowledge Using both Pseudowords and Real-word Measures. *Topics in Language Disorders,* 34/3, 210-227.
Mochizuki, Masamichi / Aizawa, Kazumi 2000. An Affix Acquisition Order for EFL Learners: An Exploratory Study. *System,* 28/2, 291-304.
Nagy, Wiliam E. / Carlisle, Joanne F. / Goodwin, Amanda P. 2014. Morphological Knowledge and Literacy Acquisition. *Journal of Learning Disabilities,* 47/1, 3-12.
Nagy, Wiliam E. / Diakidoy, Irene-Anna N. / Anderson, Richard C. 1993. The Acquisition of Morphology: Learning the Contribution of Suffixes to the Meanings of Derivatives. *Reading Behavior,* 25/2, 155-170.
Nagy, Wiliam E. / Herman, Patricia A. 1987. Breadth and Depth of Vocabulary Knowledge: Implications for Acquisition and Instruction. In M. G. McKeown & M. E. Curtis (eds), *The Nature of Vocabulary Acquisition*. Hillsdale, NJ: Erlbaum, 19-35
Nation, Paul 2013. *Learning Vocabulary in Another Language* (2 ed.). Cambridge: Cambridge University Press.
Nation, Paul & Beglar, David 2007. A Vocabulary Size Test. *The Language Teacher,* 31/7, 9-13.
Pacheco, Mark / Goodwin, Amanda P. 2013. Putting two and two together: Middle School Students' Morphological Problem-solving Strategies for Unknown Words. *Journal of Adolescent & Adult Literacy,* 56/7, 541-553.
Paribakht, Tahereh / Wesche, MMarjorie 1997. Vocabulary Enhancement Activities and Reading for Meaning in Second Language Vocabulary Acquisition. In J. Coady & T. Huckin (eds), *Second Language Vocabulary Acquisition: A Rationale for Pedagogy*. Cambridge: Cambridge University Press, 174-200.

Read, John 1993. The Development of a New Measure of L2 Vocabulary Knowledge. *Language Testing,* 10/3, 355-371.

Read, John 2000. *Assessing Vocabulary.* Cambridge: Cambridge University Press.

Reichle, Erik D. / Perfetti, Charles 2003. Morphology in Word Identification: A Word Experience Model that Counts for Morpheme Frequency Effects. *Scientific Studies of Reading,* 7/3, 219-237.

Richards, Jack. 1976. The Role of Vocabulary Teaching. *TESOL Quarterly,* 10/1, 77-89.

Sasao, Yosuke / Webb, Stuart 2017. The Word Part Levels Test. *Language Teaching Research,* 21/1, 12-30.

Schmitt, Norbert 2010. *Researching Vocabulary: A Vocabulary Research Manual.* Basingstoke, UK: Palgrave Macmillan.

Schmitt, Norbert / Meara, Paul 1997. Research Vocabulary through a Word Knowledge Framework: Word Associations and Verbal Suffixes. *Studies in Second Language Acquisition,* 19/1, 17-36.

Schmitt, Norbert / Zimmerman, Cheryl Boyd 2002. Derivative Word Forms: What Do Learners Know? *TESOL Quarterly,* 36/2, 145-171.

Singleton, David 2000. *Language and the Lexicon: An introduction.* London, UK: Oxford University Press.

Stauffer, Russell 1942. A Study of Prefixes in the Thorndike List of Establish a List of Prefixes that Should be Taught in the Elementary School. *The Journal of Educational Research,* 35/6, 453-458.

Sukying, Apisak 2017. The Relationship between Receptive and Productive Affix Knowledge and Vocabulary Size in an EFL Context. PhD Thesis, The University of Sydney, Sydney.

Sukying, Apisak 2018. Investigating Receptive and Productive Affix Knowledge in EFL Learners. In D. Hirsh (ed.) *Explorations in Second Language Vocabulary Research.* Bern: Peter Lang, 183-218.

Sukying, Apisak 2020. Word Knowledge through Morphological Awareness in EFL Learners. *TESOL International Journal,* 15/1, 74-85.

Thorndike, Edward L. 1941. *The Teaching of English Suffixes.* New York: Teachers College, Columbia University.

Tyler, Andrea / Nagy, Wiliam E. 1989. The Acquisition of English Derivational Morphology. *Journal of Memory and Language,* 28/6, 649-667.

Web, Stuart 2005. Receptive and Productive Vocabulary Learning: The Effects of Reading and Writing on Word Knowledge. *Studies in Second Language Acquisition*, 27/1, 33-52.

Web, Stuart 2008. Receptive and Productive Vocabulary Sizes of L2 Learners. *Studies in Second Language Acquisition*, 30/1, 79-95.

Wei, Zheng 2015. Does Teaching Mnemonics for Vocabulary Learning Make a Difference? Putting the Keyword Method and the Word Part Technique to the test. *Language Teaching Research,* 19/1, 43-69.

Wei, Zheng / Nation, Paul 2013. The Word Part Technique: A Very Useful Vocabulary Teaching Technique. *Modern English Teacher,* 22/1, 12-16.

Zimmerman, Cheryl Boyd 2009. *Word Knowledge: A Vocabulary Teacher's Handbook*. New York: Oxford University Press.

Zirkel, Linda 2010. Prefix Combinations in English: Structural and Processing Factors. *Morphology*, 20/1, 239-266.

Zyzik, Eve 2009. Noun, Verb, or Adjective? L2 Learners' Sensitivity to Cues to Word Class. *Language Awareness*, 18/2, 147-164.

Section 2
Studies of Language and Education

Makoto Takenoya

Pronunciation Instructions in Japanese Elementary School English Textbooks

Introduction

With the increasing significance of English in various fields, such as economics, politics, and entertainment, English has established its status as a lingua franca. To communicate in English with people from diverse first language (L1) backgrounds, it is important to develop English pronunciation skills (Derwing/Munro 2015; Levis 2018). Levis (2018) argued that it was unlikely for non-native speakers to communicate effectively when their pronunciation level fell below a certain threshold, no matter how rich knowledge of vocabulary and grammar they had. Despite being a crucial component of communication, pronunciation had long been marginalised in applied linguistics and TESOL (Derwing/Munro, 2015). Over the past few decades, however, increasing numbers of research on pronunciation have been conducted, contributing to suggest new directions in approaches to pronunciation instruction (PI) (Derwing/Munro 2015; Thomson/Derwing 2015).

There have been a variety of research themes concerning PI. One of them is about the goal of pronunciation teaching and learning. In the past, as in the heyday of audiolingualism, the goal of pronunciation was mastering native-like pronunciation, where any trace of a learner's L1 was viewed as an error to be corrected. However, this goal is now regarded as unrealistic and even unnecessary in light of the status of English as a lingua franca. Most researchers have agreed that the goal of pronunciation should be intelligible pronunciation (e.g., Derwing/Munro 2015; Levis 2005).

Another controversial topic on PI is concerned with which pronunciation features, segments or suprasegmentals, should be prioritised in PI. Some researchers have insisted on the importance of segmental features, or individual sounds of vowels and consonants (e.g., Jenkins 2000, 2002; Saito 2014; Saito/Lyster 2012). Jenkins (2002), for instance, proposed the Lingua Franca Core (LFC), a list of pronunciation features that affect intelligibility, insisting that segmental features play a crucial role in communication. On the contrary, others have suggested that suprasegmental features, such as stress and intonation, should be prioritised in PI (e.g., Hahn 2004; Tanner/Landon 2009). However, the balance and the interaction between segments and suprasegmentals are now considered important, instead of treating them separately (Zielinski 2015).

Recent studies have paid attention to the pronunciation teaching techniques and activities (e.g., Lee/Plonsky/Saito 2020). Traditional techniques employed in PI, such as minimal-pair drills, have often been criticised for being mechanical and non-communicative. Recently, however, studies have proposed teaching techniques that integrate pronunciation-related activities with other classroom activities to make them more communicative and enjoyable (Celce-Murcia *et al.* 2010; Zhang/Baills/Prieto 2020). A question to be addressed next should be exploring whether such suggestions are reflected in teaching materials.

There have been a large number of analyses for teaching materials from various perspectives, including lexical use (e.g., Brown 2011; Matsuoka/Hirsh 2010), cultural content (e.g., Davidson/Liu 2020; Shin/Eslami/Chen 2011), and pragmatics (e.g., Handford 2010). However, pronunciation is an under-researched area in the field of textbook analysis (Harwood 2014), and only a handful of studies have investigated the area. Therefore, the current study analyses pronunciation instructions in English textbooks used in Japanese elementary schools and discusses their approaches and challenges.

Literature Review

Segments vs. suprasegmentals

With the paradigm shift in the teaching of English as a Second or Foreign Language (ESL/EFL), pronunciation instruction (PI) has been integrated into the communicative approach (Murphy/Baker 2015). Along with this, the focus of PI has shifted primarily to the intelligibility from the nativelikeness (Derwing 2017). Increasing numbers of researchers on PI have explored what pronunciation features influence intelligibility. These features can be categorised to either segmental (i.e., individual sounds of vowels and consonants) or suprasegmental features (i.e., features across syllables, words, and phrases, such as stress, rhythm, and intonation).

There has been a controversial debate about which pronunciation feature should be prioritised in PI, segmental or suprasegmental features (Wang 2020; Sun/Saito/Tierney 2020). Two opposing views have arisen from this debate: some researchers suggest that segmental features should be taught preferentially in PI because they have significant impact on intelligibility (e.g., Jenkins 2002; Munro/Derwing 2006) while others argue suprasegmental features should be prioritised in PI (e.g., Tanner/Landon 2009). However, Zielinski (2015) took a different view to these arguments, questioning the assumption that segmental and suprasegmental features are independent. She argues that both features are equally important and should always be seen together. This chapter will discuss the three views.

Traditionally, pronunciation materials and curricula begin with small segmental elements and move on to larger suprasegmental features (Wang 2020). One of the advantages of segmental-based PI is its teachability (Jenkins 2000; Setter/Jenkins 2005). All segmental elements can be easily explained with three phonetic characteristics: the organ of articulation, the place of articulation, and the manner of articulation (Ladefoged 2003). In addition, many researchers have purported that segments have greater impacts on learners' intelligibility, and thus should be given emphasis in PI. Collins and Mees (2013), for instance, listed seven pronunciation elements they considered important for intelligibility, in the order in which they should be taught. The top five on the list were different segmental features and the last two were suprasegmental features. They highlighted the importance of accurate segmental production for intelligibility. In addition, Jenkins (2000, 2002), proposing the LFC, pointed out that the most common cause for communication breakdowns among non-native speakers of English was segmental problems, such as substituting a sound with another (e.g., /f/→/p/).

On the other hand, others have suggested that suprasegmental features, such as intonation and rhythm, should be given precedence over segments in PI. Fraser (2001), for example, argued that suprasegmental features should be taught first because native listeners tend to comprehend one's speech, relying on suprasegmentals rather than segmental features. She insisted that native listeners would not be able to understand what the speaker if the stress pattern is incorrect, even if pronouncing consonants appropriately. Tanner and Landon (2009) and Chela-Flores (2001) concurred with this view, and they suggested suprasegmental features should be given emphasis and priority in PI. Similarly, recent studies have supported to the importance of proper suprasegmental production to intelligibility (e.g., Gordon/Darcy 2016; Isaacs/Trofimovich 2012).

Although the segmental/suprasegmental debate arose from the premise that segmental and suprasegmental characteristics are separate, Zielinski argued that this dichotomy was inappropriate (Zielinski 2008, 2015). Zielinski (2015) claimed that the dichotomy ignored the possible interaction between the two features. Instead of debating whether it is more important to teach segmental or suprasegmental features, she insisted that both features should be regarded as part of an integrated and interactive system in which one may influence the other (Zielinski 2015). Thus, both pronunciation features should be treated as interactive and dependent features.

English education in Japanese elementary schools

In Japan, foreign language education in elementary schools was first launched in 2002 as part of the education for international understanding. Although each school could choose a language to be taught, due to the strong social demand, the majority of elementary schools selected English as the target language. In 2011, with the implement of the new course of study (i.e., the Japanese government's curriculum guideline), English language education officially started as Foreign Language Activities, which were offered for one-class hour per week (35-class hours per year) in the fifth and sixth grades. Though it was titled Foreign Language Activities, the Ministry of Education, Culture, Sports, Science and Technology (MEXT) demanded that English should be selected as the target language. In 2014, MEXT declared 'English Education Reform Plan corresponding to Globalization', which aimed to promote English education in elementary schools. The plan proposed the introduction of Foreign Language Activities in the third and fourth grades, and that of English as a compulsory subject in the fifth and sixth grades. Based on the plan, in 2017, MEXT announced the latest course of study, which has been implemented since April 2020.

Since English is a new subject for elementary schools, many teachers are worried about teaching the subject. Yonezaki, Tara, and Tsukuda (2016), who explored Japanese elementary school teachers' anxiety about teaching English, concluded that many elementary school teachers tend to have anxieties against their own pronunciation skills, teaching materials, and assessment. The findings were basically in line with previous surveys conducted in ESL (e.g., Burns 2006; Foote/Holtby/Derwing 2011) and EFL settings (e.g., Kirkova-Naskova *et al.* 2013). Considering the fact that considerable numbers of elementary school teachers in Japan lack confidence in teaching English, researchers including Uchida and Sugimoto (2020) have proposed the expansion and improvement of pre- and in-service teacher trainings to incorporate areas where teachers feel less confident.

In addition to the lack of training, a lack of teaching materials likely leads to the lack of confidence in instruction (Burns 2006; Foote *et al.* 2011). In Japan, since the textbook is the main teaching materials and plays a fundamental role in classroom, researchers have analysed textbooks from various perspectives. With regard to English textbooks, previous textbook analyses have covered a wide range of topics, including vocabulary (e.g., Brown 2011; Matsuoka/Hirsh 2010), cultural content (e.g., Davidson/Liu 2020; Shin *et al.* 2011), and pronunciation (e.g., Sugimoto/Uchida 2018; Ueda/Otsuka 2010). However, while there have been numerous analyses for high school textbooks, little analysis has been conducted on elementary school English textbooks as English recently became a subject. Hence, the present study will explore all the MEXT-approved English textbooks used in Japanese elementary schools.

Methodology

Research questions

The aim of the current study is to investigate pronunciation instructions treated in Japanese elementary school English textbooks. By exploring pronunciation features and activity types in the textbooks, the author addresses the following two research questions:

1. What aspects of pronunciation are covered in the Japanese elementary school English textbooks?
2. How are the pronunciation-related activities and descriptions presented in the Japanese elementary school English textbooks?

Textbooks for analysis

The current study analysed all seven government-approved English textbook series used that were published in 2020 and have been used in Japanese elementary schools since April 2020. Each series consists of two volumes corresponding to the two grades, fifth- and six-grade. One thing to note is that all are designed based on the Course of Study established by MEXT. The latest version of the guidelines (MEXT, 2017) describes the speech sounds that should be instructed in English classroom: i) contemporary standard pronunciation, ii) sound changes that result from the linking of words, iii) basic stresses in words, phrases, and sentences, iv) basic sentence intonation, v) basic pauses in sentences. Additionally, it includes instruction in letter-to-sound correspondences, emphasis on the differences between English and Japanese.

The target materials of the current study are 14 textbooks (seven series × two grades). Table 1 is a list of seven textbook series with the title followed by the publishers.

Abbr.	Textbook	Publisher
BS	Blue Sky elementary	Keirinkan
CJ	Crown Jr.	Sanseido
HWG	Here We Go!	Mitsumura Tosho
JS	Junior Sunshine	Kairyudo
JTE	Junior Total English	Gakko Tosho
NH	New Horizon Elementary English Course	Tokyo Shoseki
OW	One World Smiles	Kyoiku Shuppan

Table 1. Elementary school English textbooks analysed in the current study.

Procedure

To investigate which pronunciation features are covered in the textbooks, referring to MEXT (2017), Sugimoto and Uchida (2018) and Ueda and Otsuka (2010), the author prepared a list of seven labels: segments, word stress, sentence stress and rhythm, intonation, connected speech, pause, and oral interpretation. For example, the label *intonation* was prepared for practice focusing on the relation between tones and sentence types (e.g., using rising intonation on a yes-no question) and nucleus placement, and the label *oral interpretation* represents pronunciation practice that requires learners to consider how to make speech that matches meanings and emotions (Asano 2005).

The author, subsequently, conducts a pilot analysis with one of the textbook series, New Horizon (NH), which is the most common English textbook used in elementary schools in Japan. The aim of the pilot analysis is to ascertain whether the prepared labels are appropriate for the textbook analysis. The author asked a Japanese teacher of English to be a coder to assign the prepared label to pronunciation activities and descriptions in NH. Comparing how the author (Coder A) and the other coder (Coder B) assign the labels to each instance, the inter-coder reliability is confirmed with descriptive statistics. This process makes the analysis more reliable and ascertains the validity of the labels.

After the pilot study, the author peruses every textbook and collected and compiled a list of all the exercises and descriptions relevant to pronunciation. For each exercise or description, the textbook information (series, grade, page) and the contents were recorded. Each instance was then assigned a label out of the seven pronunciation features.

For the second research question, 'How are the pronunciation features presented in the Japanese elementary school English textbooks?', activity types were analysed in the same procedure as that of pronunciation features. Pronunciation activities are classified into the following three labels: *controlled*, *guided*, or *free*, as shown in Baker (2014) and Sugimoto and Uchida (2018). Based on Baker (2014), controlled activities were defined as activities where teachers take control and can predict the students' responses (e.g., repetitions, minimal pair drills, reading aloud). In contrast, free activities are communicative activities where students have room for creativity and their responses are unpredictable (e.g., role-play, discussions). Guided activities are semi-controlled and situated between the two (e.g., information gap activities, interviews). After coding and categorising the data, the frequencies of occurrence are counted and statistically analysed with tabulation. Figure 1 shows an example of labelling.

How do you say the following words in Japanese? Listen to the English pronunciation and discuss what is different with your friends. Listen again, being careful which part is strongly pronounced.
(*Original directions in Japanese; translated by the author)

Label:
Pron. feature: *Word stress*
Activity type: *Guided*

Figure 1. Labelling example 1 (JTE, 5th grade, p.15).

Data analysis

Before analysing all the textbooks, to ascertain the validity and reliability of the analysis, the author (Coder A) and the Japanese teacher of English (Coder B) respectively assigned the prepared labels to pronunciation activities and descriptions in New Horizon (NH), which is the most common English textbook series used in Japanese elementary schools. After coding the pronunciation contents of NH, using SPSS, inter-coder reliability was tested. Table 2 is the cross-tabulation table which indicates how the coders assigned labels of pronunciation features to pronunciation-related items in NH. The intercoder reliability was described with Cohen's kappa in Table 3. Table 3 illustrates symmetric measures of the agreement between the coders. It indicates the value of kappa is .803, and that of approximate significance is under .001, which means the level of agreement is strong and the intercoder reliability is substantial.

		Coder A								
		o	i	ii	iii	iv	V	vi	vii	total
	o	0	7	0	0	0	0	0	0	7
	i	1	67	0	0	0	0	0	0	68
	ii	0	0	7	0	0	0	0	0	7
	iii	0	0	0	2	0	0	0	0	2
Coder B	iv	0	0	0	0	1	0	0	0	1
	v	0	0	0	0	0	1	0	0	1
	vi	0	0	0	0	0	0	0	0	0
	vii	0	0	0	0	0	0	0	9	9
	total	1	74	7	2	1	1	0	9	95

*o: one coder assigned a label but the other did not, i: segments, ii: word stress, iii: sentence stress and rhythm, iv: intonation, v: connected speech phenomena, vi: oral interpretation.

Table 2. Cross-tabulation table of the pilot coding for pronunciation features in NH.

	Value	Asymp. Std. Error[a]	Approx. T[b]	Approx. Sig.
Measure of agreement *Cohen's kappa*	.803	.066	12.970	<.001
Number of valid cases	95			

*a. Not assuming the null hypothesis; b. Using the asymptotic standard error assuming the null hypothesis.

Table 3. Symmetric measures of agreement for pronunciation feature in NH.

In the same process, the intercoder reliability for activity types was tested. Table 4 describes how the coders assigned labels of pronunciation activity types to pronunciation-related items in NH, and Table 5 indicates measures of the agreement for activity types between the coders. It shows the value of kappa is .627, and its significance level is under .001, which means the level of agreement is strong and the intercoder reliability for activity types is high enough. These results encouraged the author to code the contents of the other textbook series. After the pilot study, the author analysed all the textbooks alone.

		Coder A				
		no*	controlled	Guided	free	total
	no*	0	7	0	0	7
	controlled	1	77	1	0	79
Coder B	guided	0	0	9	0	9
	free	0	0	0	0	0
	total	1	84	10	0	95

*no: one coder assigned a label but the other did not.

Table 4. Cross-tabulation table of the pilot coding for activity types in NH.

	Value	Asymp. Std. Error[a]	Approx. T[b]	Approx. Sig.
Measure of agreement *Cohen's kappa*	.627	.110	7.864	<.001
Number of valid cases	95			

*a. Not assuming the null hypothesis; b. Using the asymptotic standard error assuming the null hypothesis.

Table 5. Symmetric measures of agreement for activity types in NH.

Results

The current study aims to investigate what pronunciation features are covered and how they are treated in Japanese elementary school English textbooks. The study analysed all seven government-approved textbook series published in 2020. In this chapter, the author firstly presents the descriptive findings, where you can see how many pages treat pronunciation activities and involve pronunciation notes. Following the overall findings, details are illustrated by pronunciation aspects from segmental to suprasegmental features.

Overall findings

The current study first analysed the scope of pronunciation aspects in each textbook series. For a quantitative comparison, the occurrences of each pronunciation aspects were counted. Table 6 illustrates how many pages treat pronunciation activities or involve pronunciation notes, such as articulation tips. As shown in Table 6, the number of occurrences largely varies among textbook series. New Horizon (NH) and Here We Go! (HWG) treat six and five types of pronunciation aspects respectively, while Crown Jr. (CJ) addresses only two types of pronunciation features: segments and intonation.

Moreover, Table 6 highlights the most frequent pronunciation features for each textbook series in bold. Segments is the most frequent category in six textbook series, except for Blue Sky (BS), which treats sentence stress and rhythm most.

Textbook (*n* of aspects; occurrences)	**Pronunciation aspects (*n* of occurrences)**
BS (4; 62)	**Sentence stress & Rhythm (45)**, Segments (13), Intonation (3), Word stress (1)
CJ (2; 34)	**Segments (32)**, Intonation (2)
HWG (5; 56)	**Segments (21)**, Sentence stress & Rhythm (17), Intonation (9), Connected speech (7), Word stress (2)
JS (4; 30)	**Segments (21)**, Intonation (5), Word stress (3), Sentence stress & Rhythm (3)
JTE (4; 113)	**Segments (110)**, Word stress (1), Sentence stress & Rhythm (1), Intonation (1)
NH (6; 94)	**Segments (75)**, Oral interpretation (8), Word stress (7), Sentence stress & Rhythm (2), Connected speech (1), Intonation (1)
OW (4; 37)	**Segments (22)**, Sentence stress & Rhythm (10), Intonation (4), Word stress (1)

Table 6. The numbers of occurrences of pronunciation aspects in the textbooks.

These activities were assigned labels for activity type as well. As summarised in Table 7, controlled activities were dominant across all the textbook series. Only four textbook series treat guided activities: 15 in OW, 10 in NH, 2 in CJ, and 1 in JTE. Free activities were not found in any textbooks.

Textbook (*n* of occurrences)	**Activity Type (*n* of occurrences)**
BS (62)	Controlled (62), Guided (0), Free (0)
CJ (34)	Controlled (32), Guided (2), Free (0)
HWG (56)	Controlled (56), Guided (0), Free (0)
JS (30)	Controlled (30), Guided (0), Free (0)
JTE (113)	Controlled (112), Guided (1), Free (0)
NH (94)	Controlled (84), Guided (10), Free (0)
OW(37)	Controlled (22), Guided (15), Free (0)

Table 7. Distribution of pronunciation instructions by activity type.

Segments

Although the amount of treatment greatly varies, all the Japanese elementary school English textbooks treat segmental features. Segments are the most frequent pronunciation feature treated in the textbooks, while BS treats it as the second most frequent features. In this section, the author describes which vowels and consonants are addressed and how they are treated in the textbooks.

Vowels and diphthongs

The most frequent vowels covered in the textbooks are /æ/, /ɛ/, /ɪ/, /ɒ/, and /ʌ/ corresponding the alphabet letters of A, E, I, O, and U. All the textbook series treat these vowel sounds. In most cases, they are treated in phonics training. Phonics is a way of instructing reading focusing on letter-sound correspondences. Figure 2 is an example of alphabet jingle, which is commonly used in phonics training, adapted from NH, 5th grade, p.96. For this activity, teachers let students pronounce each alphabet letter's name, sound, and a word that includes a target sound after the recordings or teachers (e.g., A, /æ/, /æ/, ant; E, /ɛ/, /ɛ/, elephant).

Figure 2. Phonics training (NH, 5th grade, p.96).

In addition, two textbooks, NH and BS, offer phonetic contrast trainings, such as minimal-pair activity (e.g., cap-cup-cop, pin-pen-pan in NH, 6th grade, p.92).

Table 8 shows which vowels and diphthongs are covered in each textbook series. The mark ✓ in the table means the textbook series treats the sound, while the mark - means that it does not include the sound as a target sound. As shown in Table 8, most of the strong vowels are covered in the textbooks. However, /iː/ and /uː/ are treated only in two textbook series: New Horizon (NH) and One World Smiles (OWS), and /ɔː/ and /ɑː/ are only in Here We Go! (HWG). Moreover, no textbook series explain the schwa /ə/, /ər/ and a weak vowel /ʊ/. Additionally, the diphthongs /eɪ/ and /aɪ/ are treated in three textbooks (NH, OW, BS), and /oʊ/ is presented in two (NH, OW), though other diphthong sounds are ignored in the textbooks.

Sound	Example	BS	CJ	HWG	JS	JTE	NH	OW
/i:/	Heat	-	-	-	-	-	✓	✓
/ɪ/	Pig	✓	✓	✓	✓	✓	✓	✓
/ɛ/	Pet	✓	✓	✓	✓	✓	✓	✓
/æ/	Cat	✓	✓	✓	✓	✓	✓	✓
/ə/	wooden	-	-	-	-	-	-	-
/ʌ/	Love	✓	✓	✓	✓	✓	✓	✓
/ər/	First	-	-	-	-	-	-	-
/u:/	moon	-	-	-	-	-	✓	✓
/ʊ/	Look	-	-	-	-	-	-	-
/ɔ:/	Torn	-	-	✓	-	-	-	-
/ɒ/	Pot	✓	✓	✓	✓	✓	✓	✓
/ɑ:/	Park	-	-	✓	-	-	-	-
/eɪ/	Pain	✓	-	-	-	-	✓	✓
/aɪ/	Write	✓	-	-	-	-	✓	✓
/aʊ/	Down	-	-	-	-	-	-	-
/oʊ/	Road	-	-	-	-	-	✓	✓
/ɔɪ/	Boy	-	-	-	-	-	-	-
/ɪə/	Here	-	-	-	-	-	-	-
/eə/	Bear	-	-	-	-	-	-	-
/ʊə/	Pure	-	-	-	-	-	-	-
con-trast		*a					*b	

*a. /ʌ/-/æ/, /æ/-/ɒ/, /æ/- /ɪ/, /e/-/ɪ/, /e/-/ɒ/; b. /æ/-/ʌ/-/ɒ/, /ɪ/-/e/-/æ/

Table 8. English vowels and diphthongs covered in the textbooks.

Three textbook series (NH, JS and HWG) warn not to do vowel epenthesis, which is often seen among Japanese speakers of English. NH offers some examples of English words and the Japanese corresponding loan words to make students compare them and let them notice that the syllable structure of English is different from that of Japanese. For instance, the two-syllable English word ‘present’ is pronounced as a four-syllable word /pɯ.ɾe.zen.to/ in Japanese. JS tells not to insert /u/ sound like ball as /bɔ:lu/ and /o/ sound like bed as /bedo/. HWG warns not to pronounce the sound of ‘b’ as ‘bu’.

Consonants

Since phonics training is the most common pronunciation activity in the textbooks, most consonant sounds are covered as shown in Table 9. The table illustrates which consonant sounds are covered in each textbook. /ʃ/ and /ʧ/ sounds are treated in every textbook but JS, and a nasal sound /ŋ/ is covered only in two textbooks, NH and CJ. Furthermore, no textbook series include the sound of /ʤ/ (e.g., ju<u>dge</u>).

As syllable structure of English is different from that of Japanese and English allows consonant clusters of three consonants at onset and four at tail at maximum. NH, JTE, and BS treat the consonant cluster of 'wh', and NH includes that of 'st' as well.

Moreover, though English has some consonant sounds that do not exist in Japanese, the articulation of those sounds is largely ignored. JS and HWG explain how to articulate certain sounds. However, the explanations are too simple to instruct those pronunciations. Therefore, teachers need to know how to articulate those sounds correctly.

Four textbook series (JS, OWS, HWG and BS) present some similar sounds in one page to contrast them. The most frequent contrast is /ɹ/-/l/, which is thought as one of the most difficult sounds for Japanese EFL learners to pronounce (Saito 2014).

Sound	Example	BS	CJ	HWG	JS	JTE	NH	OW
/p/	pair	✓	✓	✓	✓	✓	✓	✓
/b/	bad	✓	✓	✓	✓	✓	✓	✓
/t/	tall	✓	✓	✓	✓	✓	✓	✓
/d/	dark	✓	✓	✓	✓	✓	✓	✓
/k/	cat	✓	✓	✓	✓	✓	✓	✓
/g/	good	✓	✓	✓	✓	✓	✓	✓
/f/	fine	✓	✓	✓	✓	✓	✓	✓
/v/	very	✓	✓	✓	✓	✓	✓	✓
/θ/	thing	✓	✓	✓	✓	✓	✓	✓
/ð/	this	✓	✓	✓	✓	✓	✓	✓
/s/	saw	✓	✓	✓	✓	✓	✓	✓
/z/	zoo	✓	✓	✓	✓	✓	✓	✓
/ʃ/	shape	✓	✓	✓	-	✓	✓	✓
/ʒ/	jam	✓	✓	✓	✓	✓	✓	✓
/h/	her	✓	✓	✓	✓	✓	✓	✓
/ʧ/	cherry	✓	✓	✓	-	✓	✓	✓
/ʤ/	judge	-	-	-	-	-	-	-
/m/	moon	✓	✓	✓	✓	✓	✓	✓
/n/	nail	✓	✓	✓	✓	✓	✓	✓
/ŋ/	sing	-	✓	-	-	-	✓	-
/l/	left	✓	✓	✓	✓	✓	✓	✓
/ɹ/	right	✓	✓	✓	✓	✓	✓	✓
/w/	way	✓	✓	✓	✓	✓	✓	✓
/j/	you	✓	✓	✓	✓	✓	✓	✓
cluster		wh				wh	St wh	
articulation notes				*a	/f/, /v/ /ɹ/, /l/			
contrast		/s/- /θ/		/ɹ/-/l/ /s/-/ʃ/	*b			*c

*a. /f/, /v/, /θ/, /ð/, /s/, /ɹ/, /l/, /w/ *b. /p/-/b/, /t/-/d/, /k/-/g/, /s/-/z/, /f/-/h/, /f/-/v/, /m/-/n/, /ɹ/-/l/ *c. /p/-/b/, /b/-/v/, /t/-/d/, /k/-/g/, /s/-/z/, /s/-/θ/, /z/-/ð/, /ʧ/-/ʃ/, /m/-/n/, /ɹ/-/l/
Table 9. English consonants covered in the textbooks.

Word stress

Six textbook series, except for CJ, include either training or notes about word stress. However, the number of them is limited. Most of the textbooks offer a handful of word stress examples. Some textbooks show the stressed part, making it bold (e.g., homework, school bag, newspaper from HWG, 5th grade, p.54), while others use the stress mark on the stressed part of a word itself (e.g., Ápril, Julý from JS, 5th grade, p.13). OW deals with word stress, but does not refer to specific words in the textbook.

NH, JTE and BS treat word stress training, while the others present some word stress examples. NH includes a word stress training, where students listen to words and fill the circle of stressed part as examples (e.g., for the word monkey, as the first syllable is stressed, students fill the first circle black). Figure 3 is a part of the page that includes the word stress training. JTE and BS present eight and six Japanese loan words respectively to let the students listen and compare them to their corresponding English words. For example, the word, orange, is a first-syllable-stressed word in English while it is pronounced as a second-syllable-stressed word [o.ɾén.ʑi] in Japanese. Figure 4 is a part of the training from BS.

Figure 3. Word stress training (NH, 5th grade, p.94).

Figure 4. Word stress training (BS, 5th grade, p.50).

Sentence stress and rhythm

English is a stress-timed language, where the stressed syllables are pronounced at approximately regular intervals, while Japanese is a mora-timed language, in which every mora is pronounced equally. Therefore, it is important for Japanese EFL learners to learn English sentence stress, or rhythm. Nonetheless, most of the textbooks treat a little or completely ignore this significant feature. HWG offers nine examples of sentence stress, making the stressed word bold (e.g., How do you spell it? from HWG, 5th grade, p.22). NH and JS present some examples with dots or stress marks on the stressed words respectively (see Figures 5). They explain that you can make your pronunciation more English-like if you pronounce the stressed part strongly. Additionally, NH and JTE give some simple sentence examples to let students think of where sentence stresses are placed. OWS also treats sentence stress but does not refer specific sentences in the student's textbook.

While these textbooks touch on sentence stress in only a few pages, BS put great focus on sentence stress and rhythm (45 out of 62 pages that treat PI). BS offers chant practice as a sentence stress training at every unit all over the textbooks. Figure 6 is one of the chant practices from BS, 6th grade. For this practice, students are asked to read dialogue aloud with chant rhythm, paying attention to English rhythm.

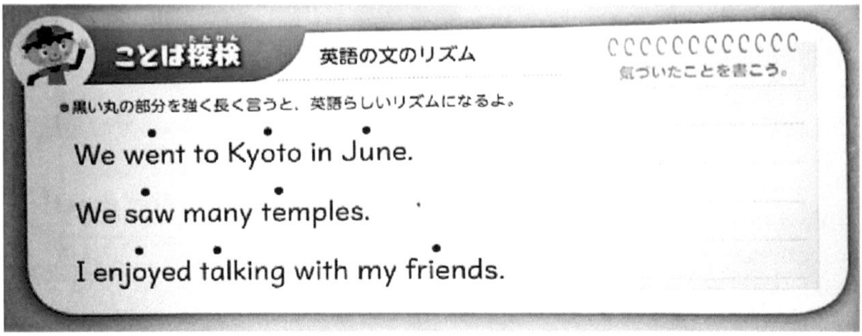

Figure 5. Sentence stress and rhythm training (NH, 6th grade, p.70).

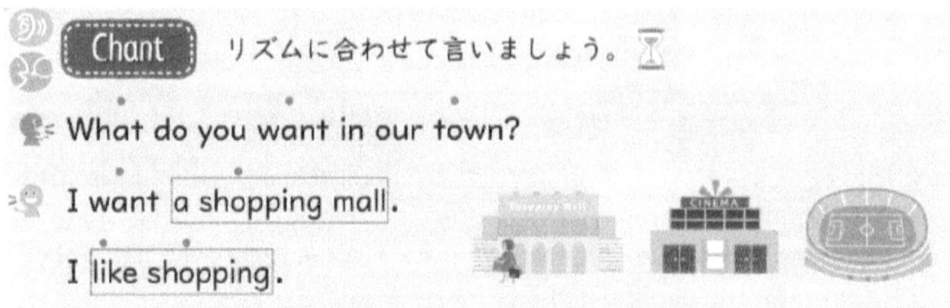

Figure 6. Chant practice (BS, 6th grade, p.34).

Intonation

Although all the textbooks include notes about intonation to some degree, only JTE has an intonation activity, where students listen to recorded speech and draw diagonal arrows in blanks. Figure 7 is a part of the intonation activity.

Figure 7. Intonation activity (JTE, 5th grade, p.15).

Other textbooks present some example sentences with a diagonal arrow (e.g., Let's pronounce sentences with paying attention to the intonation of the underlined parts. I can swim. (↘) - Can you swim? (↗) from JS, 5th grade, p.29). All the textbooks only provide examples and expect students to deduce the rules, not giving the rules explicitly. Furthermore, the treatment of intonation is restricted to the relation between tones and sentence types, and nucleus placement is not treated at all.

Connected speech

Though the connected speech phenomena appear everywhere in English and plays an important role in making English rhythm, only two textbook series, NH and HWG, give examples of connected speech. Out of the changes in connected speech, linking at a word-final consonant followed by a vowel is treated the most often (e.g., Stand‿up /stænd ʌp/ [stændʌp] from NH, 5th grade, p.64), and followed by elision (e.g., Sit‿down /sɪt daʊn/ [sɪdaʊn] from NH, 5th grade, p.64) and coalescent assimilation (e.g., Would‿you /wəd ju/ [wəʒu] from HWG, 5th grade, p.98). Figure 8 is a part of the page that includes a raising-awareness practice towards connected speech phenomena.

Figure 8. Connected speech activity (NH, 5th grade, p.64).

Oral interpretation

Although oral interpretation originally means the oralisation of literature to communicate meaning to audience, Asano (2005) defines it as how to make voice that matches meaning and emotion. Ueda and Otsuka (2010) interpret the idea and incorporate it to their textbook analysis. They set three elements for oral interpretation: 1) explanations about the interpretation of emotion or feelings (e.g., make a speech with emotion), 2) voice control instruction that pays attention to the listeners (e.g., make a speech with good speed for the listeners to follow), and 3) instructions that recognise speech is for listeners (e.g., attract audience while speech), and they exclude activities that do not have these instructions. The current study follows this idea.

Only NH has oral interpretation instructions. One is about making a pause so that audience can understand easily while a speech, another is about the speech speed and the voice clarity. NH includes instructions that raise awareness towards voice, expression, and speed at every speech activity, while the other textbook series did not include it. Figure 9 is one of the instructions for speech, which tells students to make a pause and think out of the way of speaking so that audience can understand what the speaker says easily.

Figure 9. Tips for speech (NH, 6th grade, p.64).

Discussion

The results of the current study illustrate what pronunciation features are covered and how they are presented in the Japanese elementary school English textbooks. The textbook analysis allows us to know how differently they are approached in each textbook. Key findings of specific importance and interest are:

1. The textbooks, except for Blue Sky (BS), treat segmental features more than suprasegmentals.
2. Controlled activity is the most common activity type adopted in the textbooks.
3. There is a limited number of explicit explanations about pronunciation in the textbooks (e.g., how to articulate the sound of /r/).

Each finding is discussed below and linked to the relevant previous studies to explain and comprehend the results from the current study.

Segmental features over suprasegmentals

For RQ1, 'What aspects of pronunciation are covered in the Japanese elementary school English textbooks?', the descriptive analysis clearly illustrates what types of pronunciation features are treated in the textbooks. It reveals that most of the Japanese elementary school English textbooks analysed in this study treat segmental features more than suprasegmentals, while Blue Sky (BS) devotes more pages to suprasegmental (i.e., sentence stress and rhythm) activities more than those of segments. Thus, though the treatment of each feature varies depending on the textbooks, the treatment of suprasegmentals is comparatively limited. Although there is an ongoing debate on which pronunciation features, segmental or suprasegmental, should be prioritised in PI, given the positive impact of suprasegmental instruction on intelligibility (e.g., Gordon/Darcy 2016) and the complementary role of the two features (Zielinski 2015), it might help to incorporate more activities and descriptions on suprasegmental aspects in the textbooks.

As for segmental features, they are mainly dealt with in two ways within the textbooks analysed: one is the use of phonics to draw learners' attention to the correspondences between spelling and pronunciation, and the other is to contrast vowel or consonant pairs, such as /æ/-/ɒ/ and /l/-/r/, which are known to be problematic for Japanese learners (Saito 2014; Saito/Lyster 2012), by utilising minimal pairs or simply treating contrastive pairs in the same page. Regarding the use of phonics, as MEXT (2017) stated that many junior high school students in Japan have difficulties with the phonetic differences between Japanese and English and with the relationship between English spelling and pronunciation, it seems worthwhile to use phonics technique to help them understand the relationship between spelling and pronunciation in English. However, a closer look at the results shows that only a handful of vowel sounds are treated, namely /æ/, /ɛ/, /ɪ/, /ɒ/ and /ʌ/ sounds corresponding to the letters of A, E, I, O and U and a few other vowels, whereas most of the consonant sounds are covered (see Tables 8 and 9).

Although Sugimoto and Uchida (2018) pointed out that Japanese junior high school English textbooks they analysed treated segmental features based on error prediction from contrastive analysis and did not consider functional load, the Japanese elementary school English textbooks analysed in the current study deal with vowels and consonants with higher functional loads (e.g., /æ/-/ʌ/-/ɒ/ and /p/-/b/). Conversely, although a schwa /ə/, which was regarded important for intelligibility and should not be substituted with another vowel (Jenkins 2002), was treated in most of the junior high school textbooks Sugimoto and Uchida analysed, no elementary school English textbooks analysed in this paper deal with it.

With regard to suprasegmental features, in the textbooks analysed, they are less treated in the elementary school English textbooks, compared to segmentals. Two features of specific interest, intonation and sentence stress and rhythm, are discussed here. As for intonation, it is the only suprasegmental feature that is treated in all the textbook series. All the treatments for intonation are about the relation between tones and sentence types, and there are no activities or notes for nucleus placement. Although nucleus placement plays a significant role on intelligibility (Hahn 2004; Jenkins 2000), it is neglected in the textbooks. This would be because it seems more complicated for elementary school pupils to understand and may require more knowledge to teach, compared to the relation between tones and sentence types. For nucleus placement, you firstly need to understand the distinction between content and function words, then apply the rules to each sentence, determining the placement of nucleus in the context, and finally pronouncing it with appropriate pitch movements. Therefore, though nucleus placement is important for intelligibility, as Hahn and Jenkins noted, considering the learners' age and cognitive abilities, the timing of teaching may need to be carefully taken into account. We should take a balance between what should be taught and what can be taught.

Another remarkable suprasegmental feature is sentence stress and rhythm. The feature is treated in the six-textbook series, except CJ. Particularly, BS treats it more than segments, to which the other textbook series spare the most pages. BS deals with the feature in 45 out of 62 activities and notes, while CJ does not treat it at all. The amount of its treatment varies depending on the textbook series. Thus, as each textbook places different emphasis on different pronunciation features, it is likely that learners' acquisition of pronunciation and phonological knowledge will vary greatly depending on the textbook used. Ueda and Otsuka (2010), who analysed the pronunciation instruction in Japanese junior high school English textbooks, presented a similar conclusion. They reported that most of the basic phonetic features, both on segments and suprasegmentals, were covered in each textbook series they analysed (i.e., the Japanese government-approved junior high school English textbooks). Nonetheless, they found a considerable variation across textbook series in terms of the number of explicit instructions, and therefore, concluded that the pronunciation knowledge that students gain would vary greatly depending on which textbook series they used.

Pronunciation activities in the textbooks

With regard to RQ2, how are the pronunciation features presented in the Japanese elementary school English textbooks? Each activity was assigned three activity-type labels: controlled, guided, and free. The descriptive analysis illustrates that the controlled activity is the most common and dominant across all the textbooks, whereas there are few guided activities and no free activities specifically targeting pronunciation development. Most of the pronunciation activities are designed to require learners to listen and repeat. Historically speaking, these findings are not surprising. Over the centuries, PI has employed imitative-intuitive and analytic-phonetic approaches, where controlled activities have been at the core of teaching (Baker 2014). Though these controlled techniques are often criticised for not being communicative, it has been reported that they have positive effects on phonological improvement (e.g., Saito 2014) and intelligibility development (e.g., Jenkins 2000). They are therefore not to be disregarded.

Nonetheless, according to Baker (2014), the dominance of controlled activities might lead to monotonous boring PI and raise a concern that less application of guided or free activities could prevent learners from developing comprehensible pronunciation in authentic conversations. Furthermore, research has revealed that the combined application of controlled and communicative activities has greater effects on targeted features than the use of controlled activities alone (Saito/Lyster 2012). Hence, it should be important to offer a variety of activities, not controlled activities alone as BS, HWG, and JS offer. The word stress training (Figure 1) presents a good example of guided activities that help make PI more communicative and promote active participation of learners. Although a few guided activities are included in a few textbook series, free activities are not found in the textbooks. Since MEXT has always suggested that teaching in the classroom should be textbook-driven, and teachers have no choice but to use one of the textbooks analysed in the current study, the textbook itself should include more guided and free activities on pronunciation.

A possible problem caused by a lack of explicit explanations

Another characteristic observed in the current study is a lack of explicit explanations in the textbooks. The lack of explanations could cause problems in teaching pronunciation. As the textbooks offer little or no explicit explanations about pronunciation, teachers are expected to possess pertinent knowledge on pronunciation in order to make effective use of the textbooks as PI materials. However, as the majority of elementary school teachers in Japan have not received training on teaching English, they have little knowledge on English pronunciation, nor are they confident in PI (Yonezaki *et al.* 2016). To help such teachers successfully instruct pronunciation, it might be better to have explicit explanations in the textbooks.

For example, most of the textbooks do not include any explanations on how to pronounce an English sound, though two textbook series, HWG and JS, present articulation notes (e.g., you should put the tip of your tongue to the back of your front teeth when pronouncing /l/). If teachers who lack the knowledge of English articulation use the textbook with no explanation, they may fail PI. To take another example, although the term syllable is never explained in the textbooks, several textbooks offer exercises of word stress and/or sentence stress using circles corresponding to syllables (e.g., Monkey ●○). Syllables are a difficult concept for young learners to understand, perhaps even for non-native English teachers as well. Therefore, without the knowledge of syllables, teachers may not be able to lead such activities successfully, nor can they likely create similar activities themselves. Sugimoto and Uchida (2018) expressed a similar opinion on to lack of explicit explanations in the junior high school textbooks. They reported that the textbooks they analysed had little explicit explanation concerning pronunciation. Although English teachers in Japanese junior high schools are specialists in English language teaching, unlike general teachers working in elementary schools, Sugimoto and Uchida argued that some teachers might have difficulties in teaching pronunciation due to the lack of explanation about pronunciation. This would be more so for generalist teachers working in elementary schools.

Conclusion

The content analysis of Japanese elementary school English textbooks reported findings of specific significance and interest. One of the main findings is that segmental features are treated more than suprasegmental features. More specifically, it reveals that some pronunciation features with high functional load, including the sound of /ə/ and nucleus placement, are not treated in the textbooks. It is found that controlled activity is predominant across the textbook series. Another characteristic found in the analysis is the lack of explicit explanations about pronunciation.

These findings could suggest possible ways to improve pronunciation activities and descriptions in the future textbooks. Suggestions include incorporating more suprasegmental features, such as sentence stress and rhythm training, and selecting pronunciation items based on functional loads as well as error predictions from contrastive analysis. Another suggestion is the incorporation of a wider range of pronunciation activities. The more communicative the activities are, the more difficult teachers deal with. However, they could help learners raise awareness about English pronunciation, which might enable them to understand the differences between English and Japanese pronunciation and improve their pronunciation skills. Moreover, if the textbooks had more explicit explanations, it could help teachers and learners comprehend English pronunciation more easily.

The study contributes to describing what pronunciation features are covered and how they are treated in the textbooks. However, the study still had a few limitations, even after careful consideration of the methodology. Firstly, although the author analysed all the MEXT-approved English textbooks used in Japanese elementary schools, only students' textbooks were explored for the current study. Teachers' guides and audio materials, accompanying the textbooks, were not analysed. While the content analysis of students' textbooks presented meaningful findings, analysing teachers' guides and audio materials would provide further information concerning how teachers utilise the textbooks for pronunciation instruction.

Future studies could build solidly on the current study by investigating how the textbooks are used for pronunciation instruction in real classrooms. With a teacher and student participant group, examining how they use textbooks for pronunciation teaching and learning would help understand the role of textbooks as pronunciation materials. Harwood (2014) called such studies as the textbook analysis at the level of consumption. Studies at the level of consumption, including classroom observation and teacher/student survey on pronunciation instruction, would contribute to developing the area and improving future materials.

References

Asano, Keizo 2005. Research on Teaching Oral Interpretation (1): Towards Autonomous Oral Interprets. *Nanzan Junior College Journal.* 33, 243-257.

Baker, Amanda 2014. Exploring Teachers' Knowledge of Second Language Pronunciation Techniques: Teacher Cognitions, Observed Classroom Practices, and Student Perceptions. *TESOL Quarterly*. 48, 136-163.

Brown, Dale 2011. What Aspects of Vocabulary Knowledge to Textbooks give attention to? *Language Teaching Research*. 15, 83-97.

Burns, Anne 2006. Integrating Research and Professional Development on Pronunciation Teaching in a National Adult ESL Program. *TESL Reporter*. 39/2, 34-41.

Celce-Murcia, Marianne / Brinton, Donna / Goodwin, Janet / Griner, Barry 2010. *Teaching Pronunciation: A Course Book and Reference Guide (2nd ed.)*. Cambridge: Cambridge University Press.

Chela-Flores, Bertha 2001. Pronunciation and Language Learning: An Integrative Approach. *International Review of Applied Linguistics*. 39/2, 85-101.

Collins, Beverly / Mees, Inger 2013. *Practical Phonetics and Phonology: A Resource Book for Students* (3rd ed.). New York, NY: Routledge.
Davidson, Rachel / Liu, Yongcan 2020. Reaching the World Outside: Cultural Representation and Perceptions of Global Citizenship in Japanese Elementary School English Textbooks. *Language, Culture and Curriculum*. 33/1, 32-49.
Derwing, Tracey 2017. The Efficacy of Pronunciation Instruction. In Kang, Okim / Thomson, Ron / Murphy, John (eds) *The Routledge Handbook of Contemporary English Pronunciation*. New York, NY: Routledge, 320-334.
Derwing, Tracey / Munro, Murray 2015. *Pronunciation Fundamentals: Evidence-based Perspectives for L2 Teaching and Research*. Amsterdam: John Benjamins.
Foote, Jennifer / Holtby, Amy / Derwing, Tracey 2011. Survey of the Teaching of Pronunciation in Adult ESL Programs in Canada, 2010. *TESL Canada Journal*. 29, 1-22.
Fraser, Helen 2001. *Teaching Pronunciation: A Handbook for Teachers and Trainers. Three Frameworks for an Integrated Approach*. Canberra, ACT: Department of Education Training and Youth Affairs.
Gordon, Joshua / Darcy, Isabelle 2016. The Development of Comprehensible Speech in L2 Learners: A Classroom Study on the Effects of Short-term Pronunciation Instruction. *Journal of Second Language Pronunciation*, 2/1, 56-92.
Hahn, Laura 2004. Primary Stress and Intelligibility: Research to Motivate the Teaching of Suprasegmentals. *TESOL Quarterly*. 38/2, 201-223.
Handford, Michael 2010. *The Language of Business Meetings*. Cambridge: Cambridge University Press.
Harwood, Nigel 2014. *English Language Teaching Textbooks: Content, Consumption, Production*. London: Palgrave Macmillan.
Isaacs, Talia / Trofimovich, Pavel 2012. Deconstructing Comprehensibility: Identifying the Linguistic Influences on Listeners' L2 Comprehensibility ratings. *Studies in Second Language Acquisition*. 34/3, 475-505.

Jenkins, Jennifer 2000. *The Phonology of English as an International Language*. Oxford: Oxford University Press.

Jenkins, Jennifer 2002. A Sociolinguistically Based, Empirically Researched Pronunciation Syllabus for English as an International Language. *Applied Linguistics*. 23/1, 83-103.

Kirkova-Naskova, Anastazija / Tergujeff, Elina / Frost, Dan / Henderson, Alice / Kautzsch, Alexander / Levey, David / Murphy, Deirdre / Waniek-Klimczak, Ewa 2013. Teachers' Views on Their Professional Training and Assessment Practice: Selected Results from the English Pronunciation Teaching in Europe Survey. In Levis, John / LeVelle, Kimberly (eds) *Proceedings of the 4th Pronunciation in Second Language Learning and Teaching Conference August 2012*. Iowa: Iowa State University, 29-42.

Ladefoged, Peter 2003. *Phonetic Data Analysis: An Introduction to Instrumental Phonetic Fieldwork*. Oxford: Blackwell.

Lee, Bradford / Plonsky, Luke / Saito, Kazuya 2020. The Effects of Perception- vs. Production-based Pronunciation Instruction. *System*. 88, 102185.

Levis, John 2005. Changing Contexts and Shifting Paradigms in Pronunciation Teaching. *TESOL Quarterly*, 39/3, 369-377.

Levis, John 2018. *Intelligibility, Oral Communication, and the Teaching of Pronunciation*. Cambridge: Cambridge University Press.

Matsuoka, Warren / Hirsh, David 2010. Vocabulary Learning through Reaching: Does an ELT Course Book Provide Good Opportunities? *Reading in a Foreign Language*. 22, 56-70.

MEXT 2017. *Shogakko Gakushu Shido Yoryo* [Couse of Study for Elementary Schools]. Tokyo: Toyokan Shuppan.

Munro, Murray / Derwing, Tracey 2006. The Functional Load Principle in ESL Pronunciation Instruction: An Exploratory Study. *System*. 34, 520-531.

Murphy, John / Baker, Amanda 2015. History of ESL Pronunciation Teaching. In Levis, John / Reed, Marnie (eds) *The Handbook of English Pronunciation*. Upper Saddle River, NJ: Wiley-Blackwell, 36-65.

Saito, Kazuya 2014. Experienced Teachers' Perspectives on Priorities for Improved Intelligible Pronunciation: The Case of Japanese

Learners of English. *International Journal of Applied Linguistics*. 24, 250-277.

Saito, Kazuya / Lyster, Roy 2012. Effects of Form-focused Instruction and Corrective Feedback on L2 Pronunciation Development of /r/ by Japanese Learners of English. *Language Learning*. 62/2, 595-633.

Setter, Jane / Jenkins, Jennifer 2005. State-of-the-art Review Article. *Language Teaching*. 38/1, 1-17.

Shin, Jeeyoung / Eslami, Zohreh / Chen, Wen-Chun 2011. Presentation of Local and International Culture in Current International English-language Teaching Textbooks. *Language, Culture and Curriculum*. 24/3, 253-268.

Sugimoto, Junko / Uchida, Yoko 2018. How Pronunciation is Taught in English Textbooks Published in Japan. *Seishin Studies*. 130, 3-35.

Sun, Hui / Saito, Kazuya / Tierney, Adam 2020. A Longitudinal Investigation of Explicit and Implicit Auditory Processing in L2 Segmental and Suprasegmental Acquisition. *Studies in Second Language Acquisition*. ISSN 0272-2631. (In Press).

Tanner, Mark / Landon, Melissa 2009. The Effects of Computer-assisted Pronunciation Readings on ESL Learners' Use of Pausing, Stress, Intonation, and Overall Comprehensibility. *Language Learning & Technology*, 13/3, 51-65.

Thomson, Ron / Derwing, Tracey 2015. The Effectiveness of L2 Pronunciation Instruction: A Narrative Review. *Applied Linguistics*. 36/3, 326-344.

Uchida, Yoko / Sugimoto, Junko 2020. Non-native English Teachers' Confidence in Their Own Pronunciation and Attitudes Towards Teaching: A Questionnaire Survey in Japan. *International Journal of Applied Linguistics*. 30/1, 19-34.

Ueda, Hiroko / Otsuka, Tomomi 2010. An Analysis of Pronunciation Instruction in Japanese Junior High School English Textbooks: Indications from the Early Stage of Input. *Osaka Gakuin Daigaku Kiyo*. 7, 15-32.

Wang, Xue 2020. Segmental versus Suprasegmental: Which One is More Important to Teach? *RELC Journal*. doi:10.1177/0033688220925926

Yonezaki, Michi / Tara, Shizuya / Tsukuda, Yukiko 2016. Primary School Teachers' Anxiety about Teaching English as a Compulsory Subject and Teaching English to Middle-grade Students: Structuring and Transition. *JES Journal*. 16/1, 132-146.

Zhang, Yuan / Baills, Florence / Prieto, Pilar 2020. Hand-clapping to the Rhythm of Newly Learned Words Improves L2 Pronunciation: Evidence from Training Chinese Adolescents with French Words. *Language Teaching Research*. 24/5, 666-689.

Zielinski, Beth 2008. The Listener: No Longer the Silent Partner in Reduced Intelligibility. *System*. 36, 69-84.

Zielinski, Beth 2015. The Segmental/Suprasegmental Debate. In Levis, John / Reed, Marnie (eds) *The Handbook of English Pronunciation*. Upper Saddle River, NJ: Wiley-Blackwell, 397-412.

Textbooks Analysed in the Current Study

Allen, Tamai Mitsue et al. 2020. *New Horizon Elementary English Course 5*. Tokyo Shoseki.

Allen, Tamai Mitsue et al. 2020. *New Horizon Elementary English Course 6*. Tokyo Shoseki.

Kageura, Osamu et al. 2020. *Blue Sky Elementary 5*. Keirinkan.

Kageura, Osamu et al. 2020. *Blue Sky Elementary 6*. Keirinkan.

Kanamori, Tsuyoshi et al. 2020. *One World Smiles 5*. Kyoiku Shuppan.

Kanamori, Tsuyoshi et al. 2020. *One World Smiles 6*. Kyoiku Shuppan.

Koizumi, Masashi et al. 2020. *Here We Go! 5*. Mitsumura Tosho.

Koizumi, Masashi et al. 2020. *Here We Go! 6*. Mitsumura Tosho.

Sakai, Hideki et al. 2020. *Crown Jr. 5*. Sanseido.

Sakai, Hideki et al. 2020. *Crown Jr. 6*. Sanseido.

Yorozuya, Ryuichi et al. 2020. *Junior Sunshine 5*. Kairyudo.

Yorozuya, Ryuichi et al. 2020. *Junior Sunshine 6*. Kairyudo.

Yoshida, Kensaku et al. 2020. *Junior Total English 1*. Gakko Tosho.

Yoshida, Kensaku et al. 2020. *Junior Total English 2*. Gakko Tosho.

Rahma Fitriana / David Hirsh

EFL Learner Perceptions on Translanguaging

Introduction

Recent studies in applied linguistics have examined how globalisation alters society's language practices. The development on this issue has seen the shifts on the notion that language is discrete and tied to particular countries into a paradigm that language is better viewed from user's contextual practices (Valdes *et al.* 2015). This paradigm accepts multilingual practices as a common phenomenon and has provided insights about an approach utilising these complex linguistic resources to learn a second language (L2), called *translanguaging*. Translanguaging refers to a flexible use of multiple languages, which has been widely adopted into a teaching and learning strategy (Creese/Blackledge 2011). Consequently, the studies which attempt to understand and explore translanguaging and its application have been burgeoning.

EFL classrooms in Indonesia are good examples of a multilingual learning context as there are multiple languages practised as a medium of instruction (Kartika-Ningsih / Rose 2018). In the university's English subjects, teachers and students use English, Indonesian, and if they share similar cultural background, local languages (e.g., Javanese, Sundanese, Sasak) may also be a part of classroom conversation. As noted by scholars in multilingualism, learners bring their existing linguistic knowledge to language classrooms to make meaning (e.g., Baker/Wright 2017; Cenoz/Gorter 2015). However, in Mohamed's (2013) study, such a view seems to be irrelevant since the students supported English-only practices as opposed to their national language. In another case of translanguaging practice, Carroll and van den Hoven (2016) suggest that the overt use of Arabic in English classrooms is considered taboo.

A debate on the language use in Indonesian universities was more apparent in the recent years as the government encouraged English-medium instruction (EMI) at the tertiary level (Dewi 2017). The Indonesian educational authorities view English exposure as the key to prepare generations to compete in the ASEAN economic community (The Jakarta Post 2015). In line with this, The Ministry of Research, Technology, and Higher Education planned to make English interaction compulsory as English was considered a tool to access knowledge to foster the nation's economic development (Dewi 2017). Additionally, there was an institutional policy of internationalisation which is driven by university competition to pursue world-class status and it encourages courses to be fully delivered in English. Both policies were political and some universities take the internationalisation imperative by advising teachers to use English as medium of instruction (Walker *et al.* 2019), including in the General English subject. While different stakeholders in higher education sectors may indeed have different perceptions on appropriate medium of instruction, learners' voices are significant.

Learner perceptions on language teaching aspects could affect how they approach and take action in learning (Dörnyei 2010), yet these are often overlooked. Decisions on language use should be based not only on the university expectation and teachers' perspectives, but also on empirical evidence from the learners' side. The current study attempts to contribute to the body of literature exploring students' beliefs and perceptions on the use of translanguaging. In particular, it focuses on exploring how the university students, who were enrolled in the General English classroom, perceive translanguaging strategy performed by their course instructor.

Multilingual world and language learning

The term *bilingual* or *multilingual* refers to an ability to speak two or more languages in everyday practice (Grosjean 2012). There is no consensus on these two terms with regards to how many languages are used. However, they similarly represent a plurality of languages (Garcia/Wei 2014) and as the current study does not aspire to consider the number of languages and separate them, the term *multilingual* is used, thus *bilingual* is also entailed in the concept of *multilingual*. Multilingualism is not a new phenomenon, but in today's world, it is enhanced by globalisation, technological advancement, mobility and migration (Canagarajah 2007; Cenoz/Gorter 2015).

This increasingly multilingual world provides a lens to second language acquisition (SLA). In second or foreign language classrooms where two or more languages are widely spoken and teachers share a similar first language (L1) with students, dual language use occurs on a regular basis. Cahyani, de Courcy, and Barnett (2018), who carried out an ethnographic study in Indonesian tertiary bilingual classrooms, observed that learners bring Indonesian and their local language, Javanese, into an English learning, and use both languages along with English. In the country where English is taught as a foreign language (EFL), particularly in Indonesia, complex linguistic practices are also present (Kartika-Ningsih / Rose 2018; Walker *et al.* 2019), such as Javanese and Sundanese, which diverge in each local area. This situation depicts the multilingual nature of the classroom.

As the interaction of multiple languages takes place in language classrooms, students can utilise the space to mediate learning and develop new language practices (Valdes *et al.* 2015). Thus, it is reasonable to consider that multilingual practices in the community are everyday and legitimate. A myriad of research in linguistics supported the idea that the use of mixed languages is not only common, but also meaningful for language learning (e.g., Walker 2018; Woolard 2004).

Monolingual classroom in multilingual world

Schools often disregard the multilingual nature of classrooms and constrain language use into a single acceptable language in teaching and learning, which constitutes the target language (Klapwijk / van der Walt 2016). The current dominant teaching approach in second language learning employs monolingual norms (Baker/Wright 2017; Canagarajah 2007; Carroll / van den Hoven 2016). A group of prominent scholars in multilingualism, including Palmer *et al.* (2014), pointed out that teachers are often concerned about hybrid language practices and frame such practices as undesirable in the classroom. Other evidence of monolingual ideology in schools is reported by Carroll and van den Hoven (2016), who interviewed teaching personnel of higher education institutions in the United Arab Emirates. They revealed that incorporating Arabic in the English classroom was stigmatized as breaking the rule and even could jeopardise employees' positions. This phenomenon is also known as monolingual bias (May 2014), representing an attempt to unify communities through a single common language.

Garcia and Wei (2014) discuss that the monolingual classroom does not give a wide space for students to learn since they are imposed by strict language use and suffer from language injustice. In a more extreme sense, Douglas Fir Group (2016: 35) state that this deficit orientation is "setting up second language learners for failure", considering that EFL learners frequently draw from, and work on, their home language when learning the target language. Therefore, limiting L1 resources in classroom activities, despite learners' capacity to access and shuttle between multiple linguistic varieties, remains a questionable point within language learning.

The mismatch between a multilingual world and monolingual views in language learning has been a continuing discussion. A number of research articles have examined the need for SLA to transform the norm into a more contextual and interactional pedagogy (Cook 2001; Douglas Fir Group 2016; Firth/Wagner 1997; Hall/Cook 2012). Douglas Fir Group (2016), for example, articulate strongly the transdisciplinary perspectives to rethink SLA as learners develop language proficiency by reciprocally intersecting their native and target language. To address this issue, several teaching strategies have been developed, particularly suited to bi/multilingual contexts, including translanguaging.

Translanguaging

The use of translanguaging in classrooms is proposed by Garcia (2009) to redress the language inequalities that have been practiced in ESL/EFL contexts. Translanguaging is a process by which students and teachers engage in complex discursive practices that include all the language of students in a class in order to develop new language practices and sustain the old ones (Garcia/Wei 2014). This is claimed as a transformative pedagogy theory that alters the monolingual perspective into a multilingual perspective since students are allowed to use their home languages in the classroom.

Daniel and Pacheco (2016) state that translanguaging is comparable to code-switching. Yet, translanguaging goes beyond code-switching in a way that code-switching relates to language alternation of two different code systems in speaker's utterances, while translanguaging practices approve the flexibility of two or more language practices used without a sense of language separation. Figure 1 illustrates the different models of bilingualism within code-switching and translanguaging concepts.

In code-switching, the idea is taken from an external perspective, that is, the language itself, whereby people alternate between two autonomous languages. In contrast, translanguaging considers the speaker's internal perspective and regards a student's internalised linguistic knowledge as comprising features (F) of the speaker's full linguistic repertoire with a nominal number (n), but does not name L1 or L2 (Garcia/Kleyn 2016). The concept of two separated linguistic systems is not taken into account in the translanguaging paradigm; thus, all linguistic resources belong to one language system which the speakers can select and articulate flexibly. It is quite subtle, however, to distinguish between translanguaging and code-switching in practice, as the phenomenon of language use is rarely described from a multilingual speakers' internal view (Garcia/Wei 2014).

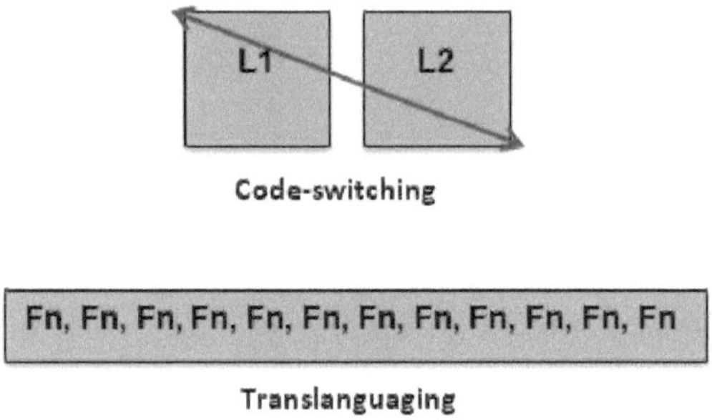

Figure 1. Differences between code-switching and translanguaging (Garcia/Kleyn 2016: 13).

There are several doubts which somewhat challenge translanguaging as a pedagogy. Involving learners' own language is considered as limiting target language exposure, and it is regarded unconstructive due to the notion that the more exposure to L2 is given, the better the target language proficiency will be (Doiz/Lasagabaster 2016; Liu/Zeng 2015; Oguro 2011). Luk and Lin (2015) observed that the Hong Kong government has blamed mixed-code teaching as the central issue contributing to students' falling achievement. This is in line with the argument of Han (2012) and Hoff (2013) who state that multilingual learners using different languages have lower academic achievement. Although the two latter studies were situated in young learner education, there are considerations for teaching and learning contexts in a general sense.

In the recent years, the translanguaging strategy is being seen more positively. A number of recent studies highlight that this strategy improves learners' understanding on the subject taught (e.g., Caruso 2018; Kleyn/Yau 2016; Rosiers 2017). Rosiers (2017) reported that the teacher and students were involved in a collaborative learning to negotiate and make meaning by switching between languages fluidly. This was better achieved in the class which was more open to other languages, creating more teacher-initiated translanguaging space to build upon students' full linguistic repertoire to comprehend the lesson. An action research study by Kartika-Ningsih and Rose (2018) in the Indonesian secondary school context support with Rosiers' (2017) findings. Kartika-Ningsih and Rose (2018) refer to this strategy as language shift, which scaffolds students' target language development significantly by making a shift between languages where appropriate. Added to this, translanguaging is also endorsed to give some positive impacts on classroom's social dimension. It can support teacher-student and student-student interactions (Ebe/Chapman-Santiago 2016; Martin-Beltran 2014; Thoms *et al.* 2005), enable students to express feelings and opinions (Garcia/Kleyn 2016; Mazak *et al.* 2016), enhance students' confidence to practice using the target language (Canagarajah 2011; Palmer *et al.* 2014), and empower students' multilingual identities (Creese/Blackledge 2015; Garcia-Mateus/Palmer 2017). Mazak *et al.* (2016), for instance, explored translanguaging in Puerto Rican classrooms and reported that the professor's translanguaging comment "You can say it in Spanish if you want" made students able to answer the question in Spanish when they were struggling to say it in English. The participants in Mazak *et al.*'s (2016) study regarded translanguaging as providing a secure space to engage in learning.

Learners' perceptions on language use

Perceptions in language learning are established under the umbrella term of beliefs, which belongs to one of the individual learner differences (Lightbown/Spada 2013). The definition of beliefs develops over time as does the approach to look at learners' beliefs. One of the significant publications in this area was Horwitz (1987), which defines beliefs as preconceived ideas on aspects of second language teaching and learning. In Horwitz's (1987) view, it is implied that a learner's belief exclusively lies within the learner's mind and is stable. Meanwhile Williams, Mercer, and Ryan (2015) suggest that beliefs can evolve over time. William *et al.*'s (2015) suggest that learners' beliefs do not only entail a cognitive dimension, but also a social construct (Barcelos 2003; White 2008) as learners interact with others and their own environment.

In the classroom contexts, Kalaja *et al.* (2016: 10) suggest that a learner's belief is a reflection on language learning and teaching aspects and assigns to these aspects "his or her own personal meanings". This contemporary definition is more contextual and dynamic in a sense that it offers a close relationship with other evolving terms of beliefs emerging in the literature, such as perceptions, attitudes, and ideologies. The constructs of beliefs and perceptions, therefore, are related and overlapping; and according to Dörnyei (2010), although beliefs are retained more tenaciously, they can be used interchangeably and both are associated with how students conceptualise their learning. The current study uses the term perception as a more dynamic construct, and adopts the aforementioned Kalaja *et al.*'s (2016) definition to illustrate learner perceptions.

There has been a surprisingly small number of studies which examine learner perceptions on the use of multiple languages in the classroom. Levine (2003) surveyed 600 foreign language learners and 163 teachers, finding that students and teachers have agreed to allow opportunities to use learner's own language and have similar perceptions on the amount of target language performed in a classroom. Unlike Levine's (2003) survey which still practices language separation by classifying them as the target and native language, Carstens (2016) examined students' perceptions on the entire multilingual practice in South African higher education context. It was revealed that students generally perceive translanguaging strategy positively, asserting its perceived benefits in acquiring English literacy.

William *et al.* (2015) suggest taking students' perception into account due to its potential consequences in learning. It has been widely discussed that perceptions are likely to affect learners' action (Borghetti/Beaven 2017; Wesely 2012; White 2008) which later may influence the outcomes of learning (Aro 2016; Kalaja/Barcelos 2003).

White (1999) and Loewen (1997), as cited in Barcelos (2003), state that the possible mismatch of what learners and teachers believe in language learning can give rise to problems with classroom interaction. As a result, students can suffer from dissatisfaction, which may lead to resistance to learning or limited learning achievement.

Methods

The current study was carried out using mixed-methods research with the explanatory sequential design, in which quantitative and qualitative phases were carried out sequentially. This design helps to obtain a thorough conclusion as a variety of data will help to validate one another in addressing research problems (Creswell 2015; Patton 2015). Quantitative data from questionnaires were firstly collected and analysed. These data aim to capture students' perceptions on translanguaging and to quickly screen participants for an interview phase. This was followed by interviews which served as the qualitative phase.

Research sites and participants

This study was conducted in a General English class of a non-English department at a university in Indonesia. English was mainly used in the General English teaching and learning process. However, learners' English proficiency is mixed so the instructor quite frequently shifts the language in classroom activities into the learner's native language, Indonesian. This setting was deemed to be a useful context to study learners' perceptions on translanguaging since the use of multiple languages in the English classroom is often considered against university administration rules (Carroll / van den Hoven 2016).

The researcher informed the students in the class about the study and there were 24 university students who agreed to participate in the research. They completed paper questionnaires and six students were invited to participate in an individual semi-structured interview. The characters of the interview participants are summarised in Appendix 1. To keep participants' anonymity, they were identified using pseudonyms.

Data collection

Gaining insights from Barcelos (2003) on approaches in investigating learner cognition, the current study combined a variety of methods to achieve a contextual understanding of learner perception. There were two data collection techniques, which were both administered in Indonesian, as participants in the study are most fluent in this language. The first technique is a close-ended questionnaire, adapting Rivera and Mazak's (2017) Language Attitude Survey. The questionnaire enquired about students' background and their general perception on the teacher's multiple language use. Prior to handling the questionnaire to participants, the questions were also examined by four colleagues in related research lines to check the question items and allow for revision. The questionnaire was then distributed in the last session of the General English course.

To explore research participants' responses, some of the students were invited to semi-structured interviews. Qualitative interviews provide flexibility to explore respondents' beliefs and attitudes (Talmy/Richards 2011). In this study, interviews were meant to clarify participants' answers, to verify researcher interpretation, and to extend the conversation which has not been elicited, yet might relate to the phenomenon in question. A set of questions was adapted from Duff and Polio (1990) which was well suited to the focus of the current study, which puts concern on the students' side. Added to this, since the qualitative interview in this study served as a confirming and elaborating tool to the quantitative result (Ivankova/Greer 2015), the question items were developed from questionnaire responses and took account of intriguing responses which require further exploration. These interview questions were previously tested with two Indonesian university students. Interviews were commenced on the day after the questionnaire completion and they were audio-recorded.

During the data collection process, the term translanguaging was not presented in the questions, but was paraphrased as a term with similar meaning in Indonesian. Ethics approval from the researcher's institution has been obtained prior to data collection procedures.

Data analysis

Questionnaire responses were analysed in a spreadsheet program and categorised using relevant codes (Dörnyei/Taguchi 2010): perceived appropriateness, perceived clarity, and language preference.

Research question: How do the students perceive translanguaging in the General English classroom?	
Themes	**Codes**
A. Students' opinion on translanguaging	1. General feeling of languages used
	2. Appropriateness
	3. Professionalism
	4. Clarity
	5. Involvement in learning
B. Perceived benefits of translanguaging	1. Understanding content knowledge
	2. Acquiring target language vocabulary
	3. Engaging
C. Perceived drawbacks of translanguaging	1. Impeding English learning
	2. Worsening English speaking skills
	3. Time-consuming
D. Language preferences	1. English
	2. English and Indonesian
E. Teaching moments to use translanguaging space	1. Reviewing materials
	2. Giving explanation
	3. Giving learning instructions
	4. Giving feedback
	5. Practising English conversation
F. Monolingual views	English learning should only use English.

Table 1. Emerging themes and codes in the interview transcripts.

The patterns from questionnaire data were identified using descriptive statistics. It provided preliminary information about students' perceptions towards translanguaging and was used to initiate the qualitative phase. Interview recordings were transcribed manually and the recurring patterns were identified. Similar patterns in the data were colour-coded and, as the interviews were conducted in Indonesian, the coding process was also performed to the transcripts using Indonesian. Coding was checked to ensure the correct interpretation and to avoid potential bias (Campbell *et al.* 2013), resulting in 86% agreement between the researcher and the inter-coder. Table 1 shows codes and themes emerging from the qualitative data.

Although quantitative and qualitative analyses were organised independently, both data analysis were then compared, linked, and integrated (Teddlie/Tashakkori 2009). A contradictory perception within individual participants was an identified problem from integrating questionnaire and interview analyses. Rather than viewing this phenomenon as problematic, Ivankova and Creswell (2009) argue that analysis from multiple data sources may not agree with one another, but could imply a deeper and more complex understanding of the phenomenon.

Results

All participants completing the questionnaire reported that the teacher switched and mixed languages during teaching and learning process. The questionnaire responses indicated that the majority of student participants, 23 respondents (96%), perceived translanguaging as a positive teaching strategy and one respondent (4%) felt 'not sure' about it (see Figure 2).

Mazak (2016) suggests a more detailed way to describe perceptions of language use by examining participants' rating on appropriateness, professionalism, clarity, and engagement impact. On average, these categorical questionnaire responses were in support of translanguaging (see Table 2).

Figure 2. Students' general perceptions on translanguaging.

Question items	Min	Max	Mean	SD
How appropriate is the teacher's language shift?	3	5	3.79	0.72
How professional is the teacher's language shift?	2	5	3.83	0.86
How clarifying is the teacher's language shift?	2	5	3.96	0.69
To what extent do you agree with the statement "language shift by the teacher affects my motivation to participate in learning activities"?	2	5	3.71	0.95
To what extent do you agree with the statement "language shift by the teacher affects my willingness to express myself"?	2	5	3.83	0.81

Table 2. Students' general perceptions on translanguaging.

To explore further on participants' responses, interview data provide a deeper insight into learners' perceptions with their own backgrounds, reasons, and experience. Students' perceptions on translanguaging are not a clear-cut phenomenon which could signify that learners perceiving it as a positive strategy consistently hold such perceptions on language mixing performed by the teacher. On the other hand, learners perceiving it as negative had an ambivalent perspective, and, in fact, regarded this translingual strategy as helpful. Four major themes resulting from examination of the questionnaires and the interviews are presented.

Perception 1: Translanguaging is a positive teaching strategy

Interview data revealed that positive attitude on language mixing was the most noticeable perception amidst other emerging themes. The data shed light on a range of different reasons underlying this perception. A shared argument from five focal participants stated that it is positive because this strategy suits their proficiency level. It was captured in Rani's statement, "For me, it's been very helpful because I am not yet fluent in English. So, I need someone to teach in Indonesian." She stated that the use of English-Indonesian in the classroom was helpful as she considered herself not really fluent in English and still needed assistance by having recourse to her first language. The participants who held a positive perception on translanguaging repeatedly mentioned the word 'helpful', 'good', 'appropriate', 'clear', 'motivating', 'comfortable', even 'caring' as they reflected on the use of mixed languages in their class.

However, determining attitudes toward language use in an English class is not always straightforward. The question eliciting participants' view of translanguaging strategy extends into the degree whether students are willing to have an English-only or mixed-language instruction. Some students were apparently enthusiastic for both options. For Eka, English was preferable because she wanted to train herself to get used to English instruction. Meanwhile, English-Indonesian was also favourable in a way that she could understand the instructor's words effortlessly. There is also another participant, Danar, who was reported to practice ambivalence by supporting mixed languages but choosing English-only instruction. It indicates that favouring mixed languages does not always imply that participants would not rather have full English instruction.

Perception 2: Translanguaging scaffolds understanding.

Another pervasive theme which emerged from the data was the perception that translanguaging enables students to understand the lesson. All interviewees agreed that the instructor's language switching helps them to make sense of English utterances in the classroom. For instance, translanguaging can facilitate students to understand grammar (Agung) and vocabulary (Danar). Danar was unique for his L1 is English, and he did not have much knowledge of Indonesian vocabulary. Language switching and mixing between English-Indonesian can lead him to understand Indonesian words and develop his Indonesian vocabulary.

(1) We learned grammar, I previously didn't understand what it meant, what those rules meant [...] something difficult was later explained using Indonesian. [Agung]

(2) I lack Indonesian vocabulary. The teacher sometimes switches to Indonesian. It makes me understand the meaning of some Indonesian vocabulary I have never encountered. [Danar]

Enabling understanding does not only deal with the content material, but can happen in any other stages of teaching, for instance when the lecturer clarified some task instructions. Rani illustrated that the teacher gave instructions in English and she felt that "Students did not really get it, then it was explained in Indonesian, so it's clearer for us." Interestingly, Melisa who held a perception that translanguaging is a negative strategy and that she prefers English-only instruction, admitted that language switching aims to make students understand the lesson better. Rani, further, juxtaposed English-Indonesian and English-only teaching by foregrounding the drawback of bringing English-only instruction in the classroom "There has been a lecturer who used full English instruction, but yeah, I could not follow learning. I was like 'I can't understand what you said!" She indicated that it constrained her to understand the lesson, thus learning became inaccessible.

Perception 3: Translanguaging accommodates learners' socio-emotional needs

The questionnaire's data suggested that translanguaging was generally perceived as affecting students' willingness to participate and communicate in the classroom. From the interviews, Agung stated that language mixing and switching is crucial to ensure smooth interaction since it can create a safe space for them to involve in the lesson, "Using both languages, we can indirectly get closer to the teacher. [...] If we are close enough, we won't feel awkward when we want to be active in class". The words *get closer* were also uttered by other participants to reflect the use of multiple languages for building interpersonal relationships between the instructor and the learners.

In addition, interview participants also said that language mixing enables them to express their feeling and ideas in a variety of learning occasions. Rani stated that teacher's language switching opens a space to show her voice, "switching between languages enables me to convey my opinions to the lecturer." Similarly, Eka reflected that the instructor's use of English-Indonesian can back her up to practice speaking English, "When I was doing a presentation, I don't know how to express some words in English. Then I was told to continue using Indonesian and later the teacher provided the English word for my previous Indonesian words." A further comment by Gita clarified her previous learning experience in a monolingual-oriented class and expressed discomfort when she felt limited to ask because she should convey it in English, "There's no way we can use Indonesian. And surely it was uncomfortable."

Perception 4: Translanguaging is not ideally performed in foreign language learning

In contrast to positive and supportive response about translanguaging practice, the interview participants pointed out that English learning ideally involves English-only instruction. Central to the perception is that mixed languages is not a standard instruction used in the English classrooms. Agung suggested that a good way to learn a foreign language is to fully use that language in the classroom:

(3) Let's say you're learning International Relations, then you switch to learning Engineering? It goes the same when you use Indonesian [in an English class]. English class uses English, Indonesian class uses Indonesian. [Agung]

Although the monolingual view was not specifically elicited by any of the questionnaire items or the semi-structured interview questions, this is a shared perception among all other interview participants. Danar, even, was reported mentioning this idea four times during interview, thus it seems to be his salient perception on language use in classroom.

Additionally, Melisa also echoed the notion that the foreign language instructor is not supposed to mix and switch languages. She suggested that this strategy is not necessary for their class. "We can understand the lesson given in English without necessarily switching into Indonesian. It must be wasting time to explain materials twice, in English and in Indonesian." Melisa reflected that it is not only irrelevant to bring translanguaging in the General English class, but the word 'wasting time' also indicated that she perceived it as inefficient. Melisa and Gita, additionally, pointed out that translingual strategy could even create such a harmful impact for language learning for it potentially worsens students' English speaking skills. Gita, for instance, worried that students will get used to mixing languages if the teacher performed translanguaging in classroom, "It's likely that the students are used to mixing Indonesian [with English]. Because the teacher lets us do that." Melissa expressed the same concern but she went further and proposed, "When we mix [English] with Indonesian, I just think that my English won't really develop." In this sense, speaking Indonesian in the English classroom was brought to attention of students as a practice of deviating the norm and was perceived to cause some potential trouble.

Discussion

Existing literature within this area has found that the use of translanguaging was deemed constructive for language learning (Creese/Blackledge 2010; Garcia/Kano 2014; Palmer *et al.* 2014). The findings in the current study reinforce this notion, suggesting that the instructor has acknowledged the students' points of view. If teachers' perception tallies with students' perception, it may result in an effective classroom management (Williams *et al.* 2015), and in a way that students hold facilitative beliefs upon what the teacher practised in classroom, these viewpoints could also have some good impact for learning.

Regardless of positive views among the participant group, their reasons varied. The most common reason behind the perceptions of teacher's translanguaging being appropriate, professional, clear, and engaging, is that this strategy can facilitate students with limited English proficiency, as also noted by Liu *et al.* (2004). The learners in Liu *et al.*'s (2004) study had been identified as having low listening and speaking ability, which to some extent can add meaning on the phenomenon being investigated in the current study, i.e., learners with lower level English proficiency hold positive attitude towards language mixing. A limitation in the current study, however, is that it is not possible to draw a broader conclusion about whether English proficiency can shape certain learner perceptions of the use of languages in classroom, as the current study only examined the learners' self-assessed proficiency level without relying on the students' score in English standardised tests. Further investigation comparing perceptions of more proficient learners with less proficient learners will contribute to a more vigorous conclusion on this matter.

Added to this, the learners' background and experience may also complicate the issue. Having been exposed to English more extensively and frequently than any of his peers, a student in the current study seems to carry English-only orientation, which might be the reason why he rejected mixed languages within teacher talk. On the other hand, another student in the participant group, who was generally neutral in responding to the questions, stated that she was conditioned to deal with mixed-language instruction in her primary and high schools. It can be inferred that their background and learning experience affect their belief system (Alannen 2003; Aro 2016; Lightbown/Spada 2013; Rivera/Mazak 2017).

Another interesting finding was the ambivalent responses from the participant group, which demonstrate students' preference and positive sense of English-Indonesian but also a liking towards English-only instruction. Learners' ambivalent perceptions pertaining to language learning have been pointed out by Mercer (2011) as a typical character of belief system. Mercer's (2011) longitudinal study of a learner's self-concept on foreign language learning revealed that the learner's beliefs about her Spanish and English ability changed based on which learning context those language skills were elicited and what others told her about her skills in each language. It seems possible to correlate this fact with the dynamic and social nature of perception (Aro 2016; Barcelos 2003; Wesely 2012). Hence, the current study adds on an understanding to the body of existing literatures outlining students' positive attitude on translanguaging, in a way that learners' positive sense on translanguaging might not be judged as a final and single conclusion. The students can have intricate or even incompatible responses if the inquiry is furthered.

In addition to feeling positive about translanguaging, the participants also expressed that this strategy is beneficial to learning. The most prominent gain they identified is associated with its resource to help students accessing content knowledge. The questionnaire and interview findings showcase that the students felt scaffolded to acquire difficult grammar and vocabulary through mixed language instruction. Interaction in learning comprises how teachers use languages and structures their talk, and through this translingual talk, they mediate learner's cognitive development (Lantolf/Thorne 2006; Lantolf/Poehner 2014). If comprehension of the target linguistic knowledge is achieved, the students are likely to develop their language skills, which marks achieving the goal of language learning.

Students' perceptions in terms of cognitive gains of translanguaging involve their views on how English-only instruction negatively affects their acquisition. One finding indicated that most participants are struggling to understand the materials if they are fully given in English. Students' low proficiency in English could impede learning if the course was delivered in EMI (Aizawa *et al.* 2020) and it is relevant with the data of the participants' self-assessed English proficiency which are mostly 'beginner'. However, the arguments of cognitive benefits of translanguaging should not be aimed to articulate that translanguaging resources must be provided in all stages of teaching, as it will make students rely on their L1 too much (Liu/Zeng 2015; Ortega 2014). Translanguaging can be performed for specific opportunities, allowing for a more effective learning using this resource. Therefore future research is suggested to explore the extent to which translanguaging space is needed and can work effectively in EFL classroom.

The current study also revealed that translanguaging was perceived by the participants as a resource to enhance learners' engagement (Canagarajah 2011; Ebe/Chapman-Santiago 2016; Martin-Beltran 2018), which signifies enabling teacher-learner communication and expressing learners' ideas. Several students in the participant group considered that the use of mixed languages allows them to communicate and they highlighted that their motivation to involve in a class is established if there is a smooth interaction between them and their teacher. It seems that students consider connectedness with the teacher played a substantial factor in learning, and thus translanguaging space could ensure this element in a target language classroom. Furthermore, the students in the current study felt assisted when they have opportunities to switch between languages if they stumbled upon several words that they found difficult to express in English. This may be the case as students mirror the teacher's talk when English was spoken with occasional recourse on Indonesian. Rather than becoming silent and leaving moments to express ideas and practice speaking English, they took a risk participating using a translanguaging space. It is clear that the inclusion of shared linguistic repertoires is perceived to reduce anxiety (Brooks-Lewis 2009; Levine 2003) to communicate and participate, thus affective benefits in learning are achieved.

Despite students' positive perceptions on the teacher's translanguaging, they evidently held monolingual perceptions by stating that English learning ideally employs English-only instruction. Although this view was only clearly observed from the interview data, the fact that all of the interview participants repeatedly expressed such an attitude without being elicited or prompted, could somewhat indicate that this is the salient perception shared by the students. This monolingual orientation was fairly entrenched in language learning (Carroll / van den Hoven 2016; Gomez *et al.* 2005), however the perspective was frequently monitored from the teacher's points of view or the researcher's observation, while the current study focuses on students' perceptions, revealing that the students might also practice monolingualism.

As a part of monolingual orientation, several students in this current study drew attention to the inefficient practice and potential harm of translanguaging, highlighting that mixing English and Indonesian is regarded uneven English performance. Therefore, it will hamper students' English speaking ability. Meanwhile, a study conducted by Al Masaeed (2016) in Arabic speaking practice sessions using English as L1 concluded that the use of L1 could improve L2 speaking performance by utilising English to mediate communication and knowledge transfer. The inclusion of students' own language does not necessarily imply limiting target language resources, nor do it limits communicative activities in the target language. It seems that students' monolingual views may be based on their vague projection about the negative impact of translanguaging, and they let that conception shapes their perception of language use in the General English classroom.

Monolingual orientation is somewhat against the proposal derived from the previous studies which suggest translanguaging pedagogies (e.g., Creese/Blackledge 2010; May 2014; Palmer *et al.* 2014). A conflict between students' multilingual resources and their monolingual views in language learning could be due to the students not being completely aware of the potential of their full linguistic resources, while their needs of translanguaging in classroom practices lead them to develop positive attitudes towards this strategy. Thus, explicit rationalisation on translanguaging and open discussion regarding the extent which this strategy is performed needs to be carried out. It does not only aim to develop an awareness that translanguaging is a legitimate phenomenon of EFL classroom, but also to make students embrace their full language repertoire and realise that they could bring that knowledge to the classroom. Building an awareness on how they are taught can deal with their preconceived ideas pertaining to a model English learning. This awareness is significant for the students before rushing to rule mixed-language instruction as an ineffective strategy, which might miss translanguaging potentials as a resource for learning.

Concluding remarks

Students' perceptions towards aspects of language learning seem to be multifaceted. It is challenging yet interesting to understand their distinct or even inconsistent perceptions, as well as the potential factors underlying those perceptions. The current study points to a view of how translanguaging was seen through the lens of university students in the Indonesian EFL context. This can provide insights on how the educators deal with language use in the General English course and enrich perspectives on translanguaging provided in teacher training programs. The results of this study seems to encourage translanguaging strategy in language classrooms, where multilingual practices are, by nature, present in this learning context. With students' acknowledgment for translanguaging's potential to optimise learning, the use of full linguistic repertoire should be embraced and taken into account. The current study suggests value for language teachers and university administration to revisit any monolingual bias which might exist, and become increasingly confident to allow translanguaging spaces where deemed necessary and useful.

References

Aizawa, Ikuya / Rose, Heath / Thompson, Gene / Curle, Samantha 2020. Beyond the Threshold: Exploring English Language Proficiency, Linguistic Challenges, and Academic Language Skills of Japanese Students in an English Medium Instruction Programme. *Language Teaching Research*. 1-25.

Alanen, Riika 2003. A Sociocultural Approach to Young Language Learners' Beliefs about Language Learning. In Kalaja, Paula / Barcelos, Ana Maria F. (eds) *Beliefs about SLA: New research approaches*. Boston: Kluwer Academic, 87-108.

Al Masaeed, Khaled 2016. Judicious Use of L1 in L2 Arabic Speaking Practice Sessions. *Foreign Language Annals*. 49/4, 716-728.

Aro, Mari 2016. Authority versus Experience: Dialogues on Learner Beliefs. In Kalaja, Paula / Barcelos, Ana Maria F. / Aro, Mari / Ruohotie-Lyhty, Maria (eds) *Beliefs, Agency and Identity in Foreign Language Learning and Teaching*. London: Palgrave Macmillan, 27-47.

Baker, Colin / Wright, Wayne E. 2017. *Foundations of Bilingual Education and Bilingualism* (6th Ed). Bristol: Multilingual Matters.

Barcelos, Ana Maria F. 2003. Researching Beliefs about SLA: A Critical Review. In Kalaja, Paula / Barcelos, Ana Maria F. (eds) *Beliefs about SLA: New Research Approaches*. Boston: Kluwer Academic, 7-33.

Borghetti, Claudia / Beaven, Ana 2017. Lingua Francas and Learning Mobility: Reflections on Students' Attitudes and Beliefs towards Language Learning and Use. *International Journal of Applied Linguistics*. 27/1, 221-241.

Brooks-Lewis, Kimberly Anne (2009). Adult Learners' Perceptions of the Incorporation of their L1 in Foreign Language Teaching and Learning. *Applied Linguistics*. 30/2, 216-235.

Cahyani, Hilda / de Courcy, Michele / Barnett, Jenny 2018. Teachers' Code-switching in Bilingual Classrooms: Exploring Pedagogical and Sociocultural Functions. *International Journal of Bilingual Education and Bilingualism*. 21/4, 465-479.

Campbell, John L / Quincy, Charles / Osserman, Jordan / Pedersen, Ove K. 2013. Coding In-depth Semi-structured Interviews: Problems of Unitization and Inter-coder Reliability and Agreement. *Sociological Methods and Research*. 42/3, 294-320.

Canagarajah, Suresh 2007. Lingua Franca English, Multilingual Communities, and Language Acquisition. *The Modern Language Journal*. 91/1, 923-939.

Canagarajah, Suresh 2011. Codemeshing in Academic Writing: Identifying Teachable Strategies of Translanguaging. *The Modern Language Journal*. 95/3, 401-417.

Carrol, Kevin S / van den Hoven, Melanie 2016. Translanguaging within Higher Education in the United Arab Emirates. In Mazak, Catherine M. / Carrol, Kevin S. (eds) *Translanguaging in Higher Education: Beyond Monolingual Ideologies.* Bristol: Multilingual Matters, 141-156.

Carstens, Adelia 2016. Translanguaging as a Vehicle for L2 Acquisition and L1 Development: Students' Perceptions. *Language Matters*. 47/2, 203-222.

Caruso, Elisa 2018. Translanguaging in Higher Education: Using Several Languages for the Analysis of Academic Content in the Teaching and Learning Process. *Language Learning in Higher Education.* 8/1, 65-90.

Cenoz, Jasone / Gorter, Durk 2015. *Multilingual Education: Between Language Learning and Translanguaging.* Cambridge University Press: Cambridge.

Cook, Vivian 2001. Using the First Language in the Classroom. *Canadian Modern Language Review*. 57/3, 402-423.

Creese, Angela / Blackledge, Adrian 2010. Translanguaging in the Bilingual Classroom: A Pedagogy for Learning and Teaching? *The Modern Language Journal*. 94/1, 103-115.

Creese, Angela / Blackledge, Adrian 2011. Separate and Flexible Bilingualism in Complementary Schools: Multiple Language Practices in Interrelationship. *Journal of Pragmatics*. 43/5, 1196-1208.

Creese, Angela / Blackledge, Adrian 2015. Translanguaging and Identity in Educational settings. *Annual Review of Applied Linguistics*. 35, 20-35.

Creswell, John W. 2015. *A Concise Introduction to Mixed Methods Research.* Los Angeles: Sage.

Daniel, Shannon M / Pacheco, Mark B. 2016. Translanguaging Practices and Perspectives of Four Multilingual Teens. *Journal of Adolescent & Adult Literacy.* 59/6, 653-663.

Dewi, Anita 2017. English as a Medium of Instruction in Indonesian Higher Education: A Study of Lecturers' Perceptions. In Fenton-

Smith, Ben / Humphreys, Pamela / Walkinshaw, Ian (eds) *English Medium Instruction in Higher Education in Asia-Pacific*. Cham: Springer, 241-258.

Doiz, Aintzane / Lasagabaster, David 2016. Teachers' Beliefs about Translanguaging Practices. In Mazak, Catherine M. / Carrol, Kevin S. (eds) *Translanguaging in Higher Education: Beyond Monolingual Ideologies*. Bristol: Multilingual Matters, 157-176.

Dörnyei, Zoltán 2010. *The Psychology of the Language Learner: Individual Differences in Second Language Acquisition.* London: Routledge.

Dörnyei, Zoltán / Taguchi, Tatsuya 2010. *Questionnaires in Second Language Research: Construction, Administration, and Processing* (2nd ed.). London: Routledge.

Douglas Fir Group (Atkinson, Dwight / Byrnes, Heidi/ Doran, Meredith / Duff, Patricia / Ellis, Nick C. / Hall, Joan Kelly / Johnson, Karen E. / Lantolf, James P. / Larsen–Freeman, Diane / Negueruela, Eduardo / Norton, Bonny / Ortega, Lourdes / Schumann, John / Swain, Merrill / Tarone, Elaine) 2016. A Transdisciplinary Framework for SLA in a Multilingual World. *The Modern Language Journal,* 100/1, 19-47.

Duff, Patricia / Charlene, Polio 1990. How Much Foreign Language Is There in the Foreign Language Classroom? *The Modern Language Journal*. 74/2, 154–166.

Ebe, Ann E / Chapman-Santiago, Charene 2016. Students' Voices Shining Through: Exploring Translanguaging as a Literary Device. In Garcia, Ofelia / Kleyn, Tatyana (eds) *Translanguaging with Multilingual Students: Learning from Classroom Moments.* New York: Routledge, 57-82.

Firth, Alan / Wagner, Johannes 1997. On Discourse, Communication, and (some) Fundamental Concepts in SLA Research. *The Modern Language Journal*. 81/3, 285-300.

Garcia, Ofelia 2009. *Bilingual Education in the 21st Century*. Oxford: Wiley-Blackwell.

Garcia, Ofelia / Wei, Li 2014. *Translanguaging: Language, Bilingualism, and Education*. New York: Palgrave Macmillan.

Garcia, Ofelia / Kano, Naomi 2014. Translanguaging as Process and Pedagogy: Developing the English Writing of Japanese Students in the U.S. In Conteh, Jean and Meier, Gabriela (eds) *The Multilingual Turn in Language Education: Benefits from Individuals and Societies*. Clevedon: Multilingual Matters, 258-277.

Garcia, Ofelia / Kleyn, Tatyana 2016. A Translanguaging Education Policy: Disruptions and Creating Space of Possibility. In Garcia, Ofelia / Kleyn, Tatyana (eds), *Translanguaging with Multilingual Students: Learning from Classroom Moments*. New York: Routledge, 181-201.

Gomez, Leo / Freeman, David / Freeman, Yvonne 2005. Dual language education: A promising 50–50 model. *Bilingual Research Journal*. 29, 145–164.

Grosjean, François 2012. An attempt to isolate, and then differentiate, transfer and interference. *International Journal of Bilingualism*. 16/1, 11-21.

Hall, Graham / Cook, Guy 2012. Own-language Use in Language Teaching and Learning. *Language Teaching*. 45/3, 271-308.

Han, Wen-Jui 2012. Bilingualism and Academic Achievement. *Child Development*. 83, 300-321.

Hoff, Erika 2013. Interpreting the Early Language Trajectories of Children from Low SES and Language Minority Homes: Implications for Closing Achievement Gaps. *Developmental Psychology*. 49, 4-14.

Horwitz, Elaine K. 1987. Surveying Student Beliefs about Language Learning. In Wenden, Anita / Rubin, Joan (eds) *Learner strategies in language learning*. London: Prentice-Hall, 119-132.

Ivankova, Nataliya V. / Creswell, John W. 2009. Mixed methods. In Heigham, Juanita / Croker, Robert A. *Qualitative Research in Applied Linguistics: A Practical Introduction*. New York: Palgrave Macmillan, 135-161.

Ivankova, Nataliya V. / Greer, Jennifer L. 2015. Mixed Methods Research and Analysis. In Paltridge, Brian / Phakiti, Aek (eds), *Research Methods in Applied Linguistics: A Practical Resource* London: Bloomsbury Academic, 63-81.

Kalaja, Paula / Barcelos, Ana Maria F. / Aro, Mari / Ruohotie-Lyhty, Maria 2016. Key Issues Relevant to the Studies to be Reported: Beliefs, Agency, and Identity. In Kalaja, Paula / Barcelos, Ana Maria F / Aro, Mari / Ruohotie-Lyhty, Maria *Beliefs, Agency and*

Identity in Foreign Language Learning and Teaching. London: Palgrave Macmillan UK, 8-24.

Kalaja, Paula 2003. Research on Students' Beliefs about SLA within a Discursive Approach. In Kalaja, Paula / Barcelos, Ana Maria F. (eds) *Beliefs about SLA: New Research Approaches* Boston: Kluwer Academic, 87-108.

Kartika-Ningsih, Harni / Rose, David 2018. Language shift: Analysing Language Use in Multilingual Classroom Interactions. *Functional Linguistics*, 5/1, 1–22.

Klapwijk, Nanda / Van der Walt, Christa 2016. English-plus Multilingualism as the New Linguistic Capital? Implications of University Students' Attitudes Towards Languages of Instruction in a Multilingual Environment. *Journal of Language, Identity & Education*. 15/2, 67-82.

Kleyn, Tatyana / Yau, Hulda 2016. The Grupito Flexes their Listening and Learning Muscles. In Garcia, Ofelia / Kleyn, Tatyana (eds) *Translanguaging with Multilingual Students: Learning from Classroom Moments*. New York: Routledge, 100-117.

Lantolf, James P. / Poehner, Matthew E. 2014. *Sociocultural Theory and the Pedagogical Imperative in L2 Education: Vygotskian Praxis and the Research/Practice Divide*. New York: Routledge.

Lantolf, James P. / Thorne, Steven L. 2006. *Sociocultural Theory and the Genesis of Second Language Development*. Oxford: Oxford University Press.

Levine, Glenn S. 2003. Student and Instructor Beliefs and Attitudes about Target Language Use, First Language Use, and Anxiety: Report of a Questionnaire Study. *The Modern Language Journal*. 87/3, 343-364.

Lightbown, Patsy M. / Spada, Nina 2013. *How Languages Are Learned* (4th ed). Oxford: Oxford University Press.

Liu, Dilin / Ahn, Gil-Soon / Baek / Kyung-Suk / Han, Nan-Ok 2004. South Korean High School English Teachers' Code Switching: Questions and Challenges in the Drive for Maximal Use of English in Teaching. *TESOL Quarterly*. 38/4, 605-638.

Liu, Yingqin / Zeng, Annie Ping 2015. Loss and Gain: Revisiting the Roles of the First Language in Novice Adult Second Language Learning Classrooms. *Theory and Practice in Language Studies*. 5(12), 2433-2440.

Luk, Gladys / Lin, Angel M. Y. 2015. L1 is Pedagogical Resource in Building Students' L2 Academic Literacy: Pedagogical Innovation in a Science Classroom in a Hong Kong school. In Jasone Cenoz / Durk Gorter (eds) *Multilingual Education: Between Language Learning and Translanguaging.* Cambridge University Press: Cambridge, 16-34.

Martin-Beltrán, Melinda 2018. "What Do You Want to Say?" How Adolescents Use Translanguaging to Expand Learning Opportunities. In Gort, Mileidis (ed.) *Complex and Dynamic Languaging Practices of Emergent Bilinguals*. London: Routledge, 98-120.

May, Stephen 2014. Discplinary Divides, Knowledge Construction, and the Multilingual Turn. In May, Stephen (ed.) *The Multilingual Turn: Implication for SLA, TESOL, and Bilingual Education*. New York: Routledge, 6-31.

Mazak, Catherine M. / Mendoza, Fiorelys / Mangonéz, Lauren Pérez 2016. Professors Translanguaging in Practice: Three Cases from a Bilingual University. In Mazak, Catherine M. / Carroll, Kevin S. (eds). *Translanguaging in Higher Education: Beyond Monolingual Ideologies.* Bristol: Multilingual Matters, 70-90.

Mercer, Sarah 2011. *Towards an Understanding of Language Learner Self-concept.* Dordrecht: Springer Netherlands.

Mohamed, Naashia 2013. The Challenge of Medium of Instruction: A View from Maldivian Schools. *Current Issues in Language Planning*. 14/1, 185-203.

Oguro, Susan 2011. Using the Target Language in Beginner Level Classroom: The Influence of Learners' Affective State on Teachers' Practice. *University of Sydney Papers in TESOL*. 6/1, 1-20.

Ortega, Lourdes 2014. Ways Forward for a Bi/Multilingual Turn in SLA. In May, Stephen (ed.) *The Multilingual Turn: Implications for SLA, TESOL, and Bilingual Education*. New York: Routledge, 32-53.

Patton, Michael Quinn 2015. *Qualitative Research and Evaluation Methods (*4th ed*)*. California: Sage.

Palmer, Deborah K. / Martínez, Ramón Antontio / Mateus, Suzanne G. / Henderson, Kathryn 2014. Reframing the Debate on Language Separation: Toward a Vision for translanguaging pedagogies in the dual language classroom. *The Modern Language Journal*. 98/3, 757-772.

Rivera, Antonio J. / Mazak, Catherine M. 2017. Analyzing Student Perceptions on Translanguaging: A Case Study of a Puerto Rican University Classroom. *HOW: A Colombian Journal for Teachers of English*. 24/1, 122-138.

Rosiers, Kirsten 2017. Unravelling Translanguaging: The Potential of Translanguaging as a Scaffold among Teachers and Pupils in Superdiverse Classrooms in Flemish Education. In Paulsrud, BethAnne / Rosén, Jenny / Straszer, Boglárka / Wedin, Åsa (eds) *New Perspectives on Translanguaging and Education*. Bristol: Multilingual Matters, 148-169.

Talmy, Stephen / Richards, Keith 2011. Theorizing Qualitative Research Interviews in Applied Linguistics. *Applied Linguistics*, 32/1, 1-5.

Teddlie, Charles / Tashakkori, Abbas 2009. *Foundations of Mixed Methods Research: Integrating Quantitative and Qualitative Approaches in the Social and Behavioral Sciences*. Thousand Oaks: Sage Publications.

Thoms, Joshua J. / Liao, Jianling / Szustak, Anja 2005. The Use of L1 in an L2 On-line Chat Activity. *The Canadian Modern Language Review*. 62/1, 161-182.

Valdes, Guadalupe / Poza, Luis / Brooks, Maneka Deanna 2015. Language Acquisition in Bilingual Education. In Wright, Wayne E. / Boun, Sovicheth / Garcia, Ofelia (ed.) *The Handbook of Bilingual and Multilingual Education*. Malden: Wiley-Blackwell.

Walker, Tony / Liyanage, Indika / Madya, Suwarsih / Hidayati, Sari 2019. Media of Instruction in Indonesia: Implications for Bi/Multilingual Education. In Liyanage, Indika and Walker, Tony (ed.) *Multilingual Education Yearbook 2019: Media of Instruction and Multilingual Settings*. Cham: Springer.

Walker, Ute 2018. Translanguaging: Affordances for Collaborative Language Learning. *New Zealand Studies in Applied Linguistics*. 24/1, 18-39.

Wesely, Pamela M. 2012. Learner Attitudes, Perceptions, and Beliefs in Language Learning. *Foreign Language Annals*. 45/1, 98-117.

White, Cynthia 2008. Beliefs and Good Language Learner. In Griffiths, Carol (ed.) *Lessons from Good Language Learner*. Cambridge: Cambridge University Press, 121-130.

Williams, Marion / Mercer, Sarah / Ryan, Stephen 2015. *Exploring Psychology in Language Learning and Teaching*. Oxford: Oxford University Press.

Woolard, Kathryn Ann 2004. Codeswitching. In Duranti, Alessandro (ed.) *A Companion to Linguistic Anthropology*. Malden: Blackwell, 73-94.

Mariana Sáez

Use of Language Learning Strategies in Textbooks: A Comparative Study

Introduction

In 1975, Rubin identified strategies linked to characteristics that "good learners" have. Some of these strategies include students linking the target language with their first language, focusing on words, structures and their meaning, seeking opportunities to practice the target language, classification of information, repetition of sounds and intonation, monitoring their process, among others (Rubin 1975: 43). The strategies mentioned, nowadays are part of the language learning strategies (LLS), which have been studied and developed by many authors such as O'Malley and Chamot (1985), Oxford (1990, 1994, 1996, 2011, 2017), and Oxford and Amerstorfer (2018).

Rebecca Oxford (1990) classified and detailed the characteristics of these strategies and how they work in practice. She highlighted the usefulness, support and empowerment the LLS provide to the learning process, enabling it to be clear, easy and meaningful for learners. Based on that, it seems indisputable that the promotion of the LLS to aid the learning process must be included in the classroom and textbooks, especially nowadays where English is a lingua franca.

The nature of the problem

Governments all over the world are aware of the importance of teaching English as a foreign language (EFL), investing in it and modifying their curricula and including EFL as a compulsory subject. In the case of Chile, the Ministry of Education has created different campaigns and programs to support students and teachers. One of these investments is through the provision of textbooks for teachers and students. However, a study found out that only 5% of teachers use them (Guernica Consultores 2016). One of the many reasons behind this is these textbooks are not linked with the curriculum proposed by the Ministry of Education. Although the solution may be simple: making textbooks based on the curriculum, other aspects need to be considered as well, such as if these textbooks are worth using with the learners, if they will positively influence the learning process. The present study analyses textbooks in terms of how these intend students to use LLS and how using these strategies aids the learning process of acquisition of English as a foreign language.

Significance of the study

The significance of the study is based on the importance and effectiveness of LLS. The use and application are considered a necessary component, especially for learners who are "less successful" (Griffiths/Parr 2001: 249). Several authors have addressed the use of LLS by successful learners and learners who struggle with the learning process (Macaro 2001; Oxford 1990; Rubin 1975). Additionally, the benefits of LLS include that the learning process becomes pleasant, and the LLS are characterized by being fast, quick, pleasant and significant for the students (Cohen 2014; Griffiths 2008; Oxford 2016). Despite the knowledge on the benefits of the LLS, there is not much understanding of how these strategies work in textbooks, how LLS aid the learning process, and how these strategies vary according to learners' proficiency levels. In EFL classrooms, textbooks are highly required; therefore, the application of LLS is essential to aid the learning process and use the textbook as a powerful classroom component.

Besides, the creation of an instrument to analyse and identify the LLS used could provide an easy and guided way to promote the use of LLS in the classroom. The instrument created for this study is based on Oxford (1990) classification of the language learning strategies. The instrument is created to identify the LLS intended to be used in the textbook. Therefore, it could be used by teachers and head of studies who select the material for their students. Finally, a recent study on the use of LLS in textbooks stated that being aware of the needs of the learners in terms of LLS allows a suitable selection of material for students (Menegale 2020). The objectives of the study are to: (1) compare the frequency of the use of language learning strategies in EFL textbooks in different courses; and (2) determine how the language learning strategies are intended to be used to accomplish a task based on the instructions given.

Research Questions:

1. How does the frequency of the use of language learning strategies change in different grades in EFL textbooks?

2. How does the intended use of the language learning strategies by students change in different grades in EFL textbooks?

Literature Review

Textbooks are considered maps for students in their learning process and guides for teachers to lead students to acquire a second or foreign language (Richards 2015). Due to their imminent influence, content analysis studies have analysed the use of Language Learning Strategies (LLS).

A study in Pakistan, 2016

In 2016, a content analysis study in Pakistan focused on grammar and language skills in English textbooks. This study aimed to analyse the frequency of communicative skills and grammars structures in English textbooks used in ninth grade (Behlol/Nasab 2016). This study used descriptive content analysis where the variables were not manipulated. The textbooks were analysed along with surveys on the perception of teachers on the textbooks. The analysis of the textbooks provided the identification of grammatical structures, their frequency and implications in the learning process, and the communicative skills used in the textbook. The study results indicated that the textbook's balance of language skills was not fair, mainly focusing on writing. Similarly, in terms of grammar structures, the overuse of present and past prevent students from being exposed to authentic communication. Even though teachers believe the textbooks are suitable for students, there are other inconsistencies in the textbooks related to the use of pictures, font type and size, which may distract the attention of students. Finally, the teachers in the study indicate that the textbooks' proficiency level is not according to the students' competencies which may alter students' proper learning process.

A study in Wisconsin, 2010

Selecting textbooks may be difficult, given the lack of information on how LLS are used in textbooks. In 2010, in the United States, a study developed in Wisconsin analysed textbooks concerning the LLS these used. The use of content analysis aided a better examination of the LLS use and its variation (Labelle 2010). The study began with a pilot study where practitioners and academicians provided feedback that allows the creation of a coding instrument to be used in the content analysis part, which was analysed in the third unit or chapter of thirty-three textbooks. The results provided the frequency of LLS and insightful notes to teachers to aid their decision to select a textbook. Out of the thirty-three textbooks analysed, six textbooks presented extensive use and variety on LLS. This study ensures that the selection of material based on the use of LLS aids the learning process, embracing the diversity of learning in the classroom.

A study in Slovakia, 2014

A third content analysis study analysed the relationship between proficiency level and the LLS promoted in Slovakia in 2014. A series of coursework textbooks were analysed to identify how LLS varies through these textbooks' different levels (Horváthová 2014). The study followed a mixed content analysis given the more profound outcomes it provides. The quantitative analysis allowed the coding of the LLS and answered the research questions on the variation and progress of the LLS. In contrast, the quantitative part involved a detailed analysis of the LLS change according to the proficiency level. The results demonstrated that cognitive strategies were highly used compared to metacognitive strategies, 63% and 32%, respectively. The use of these strategies was linked to the way students work with them in their learning process; that is to say, cognitive strategies work directly with the target language and previous knowledge to aid the learning process. Meanwhile, metacognitive strategies empower students to take control of their learning process, which is more likely to occur in learners who have been in the learning process for a more extended period of time, such as the case of teenagers and adults.

The current study

Sample

For this study, the sample selected are three textbooks used to teach English as a foreign language in Chile. The Ministry of Education provides these textbooks to schools that depend and receive support from the state. The way these textbooks were selected is based on the stratified random sample, "In which subgroups are selected from within a particular population, and samples are then generated for each of these subgroups" (Wagner 2015: 85). In Chile, English as a foreign language is a compulsory class from fifth grade onwards (Gobierno de Chile

2009). The curriculum used to teach is designed based on two-year teaching cycles; therefore, to make the sample representative, one class of the first three cycles was selected. The textbooks selected were: Think Out Loud 5, Student's Book English 7 Basico and Teens In Motion 1. The textbooks selected to be analysed only included the student's book.

Instrument

To analyse the textbooks, an instrument was elaborated based on the classification and description of the language learning strategies made by Oxford in 1990 and following her updates in 1994, 1996, 2011, 2017. The language strategies included for this study were memory, cognitive and metacognitive strategies whose detailed descriptions and classifications were the basis for creating this instrument. The instrument elaborated consisted of a diagram questionnaire, in which questions and descriptions allow the user to identify the LLS used in exercises of an EFL textbook. The creation of the instrument included a pilot test performed by two inter-raters who are language teachers completing their Master of Education studies. This process served to ensure the reliability of the instrument and make modifications to improve efficiency and management. The modifications considered three aspects such as the use of language, consideration of skills and data organisation. In terms of language, it was simplified, avoiding technical vocabulary to make the instrument friendly with the user. Even though the prospective users are ESL or EFL teachers or head of departments, it is important to provide an instrument that allows them to use their expertise and experience properly to convey accurate results.

Procedure

To use the instrument effectively, an exercise or activity of an ESL textbook is needed. First, it is a must to read the instructions and observe the exercise completely. Second, the three first questions need to be answered based on the first observation of the exercise. These three questions allow the identification of the use of memory, cognitive or metacognitive strategies. In the question where the answer is affirmative, the instrument leads to two sets of follow-up questions to identify the specific strategy being used to complete the exercise. It is important to note that the order of the questions matter. The sets of questions start by broadly referring to the LLS until they are narrowed down, and the specific LLS strategy is identified.

Coding

In the analysis, the coding process needs to start with the researcher knowing well the textbooks to analyse. This process is significant since it "helps build awareness to context and nuance, which is important in qualitative content analysis" (Drisko/Mashi 2015: 18). The researcher sets the categories previous the analysis, and this is based on the deductive coding application. The coding is based on Oxford (1990) categorisation and description of the LLS. One of the main scopes when analysing textbooks is to "Raise awareness and consciousness as well as to inform and educate" (Drisko/Mashi 2015: 7). Therefore, this study examines textbooks used in state-dependent schools in Chile to be analysed and identify how they are promoting the use of LLS to learners, which aids the identification of the LLS promoted but also how these vary based on the different levels of proficiency and ages of students.

Analysis

The present study gathers and analyses data using quantitative and qualitative approaches. Even though content analysis is usually linked to a quantitative approach, it has been stated that "Even the most sophisticated piece of quantitative research remains dependent on natural language (words), while most qualitative studies do contain some kind of quantitative information (numbers)" (Schedler/Mudde 2010 as cited by Neuendorf 2017: 10).

In terms of the quantitative data, these are represented and analysed through charts and graphs showing the frequency and trends of the LLS in the textbooks. These serve to compare the variation of the strategies used across the different textbooks analysed. Meanwhile, the qualitative approach allows deeper analysis on the use of LLS and how the learner, whether consciously or unconsciously, applies the LLS while doing an exercise of their textbook. This type of analysis is based on the grounded theory method, which in content analysis, does not develop a theory but on generating an in-depth description of theories, topics among other features (Drisko/Mashi 2015).

The analysis performed enables the researcher to address the questions given the nature of the information gathered. In terms of the first research question: How does the frequency of the use of language learning strategies change in different grades in EFL textbooks? This question is answered through the frequency of the LLS observed and registered in the textbooks analysed. The second question: How does the intended use of the language learning strategies by students change in different grades in EFL textbooks? This question is addressed through content analysis, which provides a deeper understanding of how the LLS are used to accomplish a task. The analysis of textbooks towards the use of LLS provides frequency and variation in the use of LLS, allowing an understanding of how the LLS are employed to accomplish a task.

Results and Discussion

Results of Research Question 1

The first research question proposed for this study is, "How does the frequency of the use of language learning strategies change in different grades in EFL textbooks?". To answer this question, the data gathered were analysed quantitatively and organised as presented in Table 1.

	5th grade	7th grade	9th grade
Memory Strategies	26%	19%	18%
Cognitive Strategies	58%	66%	46%
Metacognitive Strategies	16%	15%	36%

Table 1. Variation of language learning strategies frequency in 5th, 7th and 9th grade textbooks.

As presented in Table 1, the analysis of textbooks used in fifth, seventh and ninth grade to teach English as a foreign language use memory, cognitive and metacognitive strategies in exercises and activities. For instance, in the fifth grade, memory strategies are seen in 26% of exercises; meanwhile, cognitive strategies are the most used, seen in 58% of exercises and activities, and metacognitive strategies are the less observed, with only 16% of frequency. In the seventh grade, the percentage of memory strategies decreases with 19% of the frequency of their use. In comparison, cognitive strategies rise with 66%, and metacognitive strategies remain similar, being observed in 15% of activities and exercises of the textbook. Finally, in the ninth grade, memory strategies are the least seen. With only 18% of frequency, cognitive strategies are seen the most, with 46% of frequency in the textbook. Meanwhile, metacognitive strategies are observed in 36% of exercises and activities in the textbook. The variation of these results is seen in the graph presented in Figure 1.

Figure 1 presents the frequency variation of the use of LLS in fifth, seventh and ninth grade. The results evidence first that the three learning language strategies are present in the three textbooks analysed. Second, the results show that cognitive strategies are used the most in any of the levels analysed. The frequency levels are seen in at least half of the exercises and activities analysed; this frequency remains constant in any level analysed.

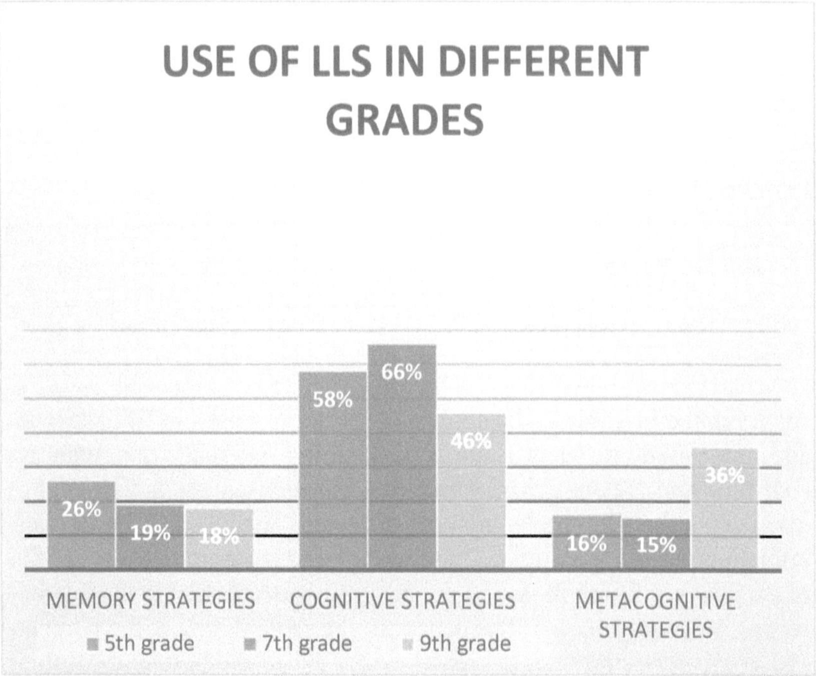

Figure 1. Use of language learning strategies in 5th, 7th and 9th grade textbooks.

In the fifth grade, the use of cognitive strategies is found in 58% of the textbook. Meanwhile, in the seventh grade, it is observed in 66% of the textbook, while in the ninth grade, in 46% of the exercises and activities analysed in the textbook. The fact that cognitive strategies are the most used suits the use of these strategies, which "Enables learners to understand and produce new language by many different means" (Oxford 1990: 37). Finally, the results in Figure 1 show the decrease of the use of memory strategies towards upper grades textbooks. For instance, memory strategies are seen in 26% of the textbook. Meanwhile, their use decreases to 19% in the seventh grade and 18% in the ninth grade. The tendency in, memory strategies are related to the fact that English as a foreign language is taught officially from the fifth grade. Therefore, learners need to use their previous memory and knowledge to connect with the target language to store and retrieve new information (Oxford 1990).

Discussion of Research Question 1

Based on the results, the strategies seen the least in the textbooks analysed were the metacognitive strategies. These strategies were seen in only 16% in fifth grade, 15% in seventh grade and an increase to 36% in ninth grade. The variation of metacognitive strategies changes significantly, being found to double in the ninth grade compared with the fifth grade. Based on the fact that metacognitive strategies enable learners to control their learning process (Oxford 1990, 2017; Oxford/Amerstorfer 2018). This process is more likely to occur in students in the education system for a more extended period of time since they have more experience in learning English as a foreign language and are more likely to be independent learners than younger learners. It is positive that despite how young students can be in the fifth grade, these strategies are still encouraged, and their use increases significantly in older grades. Metacognitive strategies are necessary to make students autonomous and in control of their learning process.

Additionally, the results reveal the predominant use of cognitive strategies. The use of cognitive strategies uses primarily the knowledge learnt and the direct use of the target language (Oxford 1990). In practical terms, cognitive strategies are seen in the application of communicative skills in authentic and non-authentic settings proposed in the exercises and activities. Likewise, identifying grammar structures, patterns, rules, keywords, and skimming and scanning to convey and understand a message. Oxford (1990, 2017) and Oxford and Amerstorfer (2018) indicated that cognitive and metacognitive strategies could work alongside supporting each other and consolidating the learning process.

In terms of the memory strategies, results show that their use is mostly seen in lower levels. This, as mentioned earlier, reinforces the idea of learners using their previous knowledge for the acquisition of a new language. In memory strategies, simple actions such as linking information and sounds, images, physical movements and mechanical techniques such as using flashcards (Oxford 1990) can be used to make the learning process dynamic and didactic, suitable for younger learners.

Results and Discussion of Research Question 2

In terms of Research Question Two, "How does the intended use of the language learning strategies by students change in different grades in EFL textbooks?", the data gathered were analysed qualitatively; therefore, the results and discussion are presented in general terms and separately by each level.

To start with, the instruction analysis identified imperative statements which explained how to complete the task. These statements contained 10 to 30 words that keywords lead to identifying the language learning strategy needed to use. Additionally, the location of exercises and activities analysed offered a better insight into the purpose of the exercise supporting identifying the language learning strategy. For instance, exercises at the beginning of the unit promoted metacognitive strategies since these exercises attempted to set goals.

Another example is found after reading passages, where exercises and activities attempt to check reading comprehension. The use of keywords such as 'read', 'write', 'true or false' indicates the use of scanning a reading passage linked to cognitive strategies such as 'Getting the Idea Quickly'. Finally, exercises where ideas need to be organised, such as exercises of mind maps, involves the use of memory strategies such as 'semantic mapping', which involves the organisation of information based on a concept given and descriptions around it.

The analysis of instructions reveal that the instructions increased in words and complexity towards upper levels. The use of keywords in the analysis of instructions provided a better identification of the strategies used along with the analysis of the exercises and activity itself. The way instructions are articulated allowed the proper identification of the strategy needed to complete the task successfully.

In the fifth grade, the textbook analysed was Think Out Loud 5. This textbook provided brief, direct instructions and simple language and keywords to explain how to do a task. This aspect allowed a clear identification of the language learning strategy that needs to be used.

It is important to note that the instructions are solely given in English and not Spanish. Additionally, the high amount of colours and pictures supports the language learning strategy used, such as 'using imagery' which is "a good way to remember what has been heard or read in the new language is to create a mental image of it" (Oxford 1990: 61).

Cognitive strategies are also identified in the fifth grade, especially when a model needs to be followed. The identification and application of formulas and patter is a cognitive strategy that allows students to use the target language to convey ideas properly in English. To support this strategy, the use of resources such as dictionaries is also encouraged to convey a clearer message or review new words learnt.

In terms of metacognitive strategies, although these are the least seen in fifth grade, it is still found primarily at the beginning of the unit or lesson while setting goals to achieve in the lesson or goal. In the fifth grade, these exercises offer tips to develop communicative skills and identify and set goals for the end of the unit. Meanwhile, in the seventh grade, the textbook analysed was Student's Book English 7 básico. This textbook has a considerable increase in the length of instructions; the use of images decreases significantly, and learners are encouraged to plan activities and monitor their learning process.

Examples observed include memory strategies, where 'Grouping' was promoted in the classification of vocabulary based on their function in language. Additionally, in cognitive strategies, 'Recognising and using Formulas and Patterns' is also identified in the seventh grade. In this level, this strategy is used to use verbs in present simple or continuous based on a specific context given. While in metacognitive strategies, two exercises are performed together using strategies such as 'Paying Attention' and 'Finding out About Language Learning'.

Finally, in the content analysis made in the ninth grade, the length of instructions increase moderately compared to the seventh-grade textbook and include several steps to complete complex tasks. Examples observed involve using memory strategies such as 'associating/elaborating' strategies, where students link new contents with familiar information (Oxford 1990, 2017). The link made between the students own traditions, and the ones celebrated worldwide strengthens the learning process, making it meaningful. Examples where cognitive strategies are found in listening exercises, where the same recording is analysed using different cognitive strategies, for instance, 'Formally practising with sounds and writing systems' where students focus on the pronunciation of specific syllables, imitate sounds and stress. The strategy used focuses on the differentiation of sounds in English, along with intonation, stress and other features, contributing to the development of the speaking skill of learners (Oxford 1990, 2017). Examples related to the use of metacognitive strategies are explicitly related to 'planning for a language task'. In this type of exercise, students are encouraged to follow specific procedures to identify the requirements of a bigger task and complete the previous steps to complete the task, such as gather information and plan with peers how to perform the task. The use of this metacognitive strategy allows learners to focus on the requirements of a task and proceed through small steps to complete the task successfully (Oxford 1990, 2017).

The content analysis results show the variation of language learning strategies in the textbooks analysed in Years Five, Seven, and Nine. The results demonstrate that memory strategies are mostly observed in younger levels than older levels. This aspect is linked to the fact that the fifth grade is the first year where English as a foreign language is taught in Chile; thus, students need to connect their knowledge between their first language with the target language. In terms of metacognitive strategies, using these strategies enables students to control their language learning process; therefore, it is more likely to be observed in older grades where students have more time of gaining linguistic experience in the education system. Last, cognitive strategies are the strategies mainly observed in all the levels studied, which is related to the nature of cognitive strategies, in which learners work directly with the target language (Oxford 1990). These aspects demonstrate the nature of EFL textbooks, which unifying thread is the target language itself.

The study showed that keywords, clear and direct instructions aid learners in completing a task successfully, leading learners to follow a plan of action, recall words, sounds and pictures, or operate the target language directly. Finally, the content analysis showed that out of the three textbooks analysed, only one promoted directly the use of learning strategies, which is the case of the fifth-grade textbook. This fact leads to the idea that if learners were taught or reminded often about the language learning strategies, they would be more likely to perform tasks easily and effectively since they would know how to approach a task. In this way, the learning process would be aided and supported by meaningful actions that enhance the acquisition of the target language.

Conclusion

The present study has been able to identify two main aspects: the use of specific language learning strategies according to the level of students and the necessity to teach language learning strategies to support the learning process. Regarding the use of LLS, the study identified using the three language learning strategies analysed, such as memory, cognitive and metacognitive strategies. However, the predominance of cognitive strategies is the most frequent and stable in all the levels analysed, which is likely to be due to the nature of cognitive strategies in direct treatment of the target language (Oxford 1990). Therefore, the use of memory and metacognitive strategies is linked to the grades and proficiency levels of the students. Memory strategies are primarily observed in the lower levels, while the use of metacognitive strategies increase in the higher levels. The use of memory strategies in the lower levels is likely because students link their previous knowledge with the target language to aid their learning process, meanwhile, metacognitive strategies provide learners with the chance to be in control of their learning process; therefore, it is most likely to be used with older students, who have been in the educational system for a longer time, and who access to being exposed to the target language in non-educative environments, such as online tools, travelling, music, television, among others. The use of metacognitive strategies allows learners to develop intrinsic motivation and learn the target language independently.

Concerning the teaching of language learning strategies, their use could improve students' learning process. The benefits of teaching and reinforcing the use of LLS allows learners to use these strategies as tools to aid their learning process. Oxford stated that teachers need to teach how to facilitate the learning process (Oxford 1990). Therefore, the job of the EFL teacher is not only related to the target language itself but also to the way students can learn effectively. Additionally, research has shown that when learners are taught strategy training, they learn better than those who do not receive such instruction (Oxford 1990). Thereupon, the necessity to teach LLS is vital to making the learning process effective and successful.

Limitations of the Study

For this study, there were two main limitations, such as time constraints and the lack of research strictly related to the topic of this study. Regarding time constraints, the nature of the research methodology and content analysis demands careful and detailed revision and analysis of the textbooks, which needs to be exhaustive to provide fruitful and accurate results. Regarding the lack of studies related to the topic of study, there are few recent studies on the topic of this study; therefore, there is no comparison on the use of LLS. However, the limitations were not a reason to dismiss the achievement of the aims proposed for this study. If this had not been the case, the present study could have provided more detail, but the aims and research questions could have been answered either way.

Recommendations for Future Research

The present study has provided a detailed analysis of how the LLS are present in EFL textbooks and how their use varies in different grades. Likewise, an instrument to analyse textbooks and identify the LLS instructions and activities have been provided. Thus, a suggestion for further research is a study based on the correlation between the strategies identified in the textbook and the ones students use in the classroom to assure that the instructions in the textbooks are promoted certain strategies and that learners identify them and use them for their benefit. This analysis could provide a deeper insight into how younger learners use LLS to identify a way to promote LLS from a young age towards older students. Finally, it would be beneficial to study how the teaching and practice of LLS in the classroom enhance the learning process.

References

Behlol, Malik / Nasab, Durri 2016. Content Analysis of English Textbook Taught at Grade 9: Focus on Grammatical Structures and Language Skills. *Journal of Research in Social Sciences.* 4/2, 122-139.

Cohen, Andrew 2014. *Strategies in Learning and Using a Second Language* (2nd ed.). London: Routledge.

Drisko, James / Maschi, Tina 2015. *Content Analysis.* Oxford: Oxford University Press.

Gobierno de Chile 2009. *Objetivos Fundamentales y Contenidos Mínimos Obligatorios de la Educación Básica y Media actualización 2009* [Fundamental Objectives and Minimum Compulsory Contents of Elementary and High School Education Update 2009]. Chile: Gobierno de Chile.

Griffiths, Carol 2008. Strategies and Good Language Learners. In Griffiths, Carol (ed.) *Lessons from Good Language Learners.* Cambridge: Cambridge University Press, 83-98.

Griffiths, Carol / Parr, Judy 2001. Language-learning Strategies: Theory and Perception. *ELT Journal.* 55/3, 247-254.

Guernica Consultores 2016. *Estudio de Uso y Valoración de Textos Escolares: Informe final. Encargado por MINEDUC y Oficina Regional de Educación para América Latina y el Caribe (UNESCO)* [Study of Use and Assessment of School Texts Final Report. Commissioned by MINEDUC and the Regional Office of Education for Latin America and the Caribbean (UNESCO)]. Chile: María Pía Olivera Vidal.

Horváthová, Božena 2014. Implementing Language Learning Strategies into a Series of Second Foreign Language Learning Textbooks. *Journal of Language and Cultural Education.* 2/1, 60-94.

Labelle, Jeffrey 2010. Selecting ELL Textbooks: A Content Analysis of L2 Learning Strategies. *Journal of Language Teaching and Research.* 1/4, 358-369.

Macaro, Ernesto 2001. *Learning Strategies in Foreign and Second Language Classrooms.* London: Continuum.

Menegale, Marcella 2020. Learning Strategies Instruction in CLIL Textbooks and Teacher-Authored Materials: A Qualitative Study. *International Journal of Linguistics.* 12/2, 186-205.

Neuendorf, Kimberly 2017. *The Content Analysis Guidebook* (2nd ed.). Los Angeles, CA: Sage.

O'Malley, J. Michael / Chamot, Anna / Stewner-Manzanares, Gloria / Kupper, Lisa / Russo, Rocco 1985. Learning Strategies Used by Beginning and Intermediate ESL Students. *Language Learning.* 35/1, 21-46.

Oxford, Rebecca 1990. *Language Learning Strategies: What Every Teacher Should Know.* Boston, MA: Heinle & Heinle.

Oxford, Rebecca 1994. *Language Learning Strategies: An Update.* Online resources: Digest.

Oxford, Rebecca 1996. *Language Learning Strategies Around the World: Cross-cultural Perspectives.* Honolulu, HI: University of Hawai'i Press.

Oxford, Rebecca 2011. *Teaching and Researching Language Learning Strategies.* London: Routledge.

Oxford, Rebecca 2017. *Teaching and Researching Language Learning Strategies: Self-regulation in Context* (2nd ed.). New York, NY: Routledge.

Oxford, Rebecca / Amerstorfer, Carmen 2018. *Language Learning Strategies and Individual Learner Characteristics: Situating Strategy Use in Diverse Contexts.* London: Bloomsbury Academic.

Richards, Jack 2015. *Key Issues in Language Teaching.* Cambridge: Cambridge University Press.

Rubin, Joan 1975. What the "Good Language Learner" Can Teach Us. *TESOL Quarterly*. 9/1, 41-51.

Wagner, Elvis 2015. Survey Research. In Paltridge, Brian / Phakiti, Aek (eds) *Research Methods in Applied Linguistics*. Bloomsbury Academy: London, 22-38.

WENJUN BU / DAVID HIRSH

To Speak or Not To Speak: Chinese International Students' Considerations of Oral Participation and Quietness in Australian Tutorials

Introduction

The classroom interaction of international students has attracted considerable research attention in recent years, reflecting in part rising levels of international student participation in universities in Australia and elsewhere. In this context, understanding the learning experience of international students has both educational and economic importance. One aspect of international student learning experience that is attracting theoretical interest is classroom oral participation. From the perspective of education practitioners and institutions with an Anglo-Saxon background, including Australian universities, in-class participation serves as a basic component of active learning, which enhances deep and independent learning through student proactive engagement in learning-by-doing (Tani 2008). As active learning involves talking and listening as well as reading, writing and reflecting (Meyers/Jones 1993), participation in class discussions is commonly perceived as a classroom norm (e.g., see Young 1991). That being said, international students are reported not to fully involve themselves in classroom discussions (Tompson/Tompson 1996), hindering instructors from completely unlocking their potential in the classroom and enhancing the communicative and educational experiences of all students (Yook/Albert 1998). According to Hodne (1997), the relatively low levels of participation of international students denote an obstacle to good performance of learning practice as well as comprehensive engagement with campus life in a foreign country. Yet there are other scholars who interpret their classroom behavior from a different perspective. Instead of viewing international students' reserved participation as underperforming involvement in class learning activities, McLean and Ransom (2005: 50) declare, albeit with no empirical support, that "silence can mean engagement in thought, not lack of ideas" and that the Western participatory style of learning is unfamiliar to international students. Hence, it is the aim of the current study to examine those statements empirically.

Research has shown that active participation in classroom activities is important for effective learning to occur (Gomez 1995; Kember/Gow 1994; Tsou 2005). Active engagement in classroom activities involves not only sitting and listening to the teacher delivering knowledge but also talking and writing about what is being learned, relating it to previous experiences and applying the processed knowledge in present situations. It is believed that in doing so the students are transferring what they learn into their own as well as enhancing critical thinking and intellectual development (Chickering/Gamson 1989; Mustapha 2010). In other words, participation is fundamental to the learning process (Murray 2018). Student oral participation being one of the most noticeable forms of class engagement, it is both reasonable and practical to study this phenomenon to facilitate effective learning.

The relatively quiet behaviour of Asian students in English-speaking classroom settings is well documented. As an example, Asian international students are described as those who "will sit silently rarely volunteering an answer unless called upon" based on Ballard and Clanchy's (1997: 16) own teaching experiences with Asian students in Australia. Biggs (1999: 3) also "found the deathly silence that preceded the start of the lecture quite unnerving, the more so when my open-ended questions met with no response" when he was teaching tertiary students in Hong Kong with English as the medium of instruction. Other researchers have emphasized the pronounced difference between Asian students' behaviour in and after class, that is, withdrawn versus active performance (e.g., Biggs 1999; Chu/Kim 1999; Kember 2000; Tani 2005). The current literature has been devoted to the exploration of the factors affecting the obvious contradiction of Asian students' behaviour, and two strands of research are identified and discussed as follows.

The role of culture in oral participation

One recurring theme in literature on classroom participation is the home culture of international students. This cultural perspective of oral participation attempts to address the issue with an essential emphasis on intercultural differences in students' learning styles and preferences. It is grounded on the hypothesis that international students, especially those from Confucian-heritage cultures or collectivist-oriented cultures such as China, Korea and Japan, do not participate to the same extent in comparison with their domestic peer students due to the obstacles and misunderstandings arising from intercultural variation (Fei 2016).

Specifically, Confucianism values collectivism over singularity, and communal voices rather than individual self-expressed opinions (Tani 2008). These cultural features are believed by Volet and Tan-Quigley (1999) to account for why Asian students feel more comfortable when asking questions in private compared to expressing opinions publicly in class. Through an examination of basic Confucian concepts, Wen and Clement (2003) conclude that Confucian values are the principal barrier for Chinese students to participate in class in the United States, which assign excessive significance to the evaluation of others who, in this case, are classmates and teachers. Thus, to speak up in class risks losing face and Asian students tend to avoid classroom communication consequently (Chan 1999; Irwin 1996; Watson 1999). On the other hand, students' oral interaction in class is prioritized in the Western tertiary institutions (Duff 2010; Ferris/Tagg 1996; Machemer/Crawford 2007), which reflects an inquiry-based tradition of teaching and learning that promotes indigenous ideas, critical thinking and learners' autonomy (Chan 1999; Durkin 2008; Speece 2002; Tweed/Lehman 2002). Utilising a Confucian-Socratic framework to analyse culture's influence on academic learning, Tweed and Lehman (2002) concluded that there was a causal relationship between Canadian tertiary students' cultural backgrounds and their learning beliefs and behaviours. While Western culture signifies the Socratic way of learning which emphasizes public questioning of generally accepted knowledge as well as beliefs by others and oneself, Chinese culture shares Confucian values that denote practical acquisition of knowledge and refinement of one's behaviour. Thus, aligning with a cultural view of participation, it is not surprising that students from a Confucian background are often characterised as silent, rote learners with passive learning styles by Western instructors (e.g., Ballard/Clanchy 1997; Durkin 2008).

Yet the above deficit views of non-Western cultures with regard to student participation are not without challenges. Some research has made counter claims either from the perspective of a culture insider or that of an outsider. From an insider's point of view, for example, Cheng (2000: 440) argues that active learning and critical thinking are also valued in Chinese education by illustrating widely accepted sayings by Confucius. One typical Confucian idiom is "qin xue hao wen", which means "(a good student should) study hard and always be ready to ask questions". Another famous motto by Confucius is "shi bu bi xian yu di zi; di zi bu bi bu ru shi", advocating that teachers need not outperform students in knowledge and students are not necessarily less learned than teachers (Cheng 2000). These proverbs reveal that, despite of the general impression of knowledge and knowledgeable teachers being highly respected by Confucianism, proactive learning through thinking and questioning is encouraged. Furthermore, Kin *et al.* (2016) refutes the perception of Japanese students as passive learners because of reserved participation in United States classrooms by highlighting the meaning those students ascribe to silence, which is ambiguous in essence and differently interpreted in Japanese and American contexts. Some Western educators also challenge the stereotypical view of international students as passive and superficial learners. From a cultural perspective, Chan (1997 as cited in Shi 2006) compares the learning beliefs and practices of Chinese and local students in an Australian university. The findings indicate that Chinese learners are highly active and monitoring their studies instead of remaining passive and doing surface learning through reproduction of knowledge. Not to aggrandize cultural differences, Biggs (1999) parallels the difficulties of international students enrolled in a Western-style university to local students moving from school to university.

By and large, scholarship with an emphasis on cultural roots of international students tends to take a culture-deterministic perspective of oral participation. While this cultural orientation helps shed light on the difficulties originated from home cultures of international students to fully participate in Western university classrooms, it oversimplifies culture as a changeless construct against time, regardless of its dynamic nature and the impact of sociocultural context on students' learning behaviour. Since the notion of Confucian-heritage culture is commonly adopted in this line of research, the diversity across Asian cultures (e.g., Chinese and Japanese cultures) is also neglected. In addition, international students' peculiarity as individuals are overlooked, such as variant language competence, which is discussed below.

The role of language competence in oral participation

Another principal theme in the literature is the English language competence of international students. This linguistic emphasis has its origin in that language competence has long been considered as a barrier in intercultural communication (e.g., Olaniran 1993). When applied to oral participation in internationalised classrooms, it is plausible to take linguistic factors into account. While some studies foreground the dominance of language proficiency from the perspectives of education practitioners, local students and international students themselves (e.g., Marginson/Sawir 2011; Morita 2004), others lend support to the strong correlation between language competence and oral participation empirically (e.g., Lee 2007; Mustapha 2010).

An insufficient view of international students' English language competence is commonly shared by students and educationists. As exemplified in Morita's (2004) study, one international student attributed the ignorance of her participation in class by both her classmates and the teacher to her limited English language level. Regarding the local students' attitudes, they are found to be reluctant to work with international students because of the latter's low English proficiency (Harrison/Peacock 2010; Osmond/Roed 2010). Some scholars and educators highlight this language insufficiency by criticizing low English entry levels set for international students. Marginson and Sawir (2011) argue that due to higher education becoming overly commercialized in countries including Australia, New Zealand and the United Kingdom, the English entry requirements for international students are problematically low to recruit more students for higher revenue, leaving the students in need of extra assistance with English. Others assert that the measurement methods for English proficiency adopted by universities (e.g., the Test of English as a Foreign Language (TOEFL) and the International English Language Testing System (IELTS)) are not valid enough to produce results that represent students' actual oral communicative skills (e.g., Cheng 2000; Coleman 1997; Liu 2000). Kim, Ablert and Sihn (2014) further articulate the seemingly contradiction between likely high scores from TOEFL Speaking Section by international students and their common difficulties in classroom participation as a result of distinctions between informal conversation and academic discussions. For the latter, not only general speaking skills are utilised, certain disciplinary knowledge and logic presentation of ideas are required as well (Kim *et al.* 2014).

There is also empirical research lending support to the impact of insufficient English competence on the degree to which international students involve themselves in classroom discussions. Mustapha (2010) has observed in two undergraduate classes at a university in Malaysia that Chinese international students with lower English language competence are less active in class discussions than those who are fluent speakers. Lee (2007) in her survey-based study of 131 East Asian students in an American university constructs linguistic factors as consisting of students' self-perceived English language proficiency, English language speaking anxiety and fear of negative evaluation. For perceived competence, appropriate use of English in terms of grammar, verb tense, vocabulary, word choice and pronunciation were graded by participants against a designed response scale. The results showed that there was a statistically significant relationship between oral participation and students' self-perceived level of English language articulation. However, the significance of English oral skills to participation was showed to be minor than that of English-speaking anxiety and fear of negative evaluation to verbal participation. Since the latter two constructs are largely influenced by individual characteristics such as personality, a close view at each individual student may provide a more comprehensive understanding of the matrix of factors behind oral participation.

Overall, difficulties related to limited language competence in classroom participation seem to be common among students studying abroad. Yet many factors other than linguistic competence or cultural influences arise while reviewing this strand of literature, such as domestic students' attitude, mastery of disciplinary knowledge, and the student's personality. It is found that even when participants are native or near native speakers, international students' participation in class remains an issue (Volet/Renshaw/Tietzel 1994). Liu (2001) argues from an emic perspective that English language deficiency is merely an assumption by Western teachers instead of a reason for reserved participation. Furthermore, language and culture are argued to be inseparable from each other (e.g., Gu 2009; Jones 1999; Straker 2016). One example is that the psycholinguistic constructs in Lee's (2007) study, speaking anxiety and fear of negative evaluation, may also be associated with losing face, which is inherent in Confucian-heritage culture. Thus, a clearly cut perspective of oral participation restricted to linguistic emphasis or cultural inheritance is too narrow to account for students' choice of speaking or not while neglecting their initiative to oral participation.

The Current Study

The present study aims to investigate the Chinese international students' perceptions and evaluation of tutorial oral participation and quietness in the classroom. In doing so, the students' agency of verbal contribution in class is respected and taken into consideration. Furthermore, the students' own motivation and expectations of tutorial oral participation will be explored, which is a vital variable that influences their oral participation. In comparison to previous research, the findings of the present study will be focused on Chinese international students' interests and needs with regard to oral participation, complementing past knowledge of disadvantageous factors they are faced with when speaking up in class. The findings will also lead to pedagogical implications that help improve international students' experience of classroom oral participation. This research project aims to explore the following questions:

1. What beliefs and expectations do Chinese international students have about oral participation in Australian university tutorials?

2. What are the views and feelings of Chinese international students towards quietness in the classroom?

Epistemology is about how knowledge is viewed. Maynard (1994: 10) argues that epistemology from the philosophical level determines what kinds of knowledge are attainable and "how we can ensure that they are both adequate and legitimate". As the methodological decisions in the course of any research are made on the basis of what epistemological position is taken, the epistemology of the study is it should be compatible with the primary inquiry and nature of the phenomenon explored, student perceptions of oral participation and reticence in class, a socially constructed behavior. Thus, regarding the present study, a constructivist paradigm of knowledge is taken.

Constructivism tends to examine a complex phenomenon as a whole and highlight how the phenomenon is shaped by the environment where it is embedded historically, culturally, and socioeconomically (Lodico/Spaulding/Voegtle 2010). Rather than taking an objectivist, mind-independent view of reality, constructivist researchers consider reality as inextricably associated with people's points of view, values and purposes because social realities are constructed and developed through human minds on the basis of their experiences, understanding and the contexts they are situated in (Scotland 2012). In this way, the result of social inquiry is never value-free and individuals' perceptions of the phenomenon are constantly subject to the change of their background or the context in which they live. On the other hand, it is stressed by Creswell (2007) that in constructivism the explored phenomenon is open to different interpretation thus manifold realities are acceptable and the complexity of the phenomenon is valued and highlighted.

Oral participation in class is a rather complex phenomenon which is under the influence of multiple factors (Ha 2014; Mack 2012). Different international students inevitably have different perceptions of oral participation in tutorials when placed in a different cultural context or a different period in time. Their understandings may be shaped by multiple factors, such as their cultural backgrounds, their language proficiency, their educational level, and the environment they are studying in. As this study aims to examine international students' perceptions of tutorial oral participation and attitudes towards silence in class, a detailed description of each participant to allow consideration of potential factors and a comprehensive synthesis of participants' viewpoints, which will be articulated below, are compatible with a constructivist epistemological position.

Setting

The present study was conducted in two university English language schools in Sydney, Australia. The schools run intensive English for Academic Purposes (EAP) courses, and students who attend these courses are largely enrolled in pathways which allow them to matriculate to the associated university when the language course is passed. EAP courses are designed to prepare students for university study, one of the demands of which is independent learning. This can be especially challenging for a learner studying in their L2, and therefore metastrategies could be particularly useful for EAP students. This setting was also chosen because it provides a useful contrast to the typical profile of teacher cognition research which is for the most part conducted in EFL environments (Borg 2012). In addition, one of the participating schools is the workplace of the researcher, and so presented a convenient context for carrying out the study.

Approach

In order to understand how Chinese international students perceive oral participation in Australian university tutorials, a qualitative research approach through diary entry and semi-structured interviews was taken. The advantage of such an approach lies in its strength to "get under the surface in order to understand people's perceptions and experience" (Silverman 2009: 5) and then, as Patton (1990 as cited in Lee 2009: 145) notes, allows us to "understand situations in their uniqueness as part of a particular context and the interactions there".

The qualitative research approach designed for this study was largely informed by the theory for grounded research (e.g., Glaser/Strauss 2017). It bears some similarity to grounded research in that no preconceptions were held in formulating research and interview questions and no pre-existing theoretical framework was used in analyzing data. This was to avoid inappropriate application of findings in different contexts and also to generate as comprehensive and context-dependent conclusions as possible. However, due to constrained time and scope for writing up a dissertation, this study did not fully follow the usual practice of grounded research, which tend to entail a longitudinal and systematic approach with several key strategies for conducting inquiry (Braun/Clarke 2006). In contrast, the present study was designed to suit tight deadline and aimed smaller compared to grounded research that generally wishes to produce a fully worked-up theory to account for the collected data (Charmaz 2014; Glaser/Strauss 2017). The thematic analysis adopted to analyze data was in some sense because it is an approach not fully committed to theory development (Holloway/Todres 2003).

Participants

Six Chinese graduate students, three female and three male students from different disciplines participated in this study. The participants were approached through personal contacts and consent forms were attained after informing them of the research procedure. Participation was completely voluntary and no monetary rewards were provided. Pseudonyms were used to protect the participants' confidentiality. Their biographical information is presented in Table 1.

	Age	Gender	Major	Stage of degree	Length of time studying abroad
Fiona	23	F	Educational Psychology	2nd semester	6 months
Alice	25	F	TESOL	1st semester	NA
Ella	29	F	Education (General)	2nd semester	NA
Leo	23	M	Applied Linguistics	2nd semester	4 years
Harry	24	M	Cross-cultural and Applied Linguistics	3rd semester	NA
Coy	32	M	TESOL	2nd semester	6 months

Table 1. Participant biodata.

Data Collection

The present study utilized questionnaires, diary prompts and semi-structured interviews to collect data. The combination of data collection methods provides a relatively rich description of subjects which allows triangulation of data and enhances research validity. In the first stage of data collection, prepared questionnaires about background information (see Appendix A) were given to participants to complete soon after they agreed to take part in the study. Then the participants were asked to write a diary entry(s) to record any impressive tutorial experience or their feelings during tutorials in the following one or two weeks. Diary prompts (see Appendix B) were provided to the participants as an instance of what might be written. The aim of writing diary entries was to keep tutorial experience fresh in students' minds and help them reflect on it, from which useful interview questions of research interest may be derived with regard to respective participant. Semi-structured interviews were carried out individually with each participant after their biographical questionnaire and diary entry were collected.

Findings

RQ1: What are the views and feelings of Chinese international students towards quietness in the classroom?

Generally, significant importance had been attached to oral participation by all participants in the study. The interview data showed that students had a highly positive evaluation of oral participation in tutorials, and more specifically, they consciously perceived its significance to be multi-dimensional: linguistically, academically, and in terms of social networking. The three differently oriented perspectives of oral participation are illustrated with related interview data as follows.

Belief 1: Oral participation in tutorial improves language proficiency

One major theme discovered from the data was the linguistic significance of oral participation. The data indicated that some of the participants recognized the linguistic benefits of speaking up in class through their own tutorial experiences. For example, Alice talked of being corrected by a classmate when the researcher asked about her impression of tutorial participation:

(1) When I communicate with him, he would reminds me of the errors that I make, like the wrong tense or word choice. For example, last night is the correct phrase instead of yesterday night. I tend to use the latter one but he told me it is incorrect, I was supposed to use last night [...] I like that. [Alice, interview]

Alice expressed how oral participation was useful in improving her English by providing more opportunities for her to get corrective feedback on speaking from other classmates.

(2) I think this is a really important role (that oral participation plays), because I consider myself weak in oral English before I came here, even though I passed all the English examinations during my college. So I think one of my goal to come here is to practice my oral English and make the language proficiency higher than before. [Harry, Interview]

Harry's response to "what role does oral participation play in tutorial" suggests that he perceived oral participation as a way to improve his oral English, which was one goal of him studying abroad. He further emphasized the importance of speaking in tutorials by relating it to his "progress in the accuracy and also the intelligibility with others" (Harry), which were among his primary concerns.

Other participants expressed a favorable attitude towards the facilitative effects of oral participation on language ability development through general statements.

(3) I think, although we are in an English-speaking environment, we speak our mother tongue for most of the time after class. Therefore, oral participation in class is a chance for us to speak and practice English. Whether it is our speaking skills or our familiarity with speaking English, oral participation activities offer us a chance to speak and practice. I think this is very good. [Coy, Interview]

(4) I think speaking up in…any possible occasions is important. First, because English is our second language, umm, just try to practice it as much as possible. It will raise your confidence, it will help you to umm, to shape your way of speaking more close or more towards the native speakers. Cause when you're communicating with them, you will be influenced…not only language wise, it's also about logic wise. Because I think Chinese, we express our ideas in a very different way with English native speakers, or at least in Australian context. When you listen to them, you can learn, or steal a little bit from, when you're having a conversation with them, when you're listening, when you're talking and you're also thinking: oh that's how he or she expresses it, that's how they convey the ideas. [Ella, Interview]

(5) I think oral participation has improved my speaking skills and because of this, I have more confidence to speak up, and have more communication with classmates. Like during a group work or discussion, you must speak up instead of just sitting there making notes. [Fiona, Interview]

These students regarded oral participation in tutorials as one occasion where they were supposed to speak English and communicate with others. While recognizing it as an academic requirement in the university, the students positively welcomed such a convention because it provides them with more opportunities to speak and practice English. Based on this shared understanding, two participants further made the suggestion that Chinese international students should be more active in tutorials even though insufficient language proficiency or speaking anxiety may be an issue.

(6) I think we should be more active in joining such oral participation activities, increasing our speeches in class. I think most of the Chinese students have good English, but they may reduce their participation because of various reasons. Some students may speak less because of bad English ability. According to me, no matter what you say can be understood by others or not, or if there are grammatical errors, expression is the important thing. That is, if you do not make any mistakes, you get no opportunity to be corrected by others. [Fiona, Interview]

(7) Sometimes it (speaking up in tutorial) can be anxious, you know, or a little bit intense, cause basically you have to stand up and speak in front of maybe twenty or thirty people, and they'll ask a lot of questions and just, you know, they're just looking at you, trying to find problems in your project of PowerPoint or those kind of stuff. So it can be, it can be moving into a nervous situation. But, yeah, I wouldn't say that's a bad thing because that's how you improve. [Leo, Interview]

By reporting the reasons why international students may not participate orally in class, participants showed their understanding of difficulties against oral participation in tutorial. Nevertheless, they still insisted on students speaking more in class as one way to improve English proficiency. Overall, the data revealed that the participants firmly believed in the significance of tutorial oral participation in terms of improving their linguistic competence.

Belief 2: Oral participation in tutorial promotes academic success

Another theme discovered from the data was the academic significance of oral participation. The data showed that participants' perceptions of the effectiveness of oral participation with regard to academic success can be classified into two categories, that is, the benefits in terms of students and teachers respectively.

Some participants ascribed the academic significance to teachers' involvement in oral participation activities in tutorial, where students' interaction with teachers and teachers' timely feedback are allowed.

(8) Oral participation is good for your study, in the long term. Considering study itself, I think oral participation can help deepen your understanding, enable you to combine theories with practice, and increase your interaction with the teacher. [Coy, Interview]

(9) I think if you have any questions, you can get feedback from the teacher quickly. It's not like when you write them down and send an email, you need to want for the answers. Oral participation gives you an answer on spot...This is a way for teachers to know each student's questions or which part of teaching is too difficult for students to understand, and they can give some feedback in time. [Fiona, Interview]

One of the participants even considered teachers' feedback or supplementary explanation of knowledge in tutorial to be the essential difference between tutorials and lectures.

(10) I think the difference between lecture and tutorial is that, lecture is a class where there are many students and the teacher elaborates on the content in general. And when it is in tutorial, the teacher is only lecturing a small amount of students, about 20, to make some points clearer or introduce more related knowledge based on students' class performance. In this way students' understanding of knowledge is deepened. [Alice, Interview]

Apart from teachers' comments from tutorial, some participants also reported that other students' speeches in class can be "inspiring" (Coy) for them. For example, when the researcher asked Coy to elaborate more on "inspiring", the word he used in the diary entry referring to one recent tutorial participation he had, Coy explained:

(11) I think first, speaking of the teacher, his whole process of scaffolding, including his final conclusion was quite inspiring. Second, it's the classmates' oral participation. Those classmates who spoke up explained theories of second language acquisition from different angles. In this view, I think it was inspiring. [Coy, interview]

Coy considered both the teacher's instruction and classmates' oral contribution in tutorial as sources of inspiration. Furthermore, Alice used one tutorial experience in her interview to exemplify the insights students may get from other classmates' oral participation in tutorials.

(12) For example, in our grammar tutorial we were asked to choose different language features to do teaching practice. Some students chose grammar feature like past tense, some chose conditional sentence with "if". For students who don't have much teaching experience like me, having those experienced teachers or those who can design interesting class activities to do some presentations or teaching practices will inspire us a lot…From simulated teaching activities designed by other students, we can learn a lot. [Alice, Interview]

According to the participants, not only other students' presentation in class may enlighten them in some way, but also the questions that other students raise and then discuss, as "the knowledge of one's own is limited" (Coy).

(13) One advantage of tutorial participation is, there are a group of students learning together. You can learn from their responses. Sometimes you may have a question and you are curious about it, but another classmate may have the same question and he brings it up for the whole class to discuss. Then they just help you solve your problem in the end. I think this is great to utilize such oral participation. [Fiona, Interview]

In further conversations with the researcher, some participants showed their consideration of how other students may benefit from their own speeches and because of this, they were willing to self-initiate oral participation in tutorial when they find their ideas worth sharing.

(14) Sometimes you are not sure whether your understanding is right or not…and some of your questions may be common among students, so if you expose them to the teacher, other students will also benefit from your questions. [Alice, Interview]

(15) I think it's (oral participation in tutorial) really important cause that's how you learn. You make up a point and you share it with others and others can learn from you and give you like advice on your project or stuff. [Leo, Interview]

(16) I will initiate a speech in tutorial from time to time. Normally under two circumstances: first, when I know the points being discussed pretty well; second, when I have some personal experiences that exemplify what the teacher talk about, which I think will contribute to the class. [Coy, Interview]

The academic benefits participants perceived of oral participation with regard to students themselves. From the perspective of teaching quality, some participants considered oral participation in tutorial to be in teachers' favor as well.

(17) I think presentation is very helpful to our study. If the teacher asks us questions and we respond based on our understanding, then the teacher will know how well we have mastered the knowledge. If the teacher keeps on lecturing without asking any questions, he will not know how well we understand the content and how should the following teaching proceed. Similarly, if we do not ask any questions, the teacher does not know how good we are at the knowledge and we are not sure if we understand it correctly. In addition, for some very specific questions, only when they are asked will the teacher realize and make the key points completely clear, which is helpful for the thorough acquisition of knowledge. [Alice, Interview]

(18) It can also help with teachers' teaching because through oral participation they can get feedback from their students in time, that is whether they understand the teaching content or not, who among the students have difficulty understanding and need more explanation and so on. [Fiona, Interview]

According to Alice and Fiona, students' oral participation reveals how well the students master the target knowledge and thus helps the teacher adjust his or her teaching to the students' needs. On the whole, oral participation facilitates teachers' teaching as well as students' learning.

Belief 3: Oral participation in tutorial facilitates social networking

Social networking emerged from the data as another significant theme related to participants' perceptions and expectations of tutorial oral participation. The transcripts of the interviews demonstrated that the participants viewed their oral participation in tutorial as a useful means to build and strengthen their social network with others, primarily their classmates and the teacher involved in the class.

(19) I feel that I was more talkative when I just came here. I guess that was because I wanted to become part of the learning community or quickly get familiar with the foreign environment. But afterwards I become more quiet in class discussion, that is to say I would not join in the participation as eagerly as before when I have a problem. At present, I won't voice any opinion when others have said the same thing and won't say that I agree with that and then share my experiences with the class and so on. [Fiona, Interview]

Here Fiona explained why her level of oral participation in class decreased over time as she studied in Australia. According to Fiona, her initiative to participate in class was largely affected by her need to expand social contacts in the environment, which was composed of the classmates and teachers. As Fiona achieved more social connections in class over time, she became less vigorous in class discussion. It was clear that Fiona held a firm belief in the active role oral participation played in building social networks. As Fiona said, speaking up in class helps her to "become part of the learning community".

Another participant Leo especially pointed out how speaking up in class can help students build connections with the teacher, who may help them with further study in the future.

(20) I guess the tutor or the professor would definitely be happier if you try to participate and get involved and they may pay more attention to you and maybe you can build up the network with them. For us who want to do a dissertation, you'd better be like participating in the tutorial. That's how you can build up the connection with your professor or tutor so you can actually, hmm, you know whenever you want to do a research, an independent research or dissertation or something like that, you can just talk to the professor, they already know you through the tutorial. [Leo, Interview]

In above interview extract, Leo argued that the more students involve themselves in class discussions, the more attention teachers will pay to them. And after students leaving an impression on teachers in this participative way, Leo considered it easier for students to seek teachers' help with study as "they already know you through the tutorial". Thus, it was natural to find Leo's perception of tutorial oral participation to be a way "you can build up the connection with your professor or tutor".

Apart from students' current social networking in the university, one of the participants Ella believed that students' future social networking in the workplace will also benefit from their experiences of oral participation in tutorial at present. For Ella, to speak up in class is a kind of social interaction, through which she can become more "comfortable" in future situations where oral presentation is needed. Thus, despite Ella's introverted personality, which was constantly preventing her from speaking up in class, she was vigorous to overcome the unease of speaking in front of the class so as to prepare herself to fulfill future social networking demands.

(21) I guess when I try to engage in the oral discussion or participation, I'm trying to, I'm consciously tying to push myself out of the comfort zone. I would say to myself there's an opportunity for you to speak up. Because in the future when you go to work, cause we're not working now, you always have to encounter such kind of situations and why not practice right now? I'd take any chance or opportunities to practice. But because of my introverted personality, I don't feel comfortable doing so. So I constantly have two little persons fighting with each other in my mind, do it, no, do it, no. [Ella, Interview]

RQ2: What are the views and feelings of Chinese international students towards quietness in the classroom?

The participant group showed mixed feelings toward quietness in classrooms. Some of the participants viewed being quiet in class discussions as one natural stage for international students to learn new things in a foreign environment and acknowledged its usefulness in learning as students are still thinking and participating even though they remain quiet. They perceived the quiet moments from a positive perspective. However, there were other participants who had a strong disfavor of not being orally engaged in classrooms and would negatively evaluate themselves if they are not proactive in class discussions. They considered quietness as a negative indicator of failing the university academic expectation as well as their own expectations of studying abroad. The participants' opposing viewpoints about quietness are illustrated with related data as shown below.

Students' positive evaluation of quietness in tutorials

One of the reasons why some participants viewed quietness in classrooms positively is that they believed it to be a natural phase for international students in the "progress to be familiar with this setting" (Harry, Interview) and think it beneficial in preparing them to be ready for later oral participation in class.

(22) I think that's (whether students are quiet in discussion or not) related to the time you study in the environment because I think, especially in first semester, you do not have so much knowledge and you just arrive here and it's a progress to be familiar with this setting. So that's why some students in their first semester, they're more afraid of speaking loud in the classroom. But you know, you see I'm in the third semester, I get more experience than others, especially those students in their first semester. So I think I'm more confident than them to speak aloud. [Harry, Interview]

Harry used his personal experience of becoming more and more interactive in class from the first semester to his third semester as an example to illustrate how student being quiet can be due to their unfamiliarity with the new environment and study content, and thus the quiet situation will be improved as their study proceeds. Aligning with Harry's viewpoint, Alice quoted one of her teachers, who also spoke English as a second language, to argue that "my current silence in class is for speaking up in the future".

(23) [The lecturer] said once in class that the first year he came here, he was unable to speak up in class because his English input was not enough. He said that he could not output when the input is not enough. I think this is very true. I believe my current silence in class is for speaking up in the future. [Alice, Interview]

Alice specifically pointed out that for international students, the more they are exposed to the English speaking environment, the more likely they are to speak up in class, and before they arrive at that point, staying quiet is their way of "learning to speak".

Another point in favor of students being quiet in class is made by Fiona, claiming that remaining silent is not the opposite side of participation; on the contrary, it is one way of participation, though quietly.

(24) I do not think that remaining silent means that I am not thinking or that I am upset. Because for me, silence is not a negative word. Actually I feel that there are many people, even including writers of the articles that we read for study, who have misunderstandings about the Asian students. Especially the previous western scholars, they tend to misunderstand Asian students, thinking they are more or less silent, inactive in class or accustomed to rote learning. That is somehow incorrect. I believe the quiet students are still thinking. They are just not speaking. [Fiona, Interview]

(25) Sometimes you may not have good ideas about what is being discussed at the moment, but when you can listen to others' opinions and get some inspirations from them. That is some advantage of being quiet. That is to say, if you listen, though you do not present anything, but you have listened, then I think it great if you find what you have listened to useful. [Fiona, Interview]

Fiona argued that when students remain quiet, it is because they are thinking. She further described how quiet thinking may work and be helpful to students' learning.

Students' negative evaluation of quietness in tutorials

Some participants considered students being quiet in class a bad phenomenon because they held the belief that to be interactive in tutorials is an academic convention in the university and students are supposed to conform to it.

(26) I think silence in tutorials is not a good sign, because the tutorial itself should be a class where there are interactions between the teacher and the students as well as among the students. Especially for language learning, I think to be orally engaged is one essential part. The whole class should be interactive. [Coy, Interview]

(27) I feel like a successful tutorial always involves a lot of participation like, I don't like the things when the lecturer just goes on like forever and students are just listening. That's not the way it's supposed to be. It's more about like people getting involved in the discussion and the information goes in and out. And creating a safe place for people to speak up and to raise up different opinions or those kind of stuff. [Leo, Interview]

Coy and Leo expressed their idea that tutorials are expected be interactive. Based on this belief, students would fail to fulfill the expectation if they remain silent in class. As Ella said, "I try to show them that I have the ability" to meet the requirement.

(28) I think it's an academic requirement or academic expectation here in this university to speak actively in class and I try to show them that I have the ability…I think it's important because…it's what the university expects us to do so. It's their educational tradition. [Ella, Interview]

Ella further refuted the above positive view that being quiet and thinking is a kind of participation. It is clear that for Ella, participation equals oral contribution in class; she negated the value of staying quiet in class discussions completely. Coy expressed a similar opinion that he doubted whether the quiet students were actually involved in class or just sitting there and waiting for the end of the class.

(29) I see it as not participating. It is not participating in oral discussions because you're not voicing yourself. You're remaining silent. How that can be participating? […] If it's a discussion, and you know, we are expected to discuss with others. Just thinking is not enough. [Ella, Interview]

(30) I see some students who have never ever spoken from the first to the last class over the whole semester. And there are a number of them. But for me, personally, I don't think they are participating in the class. Are the following the teacher? I doubt that. So I tend to think they are just sitting quietly for the end of the class. Because if you don't speak, we don't know if you are really following the class. [Coy, Interview]

Another negative point the participants made about being quiet in classrooms is in terms of their own expectations and goals of studying abroad. It was reported by the participants that quietness in class degrades their experiences of learning in a foreign country. One of the participants Harry indicated that not to be orally engaged in class would fail "my expectation for myself" when it comes to the fact that he was studying abroad in Australia. And Coy expressed some level of disappointment when he found the class was not as interactive as he had expected.

(31) I think it's more than that (the expectation of the Australian academy). It's also my expectation for myself. Because you study abroad and this is a environment, a good environment for you to practice your English and to learn some new perceptions from these educational systems. So if you just listen to teachers, I cannot say it's totally wrong, but I think when you participate in the classroom, speaking not just help you to concentrate more on the classroom but also to immerse yourself in the knowledge you need to get from the class. [Harry, Interview]

(32) I think maybe because there are many Asian students or say, Chinese students, studying in the university, and possibly some cultural factors going on, the classes seem to be too quiet. From my own personal experiences and perspective, I feel the situation is different from what I estimated before I came here. I thought it would be a very active learning environment, but in fact it is not. I feel a little bit disappointed. [Coy, Interview]

Alice and Harry took the monetary issue into consideration, adding weight to the disapproval of being orally inactive in tutorial discussions. Alice stressed that to keep silent in class prevents international students from making the best of their experiences of studying abroad and regarded it as "a waste of money", considering the expensive tuition fees. Similarly, Harry said that the cost of studying abroad was too high to allow students to idle away their class time just listening without speaking. Besides, he argued that, despite all the negative factors of oral participation, such as introverted personality or limited language proficiency, staying quiet in class is against international students' essential goal of studying abroad and should be overcome by students.

(33) Especially considering that we have spent so much money to come all the way to study here, if we keep being silent, it is a waste of money. [Alice, Interview]

(34) I don't think this is a really, uh, good phenomenon, because you pay for tuition fee, you come here from your hometown, it's so far. I don't think you should waste all the time during the classroom and I think everyone should be more brave even I know someone is shy, they're unwell to speak aloud themselves, but if they have goals or purposes to improve their oral English, I think you need to do so. That's the simplest way to improve your language proficiency…So I think that need an alternative thought of your perceptions about why you come here, why you study here, your goals, your purpose to study here, I think. [Harry, Interview]

Not only were academic requirement and personal expectations mentioned, the participants' negative evaluation of quietness in classrooms was also reflected on their unfavorable attitudes towards their own non-participative behavior in class and their participation suggestions for classmates and future Chinese international students. Most participants reported feeling upset and disappointed in themselves when they were not engaged in tutorial discussions. This was due to that they considered being quiet as a sign of "incompetence" or poor academic performance. Ella would even criticize herself because of making no oral contribution to class.

(35) I feel a little bit disappointed at myself. Like why I'm not engaged in this, like I'm not less intelligent than anybody else, incompetent in English or at least not that bad. So I would criticize myself a bit after that. [Ella, Interview]

(36) I think in most circumstances I will consider it (not being able to speak up in class) my own personal problems because maybe I didn't preview the content in advance or maybe it's just about my limitation of the knowledge…I didn't do it well and maybe I have wrong comprehension with others. [Harry, Interview]

The participants also expressed a wish for classmates and future Chinese students enrolled in Australian universities to be more active in class verbal participation, revealing their disfavor of current reticent classroom participation and preference of active participation environment over quiet classrooms.

(37) Learn English well while you are in your home country. This will increase your participation in class, otherwise, you will just keep silent. [Alice, Interview]

(38) I wish other students can speak more. [Leo, Interview]

(39) Don't get anxious, participate more, and you know, be yourself, speak up loud, that's it. Everybody makes mistakes so it's totally fine to speak up loud. [Leo, Interview]

Discussion

The present study has been developed around Chinese international students' considerations of oral participation and reticence in tutorials. The findings reveal students' comprehensive understanding and evaluation of two opposing acts, being verbally engaged in class and being reserved about speaking in tutorials. Taking both aspects into consideration helps shed light on the understanding of Chinese international students' choice to speak or not to speak in Australian tutorials.

Multidimensional beliefs with regard to oral participation in tutorials

Overall, the students believed that oral participation in class is a constructive means in improving language proficiency, facilitating academic success, and promoting social networking. Regarding the belief that verbal engagement in class activities improves students' language proficiency, the participants stressed the benefits both in terms of linguistic competence and linguistic performance, such as picking up new words or mastering English communicative skills. This is in accordance with Xue's (2013) finding that increased English group work participation helps improve international students' language proficiency. Interestingly, in spite of the participants' diverse levels of language competence, the perception of tutorial interaction as linguistically beneficial and thus worthy of attention was shared among them. This revealed the fact that the Chinese international students prioritized their identity as English language learners even though they were attending mainstream courses and one important aim for them to participate in tutorials was to improve their second language competence. What the participants believed in can find theoretical support according to Ellis and Shintani (2014:195), who emphasized the importance of interaction in second language acquisition by defining it as "a source of input and opportunities for output, which foster the internal processing that results in acquisition". Based on this point of view, Ellis and Shintani (2014) further urged that students participate actively to acquire a second language.

On the other hand, the participants of the present study also reported their unsatisfactory level of English proficiency when elaborating their intention to increase oral participation in class to improve language competence. Actually, the lack of adequate language proficiency has been reported as one primary barrier for international students to participate orally in class (Ha 2014; Wu 2011; Xue 2013). For instance, Wu (2011) found that one of the main problems that language issues posed for Taiwanese international students in an American university was verbal participation in classroom discussions. Most of Xue's (2013) participants perceived of unsatisfactory English language proficiency as one obstacle preventing them from participation during group work. Ha (2014) investigated the factors that impacted the oral classroom participation of four international students enrolled in an American graduate school through interviews, questionnaires and classroom observations over a semester, and found that language insufficiency limited students' contribution inside the classroom. It is clear that, in spite of the language issues facing the participants, Chinese international students still showed considerable motivation to improve their language proficiency though more oral participation in class discussions. Such a strong motivation deserves to be catered to by the tutees in ways such as providing more opportunities for students to speak up and giving adequate feedback on oral performance, which will help international students yield expected outcome with regard to language competence. The language proficiency gains will in turn promote international students' oral participation.

With respect to the belief that oral participation in class discussions facilitates academic success, the participants emphasized the significance of teachers' involvement in discussion activities and classmates' verbal contribution of creative ideas in class. Teachers' involvement in class discussions was considered to help students' understanding of knowledge in two aspects. First, the participants were aware of the fact that they can get timely instruction from the teacher if they raise a question during a tutorial discussion. The participants expressed a positive attitude toward self-reported inquiry in tutorial by comparing an "on-spot" answer they will get against a relatively delayed reply if they approach the teacher through other means such as writing an email after class. This demonstrated the Chinese students' autonomy in learning instead of passivity claimed by scholars of a culture-deterministic view (e.g., Ballard/Clanchy 1997; Durkin 2008). Second, the participants recognized that the tutees' elaboration of knowledge in tutorials was supplementary to lecture delivery but more interactive, practical and based on students' class performance, which they believed to be the essential differences between tutorials and lectures. The participants also showed awareness of active transition from previous quiet classes in China to participatory tutorials in Australia. Apparently, the Chinese international students adapted well to the lecture-tutorial teaching modes in the Australian university; the influence of different classroom norms were not as prominent a problem as Lee (2009) advocated in a study concerning international students in U.S. graduate seminars.

Classmates' oral contribution in tutorials was another reason why the participants considered oral participation to be a facilitative factor of academic learning. The participants declared that they can benefit from other students' speeches in tutorial by taking in different perspectives of and new information about what is being learned. Because tutorial discussions tend to involve a number of students, the whole class can learn from each other's responses to questions raised and even the questions themselves. Based on the acknowledgment of students' oral participation, the participants also showed their intention to initiate valuable presentations so that other classmates can benefit from their indigenous thinking, creating a beneficial and vibrant learning environment. This reflects that the Chinese students possess agency not only in promoting their own academic success but also that of other students. Furthermore, critical thinking, indigenous ideas and learners' autonomy that tend to be associated with western style of learning (Durkin 2008; Machemer/Crawford 2007) are actually not uncommon among Chinese international students. This implicates that to oversimplify the quietness of East Asian international students in class as a result of their Confucian-heritage cultures may be too narrow an understanding.

The third belief that the participants held about tutorial oral participation is that it facilitates their social networking. They considered tutorial participation as a means to build social connections with both classmates and teachers since to engage in class discussions is essentially a type of social interaction. According to Furnham (2004), the success of socialization resides in the kinds of contact situated in the environment where the foreign students are engaged. Thus, to expand contacts through oral participation in Australian university tutorials forms part of the international students' socialization process in the new context. Yet there is little research on the interpersonal significance of student oral participation in class. Utilizing in-depth interviews and group discussion observation, Kim (2016) examined Korean students' socialization process in a US university, focusing on their group work oral participation. Kim (2016) concluded that the students' self-perceived language proficiency, differences in socio-cultural values and educational practices were the primary factors influencing their socialization. However, Kim's (2016) study looks at international student oral participation and socialization more in terms of an academic adaptation perspective, ignoring the interpersonal social support students get from class participation. Similarly, Holmes (2016) limited the discussion of 12 international undergraduate students' socialization through oral participation to changes of academic discourse in the context of an American university.

For the present study, the participants showed high evaluation of the effects that tutorial oral participation has on fostering interpersonal relationships with classmates and teachers. This was because, as stated by the participants, that discussions in classrooms served as the major occasion where they interacted with other students in English, and where they talked to students of other nations. The participants indicated that their social interaction outside the classroom was limited. In this way, class participation was plausibly attached much interpersonal value to as oral participation can help the participants get familiar with other students and become a member of the learning community. On the other hand, the participants perceived oral participation as a way to build up their profile and leave an impression on others. One participant even reported a drop of speaking frequency in tutorials over the semester as her feeling of connectedness became strong enough and she felt it needless to remain active in class. It is clear that the Chinese international students associated their oral participation in class closely with their interpersonal needs and consciously utilized it to expand and strengthen social contacts. Yet as most current studies have focused on the academic socialization of international students in classroom oral activities, there is a dearth of research investigating the interpersonal meaning of international students' classroom oral participation, which constitutes an important part of their social networking experiences in the foreign country.

Mixed evaluation of quietness in tutorials

Moving to the findings regarding Chinese international students' evaluation of quietness in the classroom, two opposing points of view are revealed. With regard to the positive perspective of staying quiet in tutorials, two major reasons were brought up by the participants. First, the international students considered being quiet in classroom discussions as a natural stage in the process of them adapting to the new learning context. Other than issues related to culture and language, the influential factors were believed to include lack of discipline knowledge and unfamiliarity with the classroom norms. However, the students were positive that the situation would improve over time as they become more accustomed to the context. This correlates with what Kim (2016) found with Korean students enrolled in a US university, who were initially labelled as silent participants in group work oral participation became more active after they adapted over the course of a semester. In Heng's (2018: 26) study, 18 Chinese international students relearned new language skills, understood new classroom expectations and sociocultural contexts after a year studying in US higher education, most of whom used to be "unsure of the participation format" in class. These findings refute the deficit perspective of silent students in class being passive and needy; silence is a period that prepares the international students to speak actively in the future.

Another reason in favor of the student choice of remaining silent in class is that being quiet does not equal non-participation. Instead, it is another way of classroom engagement, though quietly. The participants believed that staying quiet helped them think and learn as they were listening to speeches of others in the classroom. For those participants who chose verbal silence in tutorial discussions, they challenged the idea of associating reticence with negative implications to arrive at the conclusion that Asian students were passive learners and argued it as merely a personal choice of learning style in certain contexts. This is supported by Nonnecke and Preece's (2003) argument that it lacks evidence to claim verbal expression as the only means that reflects active engagement in learning. This demonstrates that reticence does not necessarily relate to lack of engagement but can be a conscious choice of participation. However, most intercultural research evaluates the value of reticence taking the Western perspective, which tend to view reticence negatively (Scollon 1985). To avoid misinterpretation of international student silence in class especially in the Western context, therefore, more in-depth research needs to be devoted to investigations of the use and meaning of silence by international students.

While there were views affirming the value of silence in class, most of the participants evaluated classroom silence negatively. They considered to remain quiet in tutorial discussions lowers the academic expectation of the university, spoiled their experiences of studying abroad, and, in essence, is a sign of non-participation. Indeed, education in Anglo-Saxon countries takes a learner-centered approach of teaching, which values student own voices and classroom participation (Parris-Kidd/Barnett 2011; Wu 2015; Yan/Berliner 2009). Moreover, active classroom participation is generally promoted and appreciated across a variety of disciplines in higher education and is a common measurement for the evaluation of students (Tatar 2005). The fact that the participants perceive of oral participation as important academic expectation not only reveals a deep understanding of the educational goals of the university, but also a strong motivation to participate in class discussions.

The second negative view of reticence was in terms of the students' own expectations of studying abroad. They considered to be orally engaged in class activities and to have an interactive class environment as one essential part of their experiences of studying abroad while remaining quiet in class degraded such experience. For those participants themselves, they were motivated to participate actively in class despite hindering factors such as an introverted personality and limited language proficiency. For the class environment, however, the participants expressed disappointment, saying that it was not as interactive as they had expected. The third view that silence was the opposite of participation was in consistent with Western values. The participants even expressed negative evaluation of quiet students in classroom, considering them as not involved in class. It seems that the Chinese international students were well accustomed to and accepted the Western thinking of oral participation and reticence. These findings challenge the view that the influence of cultural inheritance plays a dominant role in preventing international students from oral participation (Fei 2016; Tani 2008).

Implications for theory and practice

The findings of the present study constitute a fruitful contribution to existing theory about student oral participation in that it replenishes international students' specific motives that underlie their oral participation in class. Instead of exploring reasons behind international students' low level of oral participation in class, the present study starts looks at oral participation from a motivational perspective, exploring students' motives behind and expectations of oral participation. Such a research paradigm sheds light on a holistic view of oral participation, which not only includes linguistic, cultural and contextual factors but also student agency of learning. The findings reveal that international students are driven by motivation from three dimensions, linguistic, academic and social interaction-related despite a matrix of deficit factors. The formed theoretical framework will provide better guidance for education practitioners to help international students meet the expectation of full participation.

Apart from the extension of theory, the present study bears implication for future research. Among the three orientations of motivation, social needs of international students in verbal classroom activities is under-examined. Most of current research has focused on student academic assimilation through classroom oral participation instead of the interpersonal support they aspire to get from participation in class activities. More in-depth research needs to be implemented in this direction. Another line of research is needed to further explore the use and meanings of silence by East Asian students. Participants in the present study did not explain their intension of utilizing reticence to communicate meanings in detail yet negative evaluation will take place if the teacher misinterprets students' reticence. Thus, further studies are needed in this respect.

In addition to the theoretical contributions of the present study, the findings bear important pedagogical meaning for tertiary education practitioners to promote international student oral participation in class. To encourage classroom participation, first of all, instructors should allocate some time and energy to facilitating students' language learning in oral participation activities. Since the international students think highly of language learning, English proficiency gains in oral participation should be an incentive for them to participate more in class. Second, it is suggested that practitioners embed knowledge delivery in classroom oral activities so that the students feel satisfied with academic learning through participation and this in turn will encourage their verbal behavior in oral tasks. Third, to satisfy students' social needs entails building connections with them. Therefore, practitioners are suggested to create a classroom environment conducive to oral participation by being open-minded and patient, and encouraging students to interact with each other.

International students value the class experience with active participation of not only themselves but also that of other classmates. Therefore, it is a rewarding task for the practitioners to enhance international students' college experience by making as many students to speak up in class as possible. Concerning the reticent ones of international students in class, it is meaningful to make clear their reasons behind quietness first. The student may have not adapted to the new learning environment yet and chooses to remain quiet for the time being. In this case, the instructor need not to pay much attention to urging them to speak but ensure the language input of the students. Other reasons may be that the student is actively listening and thinking or to the contrary, is in a fit of absence of mind. The practitioner needs to be careful to discern the possible reasons and apply methods accordingly to help the student participate actively in class.

References

Ballard, Brigid / Clanchy, John 1997. *Teaching International Students: A Brief Guide for Lecturers and Supervisors*. Deakin: IDP Education Australia.

Biggs, John 1999. *Teaching for Quality Learning at University: What the Student Does*. Buckingham: Open University Press.

Braun, Virginia / Clarke, Victoria 2006. Using Thematic Analysis in Psychology. *Qualitative Research in Psychology*. 3/2, 77-101.

Chan, Sally 1999. The Chinese Learner: A Question of Style. E*ducation and Training*. 41/6-7, 294-305.

Charmaz, Kathy 2014. *Constructing Grounded Theory*. London: Sage.

Cheng, Xiaotang 2000. Asian Students' Reticence Revisited. *System*. 28, 435-446.

Chickering, Arthur / Gamson, Zelda 1989. Seven Principles for Good Practice in Undergraduate Education. *Biochemical Education*. 17/3, 140-141.

Chu, Sauman / Kim, Joo Hei 1999. Comparison of the Perceptions of Classroom Participation among Asian and Non-Asian Design Students. *Multicultural Education*. 7/2, 21-24.

Coleman, Susan 1997. International Students in the Classroom: A Resource and an Opportunity. *International Education*. 26/2), 52.

Creswell, John W. 2007. *Qualitative Inquiry and Research Design: Choosing Among Five Traditions* (2nd ed.). Thousand Oaks, CA: Sage.

Duff, Patricia 2010. Language Socialization into Academic Discourse Communities. *Annual Review of Applied Linguistics*. 30, 169–192.

Durkin, Kathy 2008. The Adaptation of East Asian Masters Students to Western Norms of Critical Thinking and Argumentation in the UK. *Intercultural Education*. 19/1, 15-27.

Ellis, Rod / Shintani, Natsuko 2014. *Exploring Language Pedagogy Through Second Language Acquisition Research*. New York: Routledge.

Ferris, Dana / Tagg, Tracy 1996. Academic Oral Communication

Needs of EAP Learners: What Subject-matter Instructors Actually Require. *TESOL Quarterly*. 30/1, 31–58.
Fei, Jia 2016. The Politics of Oral Participation: The Experiences of Chinese Multilingual Speakers in Canadian University Classrooms. Doctoral Dissertation, University of Toronto, Canada.
Furnham, Adrian 2004. Education and Culture Shock. *Psychologist*. 17/1, 16-19.
Glaser, Barney / Strauss, Anselm 2017. *Discovery of Grounded Theory: Strategies for Qualitative Research*. New York: Routledge.
Gomez, Adelina M. (1995). When Does a Student Participate in Class? Ethnicity and Classroom Participation. Paper presented at the Annual Meeting of the Speech Communication Association, San Antonio, TX.
Gu, Qing 2009. Maturity and Interculturality: Chinese Students' Experiences in UK Higher Education. *European Journal of Education*. 44, 37-52.
Ha, M-J. 2014. International Students' Oral Participation in the Multicultural Classroom. *Information*. 17/12A, 6177-6182.
Harrison, Neil / Peacock, Nicola 2010. Interactions in the International Classroom: The UK Perspective. In Jones, Elspeth (ed.), *Internationalisation and the Student Voice* (pp. 125-142). London, England: Routledge.
Heng, Tang T. 2018. Different is not Deficient: Contradicting Stereotypes of Chinese International Students in US Higher Education. *Studies in Higher Education*. 43/1, 22-36.
Holloway, Immy / Todres, Les 2003. The Status of Method: Flexibility, Consistency and Coherence. *Qualitative Research*. 3, 345-357.
Holmes, Rebekah 2016. Academic Discourse Socialization through Oral Practices: The Negotiation of Participation and Identity amongst University ESL Learners. Master's Thesis, St. Cloud State University, St. Cloud, MN.
Hodne, Barbara 1997. Please Speak Up: Asian Immigrant Students in American College Classrooms. *New Directions for Teaching and Learning*. 70, 85-92.
Irwin, Harry 1996. *Communicating with Asia: Understanding People and Customs*. Kuala Lumpur: Allen and Unwin.
Jones, Jeremy F. 1999. From Silence to Talk: Cross-cultural Ideas on Students' Participation in Academic Group Discussion. *English*

for Specific Purposes. 18/3, 243–259.
Kember, David 2000. Misconceptions about the Learning Approaches, Motivation, and Study Practices of Asian Students. *Higher Education.* 40, 99–121.
Kember, David / Gow, Lyn 1994. Orientations to Teaching and Their Effect on the Quality of Student Learning. *The Journal of Higher Education.* 65/1, 58-74.
Kim, Jung Yin 2016. Group Work Oral Participation: Examining Korean Students' Adjustment Process in a US University. *Australian Journal of Adult Learning.* 56/3, 400-423.
Kim, Rina / Ablert, Lillie R. / Sihn, Hang Gyun 2014. *Reading, Writing, and Discussing at the Graduate Level: A Guidebook for International Students*. Lanham, MD: University Press of America.
Lee, Ee Lin 2007. Linguistic and Cultural Factors in East Asian Students' Oral Participation in US University Classrooms. *International Education.* 36/2, 27-47.
Lee, Given 2009. Speaking up: Six Korean Students' Oral Participation in Class Discussions in US Graduate Seminars. *English for Specific Purposes.* 28/3, 142-156.
Liu, Jun 2000. Understanding Asian Students' Oral Participation Modes in American Classrooms. *Journal of Asian Pacific Communication.* 10/1, 155-189.
Liu, Jun 2001. *Asian Students' Classroom Communication Patterns in U.S. Universities: An Emic Perspective*. Westport, CT: Greenwood.
Lodico, Marguerite G. / Spaulding, Dean T. / Voegtle, Katherine H. 2010. *Methods in Educational Research: From Theory to Practice*. San Francisco: Jossey-Bass.
Machemer, Patricia L. / Crawford, Pat 2007. Student Perceptions of Active Learning in a Large Cross-disciplinary Classroom. *Active Learning in Higher Education.* 8/1, 9-30.
Mack, Lindsay 2012. Does Every Student Have a Voice? Critical Action Research on Equitable Classroom Participation Practices. *Language Teaching Research.* 16/3, 417-434.
Marginson, Simon / Sawir, Erlenawati 2011. *Ideas for Intercultural Education.* New York, NY: Palgrave Macmillan.
Marlina, Roby 2009. "I Don't Talk or I Decide Not to Talk? Is it My

Culture?" International Students' Experiences of Tutorial Participation. *International Journal of Educational Research.* 48/4, 235-244.

Maynard, Mary 1994. Methods, Practice and Epistemology: The Debate about Feminism and Research. In Maynard, Mary / Purvis, June (eds), *Researching Women's Lives from a Feminist Perspective* (pp. 10-26). London: Taylor & Francis.

McLean, Patricia / Ransom, Laurie 2005. Building Intercultural Competencies: Implications for Academic Skills Development. In Carroll, Jude / Ryan, Janette (eds), *Teaching International Students: Improving Learning for All* (pp. 45–62). London: Routledge.

Meyers, Chet / Jones, Thomas B. 1993. *Promoting Active Learning, Strategies for College Classrooms*. San Francisco: Jossey-Bass.

Morita, Naoko 2004. Negotiating Participation and Identity in Second Language Academic Communities. *TESOL Quarterly.* 38, 573-603.

Murray, Neil 2018. Understanding Student Participation in the Internationalised University: Some Issues, Challenges, and Strategies. *Education Sciences.* 8/96, 1-10.

Mustapha, Siti Maziha 2010. Understanding Classroom Interaction: A Case Study of International Students' Classroom Participation at One of the Colleges in Malaysia. *International Journal for the Advancement of Science & Arts.* 1/2, 91-99.

Nonnecke, Blair / Preece, Jenny 2003. Silent Participants: Getting to Know Lurkers Better. In Lueg, Christopher / Fisher, Danyel (eds), *From Usenet to CoWebs* (pp. 110-132). London: Springer.

Olaniran, Bolanle 1993. International Students' Network Patterns and Cultural Stress: What Really Counts. *Communication Research Reports.* 10, 69-83.

Osmond, Jane / Roed, Jannie 2010. Sometimes It Means More Work: Student Perceptions of Group Work in a Mixed Cultural Setting. In Jones, Elspeth (ed.), *Internationalisation and the Student Voice* (pp. 113-124). London, England: Routledge.

Parris-Kidd, Heather / Barnett, Jenny 2011. Cultures of Learning and Student Participation: Chinese Learners in a Multicultural English Class in Australia. In Jin, Lixian / Cortazzi, Martin (eds), *Researching Chinese Learners* (pp. 169-187). London: Palgrave

Macmillan.
Patton, Michael Q. 1990. *Qualitative Evaluation and Research Methods*. Thousand Oaks, CA: Sage.
Scollon, Ronald 1985. The Machine Stops: Silence in the Metaphor of Malfunction. In Tannen, Deborah / Saville-Troike, Muriel (eds), *Perspectives on Silence* (pp. 21-30). Norwood, NJ: Ablex.
Scotland, James 2012. Exploring the Philosophical Underpinnings of Research: Relating Ontology and Epistemology to the Methodology and Methods of the Scientific, Interpretive, and Critical Research Paradigms. *English Language Teaching.* 5/9, 9-16.
Shi, Lijing 2006. The Successors to Confucianism or a New Generation? A Questionnaire Study on Chinese Students' Culture of Learning English. *Language, Culture and Curriculum.* 19/1), 122-147.
Silverman, David 2009. *Doing Qualitative Research: A Practical Handbook* (3rd ed.). London: Sage.
Speece, Mark 2002. Experiential Learning Methods in Asian Cultures: A Singapore Case Study. *Business Communication Quarterly.* 65/3, 106–121.
Straker, John 2016. International Student Participation in Higher Education: Changing the Focus from "International Students" to "Participation". *Journal of Studies in International Education.* 20/4, 299-318.
Tani, Massimilano 2005. *Quiet, But Only in Class: Reviewing the In-class Participation of Asian Students.* Higher Education Research and Development Society of Australia Conference, Sydney, New South Wales.
Tani, Massimiliano 2008. Raising the In-class Participation of Asian Students through a Writing Tool. *Higher Education Research & Development.* 27/4, 345-356.
Tatar, Sibel 2005. Why Keep Silent? The Classroom Participation Experiences of Non-native-English-speaking Students. *Language and Intercultural Communication.* 5/3-4, 284-293.
Tsou, Wenli 2005. Improving Speaking Skills through Instruction in Oral Classroom Participation. *Foreign Language Annals.* 38/1, 46-55.
Tweed, Roger G. / Lehman, Darrin R. 2002. Learning Considered within a Cultural Context: Confucian and Socratic Approaches. *American Psychologist.* 57/2, 89–99.

Volet, Simone / Renshaw, Peter / Tietzel, K. 1994. A Short-term Longitudinal Investigation of Cross-cultural Differences in Study Approaches using Biggs' SPQ. *British Journal of Educational Psychology*. 64, 301-318.

Volet, Simone / Tan-Quigley, A. 1999. Interactions of Southeast Asian Students and Administrative Staff at University in Australia: The Significance of Reciprocal Understanding. *Journal of Higher Education Policy and Management*. 21/1, 95–115.

Watson, Desley 1999. "Loss of Face" in Australian Classrooms. *Teaching in Higher Education*. 4/3, 355–363.

Wu, I-Ju 2011. Learning Strategies Use by International Students from Taiwan in a University Context: A Case Study. Master's Dissertation, California State University, Chico, CA.

Wu, Qi 2015. Re-examining the "Chinese Learner": A Case Study of Mainland Chinese Students' Learning Experiences at British Universities. *Higher Education*. 70/4, 753-766.

Xue, Mo 2013. Effects of Group Work on English Communicative Competence of Chinese International Graduates in United States Institutions of Higher Education. *The Qualitative Report*. 18/7, 1-19.

Yan, Kun / Berliner, David C. 2009. Chinese International Students' Academic Stressors in the United States. *College Student Journal*. 43/4, 939-960.

Yook, Eunkyong. L. / Albert, Rosita D. 1998. Perceptions of the Appropriateness of Negotiation in Educational Settings: A Cross-cultural Comparison among Koreans and Americans. *Communication Education*. 47/1, 18-29.

Young, Dolly Jesusita 1991. Creating a Low Anxiety Classroom Environment: What Does Language Anxiety Research Suggest? *The Modern Language Journal*. 75/4, 426–437.

Appendix A: Diary Entry Prompts

Please complete the questionnaire so that we can learn about you. Thank you!

Name	
Age	
Gender	
Major	
Stage of degree	It is semester _____ (e.g., 1/2) of my _____ (e.g., 1st/2nd) year of postgraduate study in Australia.
Have you studied or lived in an English-speaking environment prior to your enrolment in current postgraduate program? If applicable, please specify.	

Appendix B: Diary Entry Prompts

Please note that these prompts only give a brief idea of what a diary entry covers. You are welcome to add anything else you would like to share about your tutorial participation. Thank you!

- How did you feel about today's tutorial speech activities?
- Did you participate orally in the tutorial and in what ways (e.g., turns taken, self-initiation or response)?
- How often did you participate in each way respectively?
- How did you feel when you spoke up?
- What did you feel happy or unhappy with?
- How would you like to change your participation?
- Is there any other thing you would like to mention about your tutorial participation?

Appendix C: Interview Schedule

1) How important do you think speaking up in tutorials is and in what ways?

2) Do you intend to change your oral participation in any way and if so, how?

3) How would you describe international students' oral participation in tutorials?

4) In what situation do you prefer not to speak up in tutorials?

5) What do you think of the quiet students in class?

6) What do you perceive of the quiet moments in tutorials?

Qian Yang / David Hirsh

Academic Adaptation of International Students in Higher Education

Introduction

International students can experience a complicated academic transitional period (Cao/Zhu/Meng, 2021). Educational and cultural backgrounds are considered to affect the academic adaptation processes of international students (Campbell 2015). Although all international students experience academic disorientation, Chinese students in Anglophone universities have a particularly difficult adjustment time given the prominent cultural differences (Leong 2015). A growing number of host institutions are addressing the academic adjustment issues of international students considering their impact on the academic performance and mental health of students. However, doubts have been raised regarding whether universities provide sufficient support in assisting Chinese international students with overseas studying (Burton-Bradley 2018; Callaghan 2018; Grigg 2018).

There has been a lack of understanding of the academic adaptation experiences of Chinese international students, particularly, in their coping strategies. This qualitative study sought to fill this gap by determining the academic differences between their home and host country education systems that Chinese international students perceive while studying in English-speaking countries and, above all, how they react to such differences. Gaining insight into this aspect of academic adaptation has the potential to expand the current knowledge of acculturation. In addition, investigating the learning experiences of Chinese students in host institutions helps increase understanding of their needs in adapting to a new academic environment and offers insights for universities to optimise their services to increase the degree of satisfaction of Chinese students in their overseas studying experience.

Acculturation

Adapting to foreign society is unavoidable for international students (Zhou/Wei 2020). This adaptation process is referred to as cross-cultural adaptation, cross-cultural adjustment or acculturation. Rather than a smooth process, acculturation involves challenges and stress arising from culture shock. International students often face psychological depression and social difficulty studying overseas (Ladum/Burkholder 2019). The challenges and stress they encounter largely generate from the differences between the home and host culture. The more significant the cultural disparity is, the more challenging cross-cultural adaptation tends to be (Redmond 2000). Nevertheless, the stress and challenges can motivate individuals to develop self-learning skills and response mechanisms if effective strategies are adopted in dealing with cultural differences.

Berry (1997) proposed four acculturation strategies based on individuals' desires to maintain their own culture and to engage with the host culture: assimilation, separation, integration and marginalisation. Assimilation refers to interacting daily with the host culture with a desire to maintain one's original cultural identity, whereas separation refers to a strategy used by those who avoid interacting with the host culture and wish to maintain their cultural identity. Integration refers to maintaining one's home cultural identity while interacting daily with the host culture. In contrast, marginalisation indicates little interest in cultural maintenance or interaction with others (Behara/Khan/Hasan 2018). Among these four strategies, integration is regarded as the most functional, as it facilitates individuals adapting to the host culture. Marginalisation is considered to be a failure in the acculturation process.

Assimilation and separation are at the intermediate level (Hofhuis/Hanke/Rutten 2019). Since integration facilitates successful adaptation, it is critical to foster positive attitudes towards integration.

Chinese seem to not always adopt integration strategies. Anderson and Guan (2018) found that separation was the most commonly used strategy by Chinese international students in Australia. Meng, Zhu and Cao (2017) also found that almost half of Chinese international students used separation strategies. Although inconsistent results have been found in other studies (e.g., Zheng/Berry 1991), Chinese international students may face difficulties in attempting to integrate two cultures. Shafaei, Abd and Nejati (2016: 48) argued that "the lower the gap between the cultural values and norms of ethnic and host countries, the higher the tendency by international students both to adapt to the host country's culture and to keep the ethnic country's culture". The extent to which norms and values differ from one country to another is defined as cultural distance (Hofstede 1980). Cultural distance can be reflected by differences in cultural values such as power distance, individualism/collectivism and uncertainty avoidance (Hofstede 2001).

Western countries, such as Australia, are characterised as low in power distance and uncertainty avoidance but high in individualism, whereas East Asian countries, such as China, are rated high in power distance, collectivism and uncertainty avoidance (Eringa *et al.* 2015; Loh/Teo 2017; Yang *et al.* 2018). "In high power distance cultures [...] people are more likely to accept a hierarchical structure and demonstrate greater respect for position, age, and/or authority than do those in low power distance cultures" (Zhang 2013: 242). In individualistic cultures, individuals are expected to pursue their personal goals. In collectivistic cultures, people are encouraged to value group integrity more than personal achievements (Lee/Ciftci 2014). Cultures with low uncertainty avoidance possess higher tolerance towards unknown or ambiguous situations and are thus more innovative than societies with high uncertainty avoidance, which are less tolerant to ambiguities and less receptive to changes and innovations (Adair/Xiong 2018).

East Asian students in Western countries inevitably have more challenging adaptation experiences due to the high cultural distance since it is less likely for their home culture to offer much insight into the characteristics of the host culture (Guan *et al.* 2018). One of the prominent adaptation challenges that East Asian international students face is the adjustment to a Western educational environment (Park 2016). Academic life is a major concern among international students (Ward/Bochner/Furnham 2001). Academic adjustment plays a significant role not only in the academic success of international students but also in their overall cross-cultural experience (Wu/Garza/Guzman 2015). Therefore, academic adaptation to the host institution should be regarded as an important facet for the acculturation of international students.

Academic adaptation

The phenomenon of international students adjusting academically to a host culture is referred to as academic adjustment or academic adaptation (Yu/Wright 2017). It is a complex process of appreciation and acquisition of the host culture in academic settings (Kim 2012). Previous research on academic adaptation of international students has adopted a "deficit frame" (Tran 2013: 2), emphasising weaknesses in adapting to a foreign educational culture (Ge/Brown/Durst 2019) and attributing such weaknesses to the academic shock caused by disparities between the new and prior educational environments (Gu/Maley 2008). Academic shock presents in various forms, including unfamiliarity with teaching and learning approaches, uncertainty regarding academic requirements and expectations. (Robertson *et al.* 2000; Zhang 2002). International students experiencing academic shock encounter challenges and difficulties during academic adaptation, which may hinder their academic performance. A number of studies found that the home culture influences the ability and inclination of international students to adapt to new ways of thinking and behaving (Gahan/Abeysekera 2009; Tan/Liu 2014). Academic adaptation challenges of Chinese students studying in Australia may arise from the distinct disparities in the education culture between the two countries. It has been argued that different teaching and learning styles, social integration difficulty and attitudes towards support challenge Chinese international students (Heng 2017; Le/McKay 2018).

Teaching and learning style differences

Western classes are more interactive and student-centred than those in Eastern countries (Ma *et al.* 2020). Many Chinese students are unfamiliar with such instructional and learning styles (Cheung 2013). Students from highly individualistic cultures tend to be more independent, more open to competition and more active in debates (Ozer 2015). Meanwhile, students from cultures characterised by high collectivism and power distance, such as Chinese culture, tend to be more compliant, quieter in class and more reserved in expressing their thoughts and asking questions (Wang/Mallinckrodt 2006). The verbal passiveness of Chinese students in Western classrooms has received great attention from researchers. Xing, Bolden and Hogenkamp (2019) attributed Chinese students' quietness in class to their language disadvantage. Wang and Shan (2006) suggested that Chinese students prefer to obtain accurate answers directly from teachers rather than through class discussion or laborious research, which might be related to the academic norm of teachers giving clear and ample instructions in China (Valdez 2015).

Yan and Berliner (2011) ascribed Chinese students' quietness to the cultural value that questioning teachers equates to challenging their authority, which hampers social harmony (Guan/Meng 2007). The silence of Chinese students has also been suggested to indicate their disinterest in learning or deficiency in cognitive skills (Rear 2017). In response, Banks (2016) argued that Asian students may utilise silence as a deep-thinking tool and as a way to discover the truth inside themselves. Another explanation is that Chinese students prefer to have discussions with teachers outside of the classroom to avoid "interrupting the flow of the lecture" (Jackson/Chen, 2018: 298).

Aside from the influence of Chinese academic norms, challenges to academic adjustment may also "stem from a lack of tacit knowledge of teaching, learning and assessment cultures in the new environment"

(Yu/Wright 2017: 350). Blasco (2015) conducted a study on Master's-level international students at a Demark university. She found that a major source of confusion regarding the teaching/learning culture was the "taken for granted" practices that are not explained to international students and that they therefore fail to incorporate in their learning. She proposed that *tacit knowledge,* such as how to interpret course plans and what is expected from teachers, is regarded as "common knowledge". Teachers and domestic students may not realise the existence of such unrecognised tacit knowledge. For instance, teachers expect students to know the format and logic of written assignments without realising that these characteristics can be quite divergent from what is customary in international students' home countries.

One of the major sources of confusion for Chinese international students regarding assessment requirements is the demonstration of critical thinking in academic tasks. While it is highly valued in Western education systems, critical thinking has always been claimed to be absent from Chinese students (Heng 2018). The literature ascribes its absence to the difference in the Chinese educational culture, suggesting that the teacher-centred Chinese classroom emphasises unquestioning respect for teacher authority, and students are expected to listen quietly and do as teachers say (Han/Han 2019). Thus, Chinese students inevitably have difficulty understanding and practising critical thinking, which values questioning. Nevertheless, many researchers doubt that critical thinking is a sole Western attribute (Li/Wegerif 2014; Rear 2017; Wang/Liyanage/Walker 2019). Tan (2017: 339) believed that Confucianism fosters critical thinking by encouraging individuals "to exercise judgement appropriately [...] to particular action-situations judiciously". This definition of critical thinking is not necessarily antagonistic towards the Western concept of critical thinking, which advocates linear, deductive and inductive reasoning and questioning.

Lu and Singh (2017) argued that Chinese people express critical thinking obliquely to avoid unwarranted confrontation. Based on Hall (1976), China is categorised as a "high-context culture", in which communication tends to be indirect. This indirectness is embodied in Chinese rhetoric, which presents arguments in a circular way, distinct from linear English rhetoric (Yeung 2019). The discrepancy in the interpretations and demonstrations of critical thinking may explain the struggle of Chinese students in attempting to meet the expectations of teachers at Western universities.

International students may be willing and able to adapt to new academic norms as they become more familiar with the host educational culture (Cheung 2013). Loh and Teo (2017) ascribed Chinese students' willingness to do so to the high power distance that characterises Chinese culture. They suggested that Chinese students tend to recognise the academic norms that are favoured by teachers and attempt to adjust to them. In addition to students' efforts, external support also matters. Most international students study overseas for a short period of time and start the semester shortly after their arrival, when they are overwhelmed by a series of other acculturation issues (Li *et al.* 2017). To avoid academic stress compounding the problem, it is necessary to offer sufficient academic support. The current study aimed to determine whether Chinese international students perceived educational differences between Chinese and Australian education systems and the logic behind these differences, as well as their responses to the new education system.

Social integration difficulty

The degree of social integration of international students describes how well they initiate and maintain interpersonal relations in host countries (Galchenko / van de Vijver 2007). International students normally have three social networks: personal ties with people from the same country (co-national network), with international students from other countries (multi-national network) and with people from the host country (host national network) (Cao/Zhu/Meng 2016). Social networks play an important role during the transitions of international students, and social support stemming from social networks helps students to alleviate acculturative stress and facilitates positive adaptation (Forbush/Foucault-Welles 2016). Research has shown that Chinese international students develop the closest relationships with their co-nationals (Bertram *et al.* 2014). Kim (2001) argued that co-national interaction might negatively affect adaptation in the long term. Surrounding themselves solely with co-nationals prevents international students from adapting successfully to the unfamiliar foreign environment. In contrast, building social networks with host nationals benefits international students predominantly in terms of academic adaptation (Pho/Schartner 2021).

International students face challenges in social integration with host nationals (Marangell/Arkoudis/Baik 2018). English deficiency is often claimed as a factor that discourages social interaction with host nationals (Akhtar / Kröner-Herwig 2015). Students with limited English language proficiency find it difficult to befriend native English speakers, as they struggle to convey clear and accurate messages. In addition, Chinese students might feel ashamed of their broken English and therefore avoid occasions involving English speaking. Cultural difference also plays a role in social difficulty. Wang (2018) noted that Chinese students struggle to develop friendships with British people, as the more they interact with locals, the more cultural and lifestyle differences they perceive.

They feel stressed attending social events and making friends with host nationals. Another culture factor that prevents Chinese students from enjoying social life is their worries about having too much fun and that enjoyment in community life will affect their studying (Arambewela/Hall 2013). Given that academic success is the primary goal of Chinese international students, they might withdraw themselves from certain social events. Poor social integration can lead to loneliness and homesickness, which can be detrimental to academic adaptation (Yan/Berliner 2011). Many studies have suggested that international students should build stronger social networks in host countries, but few have discussed the implementation and effectiveness of such strategies. The current study gathered narrations of Chinese international students on their experiences in this regard.

Attitudes towards support

In response to academic differences and challenges, Chinese students tend to be self-reliant (Wei *et al.* 2012). Meng, Zhu and Cao (2018) ascribed such self-reliance to Chinese collectivism advocating endurance and sacrifice. Li (2016) believed that Chinese people view seeking help from acquaintances as burdening and jeopardising social relationships. Feelings of stigma and shame prevent Chinese people from seeking professional help (Ma/Zhu/Bresnahan 2021). Forbes-Mewett and Sawyer (2016) found that Chinese students suffering from acculturative stress and mental issues have trouble in recognising the need for professional help and seeking such help. They claimed that Chinese tend not to treat psychological counselling as normal and often deny depression or any negative experiences. Some international students hold a negative view of psychological counselling and believe that only those with special disabilities or problems need counselling. In addition, Asian students are reserved about expressing their personal issues to people they are not familiar with and prefer to turn to family and friends for help (Heng 2018; Zhang 2013).

McMahon (2011) found that Chinese students ask favours from their teachers for issues beyond academic problems. This practice might be related to the Chinese teacher-student relationship, which usually extends to personal matters. In China, a monitor is assigned to each class who provides help with students' learning and their everyday lives (Li/Pitkänen 2018). In Western countries, teacher-student relationships are bound by professional needs and interests. Chinese international students are often frustrated in attempting to find the appropriate way to interact with their teachers at the early stage of their studies (Banjong 2015). The weak teacher-student relationship decreases students' sense of belonging (Chiu *et al.* 2016), which can cause psychological and behavioural problems (Baumeister/Leary 1995).

Criticisms have been made regarding the lack of sufficient university support (Roberts/Boldy/Dunworth 2015). Some researchers have questioned the availability and accessibility of mental health services (e.g., Blignault *et al.* 2008). Many international students are not aware of the existence of counselling services and are unfamiliar with the concept and process of such services. They may hold distrustful attitudes towards counsellors and be uncertain of the effectiveness of counselling (Zhang 2013). Researchers have suggested that host institutions increase international students' awareness of and access to supportive services. Xue (2018) proposed that universities should educate international students about the benefits of counselling and employ counsellors with a high-level of cross-cultural sensitivity. Teachers and university staff could also recommend other university services, such as orientation programmes, language courses, workshops and seminars. The key is for universities to consider the difficulties in acculturation and academic adjustment that international students might encounter to create a more inclusive and supportive environment.

The Current Study

The current explored the academic adaptation experiences of Chinese students studying at an Australian university. It investigated two research questions using qualitative methodology:

1. What academic differences between Chinese and Australian education systems are perceived by Chinese international students at an Australian university?
2. How do Chinese international students at this Australian university respond to such differences?

This research used a qualitative design to provide rich, descriptive and exploratory data. Qualitative research elicits understandings that are difficult to gain through a quantitative approach by providing thick and in-depth descriptions (Gephart 2004) of the thought processes, emotions and experiences of participants (Strauss/Corbin 1998). A qualitative design was considered to be most appropriate to permit the researcher to reveal the underlying assumptions, beliefs and values (Yauch/Steudel 2003) of Chinese international students' academic adaptation experiences. An exploratory study allows the researcher to collect and analyse data without imposing predetermined concepts and viewpoints on participants (Azungah 2018). The inductive data collection and analysis approach in this study was informed by grounded theory. Grounded theory refers to the process of collecting, analysing and formulating theory explicitly from the data rather than from pre-existing theoretical frameworks (Strauss/Corbin 1998). Grounded theory is based on the data rather than preconceived ideas, allowing the voices of participants to be heard while encouraging patterns and themes to emerge.

Participant selection and recruitment

The population of interest was enrolled Chinese international students at an Australian university. A purposive sampling method was used to identify 6 participants. Purposive sampling allows participants to be selected based on specific characteristics that are critical for addressing the research questions (Patton 2001). The sample size was decided based on the recommendation of Guest, Bunce and Johnson (2006) that six to twelve participants are sufficient for qualitative interviews to reach data saturation, especially in regard to a highly homogeneous group. Participants of this study were selected based on the following criteria:

1. Participants must be mainland Chinese students.
2. Participants must have no/little (less than 3 months) overseas studying experience prior to studying at the Australian university under study.
3. Participants must have studied for over 6 months at the Australian university (excluding pre-enrolment courses).

A background questionnaire of 10 questions to address these criteria was used to select 6 qualified participants. The questions concerned the students' English proficiency, region of origin, previous educational background and stage of overseas study and other demographic information (see Appendix A for the background questionnaire). Qualified respondents were invited to schedule an interview upon completing the questionnaire. Of the 6 students who completed the background questionnaire, 6 were eligible for the interview. All 6 attended their interviews. Each participant was given a pseudonym to protect confidentiality and anonymity (see Appendix B for the demographic data of the participants).

Data collection and data analysis

Semi-structured interviews were conducted to collect data. An interview schedule consisting of 10 questions was designed by the researcher based on the research questions and literature review (see Appendix C for the interview schedule). Interview Questions 1-5 were designed to address Research Question 1, and Interview Questions 6-9 targeted Research Question 2. Interview Question 10 invited participants to share any relevant thoughts regarding the topic. The interviews lasted from 40 to 90 minutes and took place from May 6th to May 13th, 2019, when all participants were at a late stage in their second semesters. All interviews were audio-recorded. The interviews were conducted in Chinese based on the interviewees' preferences. The researcher collected and analysed the interview data concurrently, which allowed for the adjustment of the interview approach and questions. Considering its exploratory nature, this study analysed data following the inductive qualitative data analysis procedures outlined by Thomas (2003) and the grounded theory analytical steps proposed by Eaves (2001) (see Appendix D for phases of data analysis).

Results

Perceived academic differences

Research Question 1 aimed to determine the academic differences that Chinese international students perceived regarding Chinese and Australian universities. The differences, although not necessarily negative, affected participants' experiences studying at the Australian university under study.

Teaching and learning philosophy

The participants claimed that Chinese classrooms are more structured and teacher-oriented and that it is not conventional for students in China to take the initiative in studying. They believed that Chinese students tend to situate themselves at the receiving end and are accustomed to knowledge being delivered directly by teachers; in contrast, in Western classrooms, teachers and students are encouraged to work collaboratively. The participants shared their thoughts about their experiences with the more interactive, autonomous Western education mode.

Interactive classes: concerns about wasting time

The participants indicated their reluctance to take the initiative to raise and answer questions in class or to join class discussion, fearing their incompetence in English would prolong their speech and thus waste others' time.

(1) If I get stuck in English, I would be the one who wastes time of the whole class. Imagine how much time would I waste if everyone loses one minute because of me? [Daisy]

The participants reported their less proactive involvement in class discussion compared with that of their Western counterparts. They stated that in the Chinese classroom, speaking out too much can be considered disruptive behaviour that slows down the teaching and learning progress. In contrast, the participants perceived that their Australian university valued interactive classrooms in which discussion and debate are encouraged.

(2) If you speak too much in a Chinese classroom, you are hindering other classmates' learning process, which could lead to an inability to complete a teaching task. So, we don't have much chance to voice our thoughts [...] But the culture here encourages people to voice their thoughts. [Heidi]

The difference in classroom interaction was not always welcomed by participants. Many raised their doubts about excessive class discussion. They noticed that some discussions between Westerner students and teachers were off-topic. In addition, they suggested that discussion time could be used for more important, relevant points. May acknowledged that discussion inspires novel ideas and critical thinking but questioned the necessity of covering irrelevant topics.

(3) The good side is that we can indeed get many new ideas through discussion [...] But sometimes it takes half of the lesson time when a lot of content on the PPT has not been covered yet. So, we are not taught what we are supposed to learn. I think it's a waste of time to spend so long on irrelevant, less important stuff. [May]

Autonomous learning: self-initiated learning

The high degree of student autonomy at the Australian university was indicated to be challenging by the participants. They found themselves to be fully responsible for their study, which required a high level of independence and self-control. In comparison, the participants claimed that teachers in China provide abundant learning resources and instructions. Cathy described the difference using an analogy.

(4) If we compare the education mode to playing computer games, Chinese teachers would give students game guides, maps and strategies. They would help with knocking down mini bosses and instruct students in how to fight with the final boss whereas Western teachers would just assign the task of nailing the final boss, period [...] It's easier to study in China because students can just use what they have been taught directly on the exams [...] Here, students have to construct their own knowledge framework. [Cathy]

The challenge related to autonomy for the participants was that they had to manage multiple assignment deadlines throughout the academic year. The participants needed to ensure that they completed assignments before the due dates. May emphasised her fear of deadlines and explained that in China, she had sufficient time to prepare for the sole major assessment at the end of each semester.

(5) Too many deadlines. It's killing me [...] Here, I know I should never procrastinate. Procrastination is fatal [...] I feel a lot of pressure. I know I have to plan ahead and do it. Unlike in China, I may just relax at first and concentrate on my study before the final exam [...] [May]

Despite the concerns, the participants claimed to have no bias against either mode. They commented on the pros and cons of each mode and described their endeavors to adjust themselves to the teaching and learning mode at the Australian university.

Evaluation culture

Participants identified significant differences between Chinese and Western university evaluation cultures, which mainly varied in the expectations of essay writing and the explicitness of assignment requirements.

Essays: English rhetoric and critical thinking

The participants reported that essay writing is a major assessment tool in Australia and that the expectations for essay writing are challenging to meet. They highlighted the difficulty of grasping and applying the essence of Western academic writing, which values meticulous logic and critical thinking. They claimed that the structure of Chinese writing more resembles a spiral circling around a point, whereas English writing is more linear and direct. The participants stated that they endeavoured to present their writing in a less implicit, more straightforward way. Moreover, they shared their struggles to understand and demonstrate critical thinking, which is less stressed in Chinese writing.

(6) Chinese writing doesn't really require critical thinking [...] At most, they will ask you to answer "what", "why" and "how" in the body paragraphs. As long as these three questions are addressed and elaborated, the writing is considered to be good [...] I think critical thinking is more of questioning [...] But if I question too much, I receive the feedback of being too subjective [...] if I question less, teachers say I am not critical enough [...] Locals might be born to be questioning [...] I am so confused. [Cathy]

Assignments: implicit requirements

Understanding the requirements and expectations of academic tasks in Australia was considered to be difficult by the participants. They claimed to receive less explicit assignment instructions than in China. They noted that even when assignment instructions were listed in unit outlines and explained by teachers in class, some of the hidden expectations remained ambiguous. They noted that teachers who claimed to provide broad and general assignment frameworks to allow freedom in writing were not as inclusive and open-minded as the participants expected, and they were marked based on the teachers' implicit expectations. Heidi argued that these teachers were self-contradictory and that the marks they gave were similar to the scenario of Schrödinger's cat.

(7) You never know what is in their mind [...] Even if you email them and ask them in person about what they want, they still grade you by instinct [...] Before you see the mark, you never know if it's high or low; it's Schrödinger's grades... [Heidi]

Although all participants agreed that a step-by-step guide is unnecessary for postgraduate level students as it hinders the development of their self-study abilities, they still preferred clearer instructions.

Responses to academic differences

Research Question 2 was based on Research Question 1 and aimed to explore the coping strategies of Chinese international students in response to the academic differences that they perceived. The participants generally took proactive actions to achieve more desirable academic performance. They reported three responses approaches: self-facilitated, peer-facilitated and university-facilitated strategies.

Self-facilitated strategies

All participants reported most frequently using self-facilitated support strategies. They indicated their reluctance to trouble others with their personal issues. The participants made use of (a) internet resources, (b) self-developed language learning strategies, (c) time management, and (d) self-counselling.

Internet resources
In response to the highly autonomous learning environment, the participants made attempts at self-initiated studying. The internet was reported to be an indispensable tool for self-study. The participants searched online for academic resources, including academic papers,

reference styles, concept elaboration. Daisy considered internet research to be the most straightforward and time-saving way to solve academic problems.

Self-developed language learning strategies

To adjust to an interactive classroom, the participants previewed the lesson contents and drilled their English skills to be able to better participate in class discussion and avoid wasting class time. They developed their own learning strategies targeting their English insufficiencies. The participants also indicated that they previewed course readings to grasp the gist of the lesson. They noted that such strategies are uncommon in Chinese university classes where information in Chinese can be understood promptly. They argued that in Australia, it can be overwhelming to absorb and internalise lesson content without sufficient preparation.

(8) Before the lesson, I would go through readings that teachers provide and look up unknown words and terms in the dictionary [...] I feel that here I don't have time to look it up in the dictionary if there is a new word that I come across in class. [Daisy]

These learning strategies were considered to be effective by the participants. Meanwhile, they never stopped exploring new ways to manage a variety of academic issues.

Time management

The participants indicated that time management was central for successful academic task completion. The amount and intensity of assignments were considered to be overwhelming. The participants claimed to have experienced crises related to deadlines in the first semester and thus learned their lesson to plan ahead in the later semester. To prevent procrastination, they generally set schedules, avoided distractions and committed to their plans. The participants thought they had made progress in overcoming procrastination. Notably, the participants' study partners (if they had any) were all Chinese, whom they said they had no language barrier with.

Self-counselling
The participants reported that academic differences and challenges caused them psychological stress to varying extents. The participants had the propensity to solve their emotional problems on their own. They preferred not to burden their families and friends with personal issues. They also ruled out the option of seeking professional help. Five of the six participants indicated their awareness of university counselling services but viewed them as unnecessary. Some also questioned the effectiveness of counselling.

(9) Everyone is pressured. I don't think it's proper to spread negative energy to others [...] My family would worry about me if I tell them [...] I doubt if counselling works [...] Nobody can help you to solve your problems except for yourself [...] A counsellor is a stranger who knows nothing about you [...] It is very hard for him/her to help you out [...] too hard. [Heidi]

Nonetheless, all participants emphasised the importance of cultivating friendships. They believed that friends could comfort, encourage and support them when in need.

Peer-facilitated strategies

The participants reported seeking out friends and classmates for help when self-coping strategies failed. All participants turned to their co-nationals first rather than non-Chinese peers. The major concern raised was the language barrier. However, when necessary, low confidence in English competence would not prevent them from asking for favors from their non-Chinese peers.

Peer learning
All participants reported experiences of learning from peers. They described exchanging information such as learning strategies, teaching content, assignment requirements. They regarded reading highly marked writings of classmates as the quickest way to understand teachers' expectations and preferences regarding assignments.

(10) I don't think the time is enough for me to learn how to write systematically. So, the quickest way is to read others' work, I think. [Daisy]

Interestingly, the peers in discussion were all Chinese. The participants believed that the writings of Chinese classmates who shared similar education backgrounds and English language proficiency were instructive and helpful. They claimed that discussing issues with peers in Chinese alleviates any possible misunderstanding caused by language barriers. Communication with peers allows for the circulation of information, which was considered by participants to facilitate their study.

Peer counselling

The participants described experiences of seeking comfort from their friends and classmates. They valued their friends' company and acknowledged their help to be a psychological comfort. The participants indicated that they generally exposed their inner feelings only to co-nationals and built stronger ties with Chinese peers than with peers of other nationalities.

University-facilitated strategies

The participants shared their experiences of seeking institutional support, including asking teachers questions and attending university-organised workshops and events.

Teacher support

The participants reported that, to clarify confusion about assignment requirements and seek general academic advice, they approached teachers, regardless of their concerns about their English incompetence. They stated that most teachers showed willingness to offer academic support, such as by providing academic resources and assignment feedback. Victoria expressed her general satisfaction with the help received from teachers.

(11) Most teachers are quite responsible. My project supervisor would even read my writings line by line and give detailed feedback. [Victoria]

Nonetheless, the participants also received late or no responses from teachers, which they claimed negatively affected their studying. Daisy emphasised how it hindered her learning motivation and performance.

(12) You would overthink when teachers did not reply you [...] I would think, why is this happening to me? What could I do? I was really upset. I was really panicked. I was really angry. I became very emotional. Even my studying motivation dropped. [Daisy]

The participants also indicated that when they encountered such an issue, they did not know whom to turn to for help. In the end, they simply gave up or determined a way forward by themselves.

University services

University academic services were considered to be comprehensive and useful to a certain extent. The participants reported attending academic workshops regarding English language or academic writing at least one time. They acknowledged the workshops to be helpful in addressing *surface* problems in terms of language use and reference styles. However, the workshops failed to shed light on *underlying* issues such as critical thinking.

(13) They (academic workshops) are effective for addressing surface problems. But when it comes to "thought", they just don't work [...] They are helpful to some extent [...] At least, I think the university knows what we are confused about [...] but they failed to address the problems by providing sharp and direct answers. [Cathy]

The participants reported very little use of non-academic services, including counselling. They claimed to have experienced some stress arising from studying but considered it unnecessary to approach counsellors. The participants believed that only those who are deeply troubled by psychological stress would seek professional help. They preferred to rely on themselves or their friends to manage stress.

(14) I know about counselling services, but I don't think I need it [...] If I am so depressed that my life and study get stuck, then I will go [...] I think Chinese turn to friends for help more, someone we know well. [Hana]

In general, the participants expressed their overall satisfaction with university services but indicated room for improvement.

Discussion

Perceived academic differences

In comparing their previous and present learning experiences, the participants noted a stark contrast between Chinese and Australian education systems. The contrast was embodied in the differences in the teaching and learning philosophy as well as in the evaluation culture. These differences affected the participants' learning in many aspects, from class participation, interactions with teachers and peers to academic task completion.

Teaching and learning philosophy

The findings showed the different teaching and learning philosophies between Chinese and Western universities. The interpretation of the participants' narratives revealed that Western education is more student-centred, whereas Chinese education is more teacher-centred. The participants reported having experienced challenges adapting to an interactive, autonomous education mode at the Australian university.

Interactive classes: concerns about wasting time

The participants attributed their reticence in class to strong concerns about wasting others' time. The researcher argues that collectivism, which places the collective interest over that of individuals, may explain their quietness. In China, where collectivism is highly valued, individuals are expected to give priority to the needs of the group. The participants feared using their "clumsy" English and that speaking out too much would take up the time of teachers and peers. There is a general consensus in the literature that English disadvantages prevent Chinese students from engaging in classroom discourse (Xing/Bolden/Hogenkamp 2019). It is believed that the Chinese culture of avoiding "losing face" intimidates students in regard to exposing their weakness in English language. This concern, however, was not mentioned by the participants of this study. Instead of "saving face", the participants seemed to attempt "saving time". Their silence did not indicate a disinterest in learning or a deficiency in cognitive skills (Rear 2017); rather, it might have been related to their reluctance to disturb others with their personal issues.

Aside from the linguistic factor, students' unwillingness to speak out in class has been suggested to be a product of the high power distance of Chinese culture and the fact that students in China view teachers as bastions of knowledge and are accustomed to the "teachers talk, students listen" mode (Guan/Meng 2007). Nevertheless, a claim that Chinese students listen without thinking should be made cautiously. In fact, Asian students regard silence as an essential component of deep thinking (Rear 2017). It is through silence that one can discover the truth inside oneself (Banks 2016).

The participants also expressed disapproval of their learning time being hampered. They indicated their reservations about prolonged and irrelevant class discussions often taking place between teachers and students of Western cultures. The Western education system encourages students to contribute to the class (Blasco 2015). Western students are accustomed to the discussion-based pedagogy and often proactively initiate and engage in class discussion. The participants were aware of such an educational difference and acknowledged certain benefits. Nonetheless, they stated their preferences for a more didactic classroom. In-class discussion was welcomed by the participants on the condition that it was short and to the point. They claimed that discussion between teachers and Western students often ended up straying from the topic. The participants found such discussion disruptive and questioned the meaning of excessive class discussion.

Jackson and Chen (2018: 298) suggested that Chinese students have an implicit understanding that they should have discussions with teachers outside of the classroom "to avoid interrupting the flow of the lecture". The word "interrupt" was also used multiple times by the participants in this study, suggesting their reluctance to slow the teaching and learning progress because of individuals' speaking out.

Autonomous learning: self-initiated learning

In Western education, autonomous learning is advocated, and students are expected to be independent and self-responsible. In China, students often face pressure from teachers to study hard. A monitor is assigned to each class to provide students with abundant academic resources and help (Li/Pitkänen 2018). In contrast, teachers in Western universities serve as guides. The students had to be self-initiated and highly disciplined. It seems that the sharp transition from a teacher-dominant culture to a student-oriented environment overwhelmed the participants. They reported a range of issues, such as lacking time management and research skills.

Despite the challenges, the participants showed no bias against the differences. For instance, the participants perceived benefits of the much-criticised Chinese spoon-feeding pedagogy in providing them with well-rounded support from teachers. However, the participants also indicated their willingness to adjust to the Western education culture. Loh and Teo (2017) argued that the openness Asian students show towards a student-centred approach reveals the influence of a high power distance culture; that is, if teachers adopt a particular teaching approach, Asian international students endeavour to adapt to it.

Evaluation culture

Data analyses revealed the participants' unfamiliarity with Western evaluation culture, particularly with the expectations for essay writing and assignment requirements. Reported to be the major assessment instrument, academic essay writing posed a great challenge to the participants. They struggled to practise English rhetoric and critical thinking in their writings. They claimed that vague assignment requirements compounded the situation.

Essays: English rhetoric and critical thinking

The participants noticed a difference between Chinese and English rhetoric and shared a view that Chinese writing has an indirect structure and presents the arguments in a circular way, whereas English writing is linear and direct. Their perceptions coincide with that of Yeung (2019: 52), who argued that Chinese rhetoric tends to "switch back and forth in positions before reaching an overarching resolution of conflict". This structure can be baffling for English readers who are accustomed to the linear patterns of development. Hall (1976) first proposed the concepts of "high-context culture" and "low-context culture". People in high-context cultures, such as Chinese culture, tend to communicate in an indirect and implicit way, whereas those in low-context cultures, such as that of Australia, prefer direct messages. The deep-rooted cultural difference may explain why the participants of this study struggled to adjust to English rhetoric. The participants also stated a constant endeavour to define, understand and practise critical thinking in their writing.

Critical thinking emphasises questioning and independent dispositions (Heng 2018). The idea that Chinese students lack critical thinking ability might not be true, considering that Chinese Confucianism encourages individuals to judge appropriately and judiciously (Tan 2017). The Western way of demonstrating critical thinking through linear, deductive and inductive reasoning (Tan 2017) and the Chinese way of indirectness may explain the apparent absence of critical thinking among Chinese students (Lu/Singh 2017). The participants of this study interpreted critical thinking in nuanced ways. They seemed to understand the concept of critical thinking but all struggled with its application. Since critical thinking was a key factor under evaluation, unsuccessful demonstration of critical thinking could dishearten students who strove for satisfactory academic performance.

Assignments: implicit requirements

Differences in the explicitness of the teacher's instructions on assignment requirements perplexed the participants. In China, teachers usually provide clear and ample instructions to assist students' learning (Valdez 2015). At the Australian university, the participants claimed that the assignment requirements were rather vague, which hindered their understanding of their teachers' expectations. Blasco (2015) ascribed such a lack of understanding to a lack of tacit knowledge of the host education culture. She believed that when implicit academic norms and culture are assumed to be well acknowledged by teachers in one culture, teachers may not realise that students from other cultures might not be aware of such "taken for granted" knowledge. Teachers' expectations and students' understanding of assignments could be very different. Another explanation could be related to the high uncertainty avoidance that characterises Chinese culture, in which ambiguity and uncertainty are not greatly tolerated (Ching *et al.* 2017). Chinese students prefer a direct and clear answer from the teacher. The participants agreed that step-by-step instructions were unnecessary at a postgraduate level, but they indicated their dissatisfaction with overly vague assignment requirements. In contrast, Western culture is more receptive to changes and innovations, so Western students are familiar with a less constrained framework.

Responses to academic differences

In response to the perceived academic differences between Chinese and Australian education systems, all participants developed coping strategies, including self-facilitated, peer-facilitated and university-facilitated strategies.

Self-facilitated strategies

The participants in this study tended to solve problems by themselves. This finding is consistent with the existing literature, which suggests self-coping to be the most favoured coping strategy by Chinese international students (Wei *et al.* 2012). The participants relied on internet resources, self-developed learning strategies, time management skills and self-counselling to address language issues, academic differences and psychological stress derived from academic challenges. The participants' narratives resonated with Li's (2016) finding that Chinese people feel that they are a burden and are jeopardising social relationships when seeking help from others. The participants in this study expressed a strong unwillingness to bother others with their personal issues. The Chinese collectivistic culture often encourages sacrifice and endurance to achieve and maintain social harmony (Cao/Zhu/Meng 2018). Thus, Chinese students are used to minimising and concealing their concerns and stress to avoid troubling others. In contrast, students from Western individualistic countries feel freer to seek support from others since their culture highlights individuals' freedom to pursue their well-being. Through continued efforts, the participants reported progress in academic performance and self-adjustment.

Peer-facilitated strategies

The participants approached peers for help and built rapport mostly with co-nationals. They turned to their student peers for academic support (peer learning) and psychological solace (peer counselling). All participants emphasised the importance of establishing friendships in Australia. The finding concerning their preference to seek help from Chinese peers is consistent with those of previous studies (Bertram *et al.* 2014; Meng/Zhu/Cao 2018). A number of reasons might explain such a preference. First, English incompetence hinders Chinese students from effectively communicating with English speakers, but a shared mother tongue facilitates mutual understanding. Second, cultural discrepancy can frustrate and intimidate Chinese students and discourage them from befriending host nationals and multi-nationals. In addition, Chinese students experience unique academic adjustment difficulties that people from other cultures may not find relatable, which leads to a lack of emotional resonance. Third, the large Chinese international community at the university allows Chinese students help and support each other to better adjust to the foreign culture. When students' needs can be met through the support of the Chinese community, their interest in forming cross-cultural friendships may decrease.

University-facilitated strategies

The participants held mixed attitudes towards the academic and non-academic services provided by teachers and the university. The participants highly disapproved of teachers' late or lack of responses regarding academic inquiries. They demonstrated strong feelings of frustration and confusion, which negatively affected their learning in a number of ways. First, Chinese have low tolerance of ambiguity and uncertainty. When the participants reached out to teachers with questions and received no response or late responses, the ambiguity perplexed them. Second, delayed or a lack of responses demotivated the participants. China is a country characterised by high power distance where teachers are respected as authorities. Chinese students attach great importance to the teacher-student relationship. When students do not receive a response or receive a late response from a teacher, they may assume that the teacher has a bias against them or against Chinese students. In addition, the participants in this study were unaware of who else they could approach to report such issues. The weak teacher-student relationship could reduce Chinese students' sense of belonging (Chiu *et al.* 2016), leading to psychological and behavioral problems. (Baumeister/Leary 1995). Despite the criticism of certain teachers' irresponsibility, the participants indicated that most teachers were nice and helpful.

The findings also included the participants' perceptions of academic workshops and other services, including counselling provided by the university. The participants appreciated the university's effort to offer a wide variety of workshops aimed at language use, writing and critical thinking. However, these workshops were not as effective as they expected, especially in addressing deep-rooted, cultural issues such as critical thinking. This finding suggests that problems that emerge from educational cultural differences require more time and effort to solve. Counselling services were reported to be heard of but never used. Heng (2018) noted that, in decreasing order, international students prefer to seek help from friends, academic staff, and then healthcare professionals. The literature has ascribed the reluctance of Chinese students to seek professional support to cultural stigma (Ma/Zhu/Bresnahan 2021). Analyses of the participants' narratives found no support of such a statement. Instead, the participants viewed their stress as mood swings that are common among students and deemed it unnecessary to seek professional help. Their narratives suggest their lack of proper understanding of counselling. They seemed to believe that their issues were not "serious" enough to ask professional help.

Academic adaptation model

This study explored the academic adaptation experiences of Chinese international students at an Australian university. The interpretation of the findings revealed academic differences in teaching and learning philosophy and evaluation culture between China and Australia. The differences originate from the distinctive education systems and cultural values, which posed challenges to the participants. In response, the participants adopted self-facilitated, peer-facilitated and university-facilitated strategies. Berry (1997) proposed four acculturation strategies: marginalization, separation, assimilation and integration. This study finds that the participants adopted an assimilation strategy. They noticed the difference between Chinese and Australian academic norms without judging one to be necessarily better than the other. They respected and endeavored to adjust to the host culture. However, they interacted more with co-nationals and relied heavily on the Chinese student community.

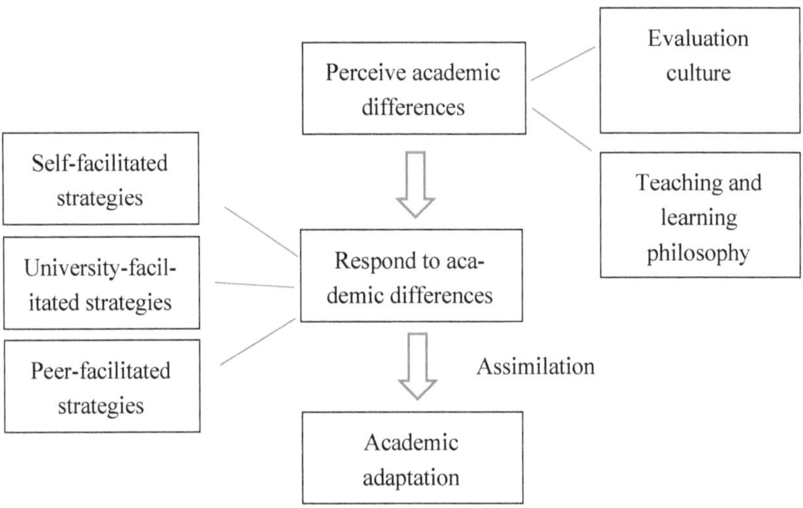

Fig. 1. Chinese international students' academic adaptation model.

Thus, the strategy used by the participants is best categorised as assimilation and was proven to be fairly effective in promoting their academic adaptation. Based on the findings for the participant group, the researcher proposes an academic adaptation model of Chinese international students, suggesting that Chinese students first perceive academic differences and then respond to the differences using an assimilation strategy that facilitates successful academic adaptation (see Figure 1).

Conclusion

This study investigated Chinese international students' academic adaptation experiences at an Australian university. The study revealed how cultural differences impact students' academic adjustment, providing Australian educators with insight into Chinese international students' experiences. The developed academic adaptation model contributes to cross-culture theory by providing a new perspective in understanding how Chinese students experience their academic transitions from China to Australia. This study provides a basis for further research to gain a more comprehensive and holistic picture of Chinese international students' cross-cultural experiences. Further research can test the model developed by the researcher with a larger number of Chinese students across universities in Australia. Both male and female students from different disciplines should be involved. Quantitative methods can be used to verify the findings of this study. In addition, future studies could obtain a broader picture from the perspectives of teachers, universities and local students. Comparing views of Chinese students with people who interact with them may identify possible misunderstandings and barriers, which could contribute to bridging communication gaps.

References

Adair, Wendi L. / Xiong, Tracy X. 2018. How Chinese and Caucasian Canadians Conceptualize Creativity: The Mediating Role of Uncertainty Avoidance. *Journal of Cross-Cultural Psychology*. 49/2, 223-238.

Akhtar, Mubeen / Kröner-Herwig, Birgit 2015. Acculturative Stress among International Students in Context of Socio-demographic Variables and Coping Styles. *Current Psychology*. 34/4, 803-815.

Anderson, Joel R. / Guan, Yao 2018. Implicit Acculturation and the

Academic Adjustment of Chinese Student Sojourners in Australia. *Australian Psychologist*, *53*(5), 444-453.

Arambewela, Rodney / Hall, John 2013. The Interactional Effects of the Internal and External University Environment, and the Influence of Personal Values, on Satisfaction among International Postgraduate Students. *Studies in Higher Education*. 38/7, 972-988.

Azungah, Theophilus 2018. Qualitative Research: Deductive and Inductive Approaches to Data Analysis. *Qualitative Research Journal*. 18/4, 383-400.

Banjong, Delphine N. 2015. International Students' Enhanced Academic Performance: Effects of Campus resources. *Journal of International Students*. 5/2, 132-142.

Banks, Sachie 2016. Behind Japanese Students' Silence in English Classrooms. *Accents Asia*. 8/2, 54-75.

Baumeister, Roy F. / Leary, Mark R. 1995. The Need to Belong: Desire for Interpersonal Attachments as a Fundamental Human Motivation. *Psychological Bulletin*. 117/3, 497-529.

Behara, Jita / Khan, Khan Abraruzzaman / Hasan, Basheer 2018. Predicting Effects of Acculturation Strategies on Acculturative Stress. *Indian Journal of Positive Psychology*. 9/1, 190-192.

Berry, John 1997. Immigration, Acculturation, and Adaptation. *Applied Psychology*, 46/1, 5–34.

Bertram, David M. / Poulakis, Mixalis / Elsasser, Betsy Shaw / Kumar, Ekta 2014. Social Support and Acculturation in Chinese International Students. *Journal of Multicultural Counseling and Development*. 42/2, 107-124.

Blasco, Maribel 2015. Making the Tacit Explicit: Rethinking Culturally Inclusive Pedagogy in International Student Academic Adaptation. *Pedagogy, Culture & Society*. 23/1, 85-106.

Blignault, Ilse / Ponzio, Vince / Rong, Ye / Eisenbruch, Maurice 2008. A Qualitative Study of Barriers to Mental Health Service Utilization among Migrants from Mainland China in Southeast Sydney. *International Journal of Social Psychiatry*. 54/2, 180-190.

Burton-Bradley, Robert 2018. Poor English, Few Jobs: Are Australian Universities Using International Students as 'Cash Cows'? *ABC News*, November 27.

Callaghan, Ruth 2018. Are International Students Customers, Clients or Cash Cows? *The 268,* September 11.

Campbell, Throy A. 2015. A Phenomenological Study on International Doctoral Students' Acculturation Experiences at a US University. *Journal of International Students*. 5/3, 285-299.

Cao, Chun / Zhu, Chang / Meng, Qian 2016. An Exploratory Study of Inter-relationships of Acculturative Stressors among Chinese Students from Six European Union (EU) Countries. *International Journal of Intercultural Relations*. 55, 8-19.

Cao, Chun / Zhu, Chang / Meng, Qian 2021. Chinese International Students' Coping Strategies, Social Support Resources in Response to Academic Stressors: Does Heritage Culture or Host Context Matter? *Current Psychology*, *40*(1), 242-252.

Cheung, Alan C. K. 2013. Language, Academic, Socio-cultural and Financial Adjustments of Mainland Chinese Students Studying in Hong Kong. *International Journal of Educational Management,* 27/3, 221-241.

Ching, Yuerong / Renes, Susan L. / McMurrow, Samantha / Simpson, Joni / Strange, Anthony T. 2017. Challenges Facing Chinese International Students Studying in the United States. *Educational Research and Reviews*. 12/8, 473-482.

Chiu, Ming Ming / Chow, Bonnie Wing-Yin / McBride, Catherine / Mol, Stefan Thomas 2016. Students' Sense of Belonging at School in 41 Countries: Cross-cultural Variability. *Journal of Cross-Cultural Psychology*. 47/2, 175-196.

Eringa, Klaes / Caudron, Laura N. / Rieck, Kathrin / Xie, Fei / Gerhardt, Tobias 2015. How Relevant are Hofstede's Dimensions for Intercultural Studies? A Replication of Hofstede's Research among Current International Business Students. *Research in Hospitality Management*. 5/2, 187-198.

Forbes-Mewett, Helen / Sawyer, Anne-Maree 2016. International Students and Mental Health. *Journal of International Students.* 6/3, 661-677.

Forbush, Eric / Foucault-Welles, Brooke 2016. Social Media Use and Adaptation among Chinese Students Beginning to Study in the United States. *International Journal of Intercultural Relations*. 50, 1-12.

Gahan, Peter / Abeysekera, Lakmal 2009. What Shapes an Individual's Work Values? An Integrated Model of the Relationship between

Work Values, National Culture and Self-construal. *The International Journal of Human Resource Management*. 20/1, 126-147.

Galchenko, Irina / van de Vijver, Fons 2007. The Role of Perceived Cultural Distance in the Acculturation of Exchange Students in Russia. *International Journal of Intercultural Relations*. 31/2, 181-197.

Ge, Lin / Brown, Douglas / Durst, Douglas 2019. Chinese International Students' Experiences in a Canadian University. *Journal of International Students*, *9*(2), 582-612.

Gephart, Robert 2004. Qualitative Research and the Academy of Management Journal. *Academy of Management Journal*. 47/4, 454–462.

Grigg, Angus 2018. Chinese Students Treated as Cash Cows at Australian Universities. *Financial Review,* August 28.

Gu, Qing / Maley, Alan 2008. Changing Places: A Study of Chinese Students in the UK. *Language and Intercultural Communication*. 8/4, 224-245.

Guan, Qun / Meng, Wanjin 2007. China's New National Curriculum Reform: Innovation, Challenges and Strategies. *Frontiers of Education in China*. 2/4, 579-604.

Guan, Yanjun / Liu, Shengming / Guo, Michael Jie / Li, Mengyu / Wu, Mengyi / Chen, Sylvia Xiaohua / Xu, Sabrina Lingxiao / Tian, Lin 2018. Acculturation Orientations and Chinese Student Sojourners' Career Adaptability: The Roles of Career Exploration and Cultural Distance. *Journal of Vocational Behavior*. 104, 228-239.

Guest, Greg / Bunce, Arwen / Johnson, Laura 2006. How Many Interviews are Enough? An Experiment with Data Saturation and Variability. *Field Methods*. 18/1, 59-82.

Hall, Edward 1976. *Beyond Culture*. Garden City, NY: Anchor Press.

Han, Jinghe / Han, Yu 2019. Cultural Concepts as Powerful Theoretical Tools: Chinese Teachers' Perceptions of their Relationship with Students in a Cross-cultural Context. *International Journal for the Scholarship of Teaching and Learning*. 13/1, 8.

Heng, Tang T. 2017. Voices of Chinese International Students in USA Colleges: 'I Want to Tell Them That …'. *Studies in Higher Education*, 42/5, 833-850.

Heng, Tang T. 2018. Different is Not Deficient: Contradicting Stereotypes of Chinese International Students in US Higher Education.

Studies in Higher Education. 43/1, 22-36.

Hofhuis, Joep / Hanke, Katja / Rutten, Tessa 2019. Social Network Sites and Acculturation of International Sojourners in the Netherlands: The Mediating Role of Psychological Alienation and Online Social Support. *International Journal of Intercultural Relations*. 69, 120-130.

Hofstede, Geert 1980. Culture and Organizations. *International Studies of Management & Organization*. 10/4, 15-41.

Hofstede, Geert 2001. *Culture's Consequences: Comparing Values, Behaviors, Institutions, and Organizations Across Nations* (2nd ed.). Thousand Oaks, CA: Sage publications.

Jackson, Jane / Chen, Xinren 2018. Discussion-based Pedagogy through the Eyes of Chinese International Exchange Students. *Pedagogies: An International Journal*. 13/4, 289-307.

Kim, Young Yun 2001. *Becoming Intercultural: An Integrative Theory of Communication and Cross-cultural Adaptation*. Thousand Oaks, CA: Sage.

Kim, Young Yun 2012. Beyond Cultural Categories: Communication, Adaptation, and Transformation. In Jane Jackson (ed.) *The Routledge Handbook of Language and Intercultural Communication.* New York, NY: Routledge, 229–243.

Ladum, Ariel / Burkholder, Gary 2019. Cultural Distance, Acculturative Stress, Functional Social Support, and Psychological Adaptation of International Students. *Higher Learning Research Communications*. 9/1, 28-46.

Le, Huong / McKay, Jade 2018. Chinese and Vietnamese International Students in Australia. *International Journal of Educational Management*, 32/7, 1278-1292.

Lee, Ji-Yeon / Ciftci, Ayse 2014. Asian International Students' Sociocultural Adaptation: Influence of Multicultural Personality, Assertiveness, Academic Self-efficacy, and Social Support. *International Journal of Intercultural Relations*. 38, 97-105.

Leong, Pamela 2015. Coming to America: Assessing the Patterns of Acculturation, Friendship Formation, and the Academic Experiences of International Students at a US College. *Journal of International Students*. 5/4, 459-474.

Li, Hanwei / & Pitkänen, Pirkko 2018. Understanding the Integration of Mainland Chinese Students. *Nordic Journal of Migration Research.* 8/2, 107–115.

Li, Jian 2016. A Cultural Hybridization Perspective: Emerging Academic Subculture among International Students from East Asia in US. *Universal Journal of Educational Research.* 4/9, 2218-2228.

Li, Li / Wegerif, Rupert 2014. What Does it Mean to Teach Thinking in China? Challenging and Developing Notions of 'Confucian Education'. *Thinking Skills and Creativity.* 11, 22-32.

Li, Zhen / Heath, Melissa / Jackson, Aaron P. / Allen, G. E. Kawika / Fischer, Lane / Chan, Peter 2017. Acculturation Experiences of Chinese International Students Who Attend American Universities. *Professional Psychology: Research and Practice.* 48/1, 1-26.

Loh, Chee Yen Raymond / Teo, Teck Choon 2017. Understanding Asian Students Learning Styles, Cultural Influence and Learning Strategies. *Journal of Education & Social Policy.* 7/1, 194-210.

Lu, Siyi / Singh, Michael 2017. Debating the Capabilities of "Chinese Students" for Thinking Critically in Anglophone Universities. *Education Sciences.* 7, 1-16.

Ma, Kyunghee / Pitner, Ronald / Sakamoto, Izumi / Park, Hyun Y. 2020. Challenges in Acculturation among International Students from Asian Collectivist Cultures. *Higher Education Studies, 10*(3), 34-43.

Ma, Siyuan / Zhu, Yi / Bresnahan, Mary 2021. Chinese International Students' Face Concerns, Self-Stigma, Linguistic Factors, and Help-Seeking Intentions for Mental Health. *Health Communication*, 1-9.

Marangell, Samantha / Arkoudis, Sophie / Baik, Chi 2018. Developing a Host Culture for International Students: What Does it Take? *Journal of International Students.* 8/3, 1440-1458.

McMahon, Patrick 2011. Chinese Voices: Chinese Learners and Their Experiences of Living and Studying in the United Kingdom. *Journal of Higher Education Policy and Management.* 33/4, 401-414.

Meng, Qian / Zhu, Chang / Cao, Chun 2017. The Role of Intergroup Contact and Acculturation Strategies in Developing Chinese International Students' Global Competence. *Journal of Intercultural Communication Research.* 46/3, 210-226.

Meng, Qian / Zhu, Chang / Cao, Chun 2018. Chinese International Students' Social Connectedness, Social and Academic Adaptation:

The Mediating Role of Global Competence. *Higher Education*. 75/1, 131-147.

Ozer, Simon 2015. Predictors of International Students' Psychological and Sociocultural Adjustment to the Context of Reception While Studying at Aarhus University, Denmark. *Scandinavian Journal of Psychology*. 56/6, 717-725.

Park, Eunjeong 2016. Issues of International Students' Academic Adaptation in the ESL Writing Class: A Mixed-methods Study. *Journal of International Students*. 6/4, 887-904.

Patton, Michael Quinn 2001. *Qualitative Research & Evaluation Methods* (3rd ed.). Saint Paul, MN: Sage.

Pho, Hanh / Schartner, Alina 2021. Social Contact Patterns of International Students and Their Impact on Academic Adaptation. *Journal of Multilingual and Multicultural Development*, *42*(6), 489-502.

Rear, David 2017. Reframing the Debate on Asian Students and Critical Thinking: Implications for Western Universities. *Journal of Contemporary Issues in Education*. 12/2, 18-33.

Redmond, Mark V. 2000. Cultural Distance as a Mediating Factor between Stress and Intercultural Communication Competence. *International Journal of Intercultural Relations*. 24/1, 151-159.

Roberts, Pam / Boldy, Duncan / Dunworth, Katie 2015. The Views of International Students Regarding University Support Services in Australia: A Case Study. *International Education Journal: Comparative Perspectives*. 14/3, 122-137.

Robertson, Margaret / Line, Martin / Jones, Susan / Thomas, Sharon 2000. International Students, Learning Environments and Perceptions: A Case Study using the Delphi Technique. *Higher Education Research & Development*. 19/1, 89-102.

Shafaei, Azadeh / Abd Razak, Nordin / Nejati, Mehran 2016. Integrating Two Cultures Successfully: Factors Influencing Acculturation Attitude of International Postgraduate Students in Malaysia. *Journal of Research in International Education*. 15/2, 137-154.

Strauss, Anselm / Corbin, Juliet 1998. *Basics of Qualitative Research Techniques*. Thousand Oaks, CA: Sage.

Tan, Charlene 2017. A Confucian Conception of Critical Thinking. *Journal of Philosophy of Education*. 51/1, 331-343.

Tan, Su-Ann / Liu, Shuang 2014. Ethnic Visibility and Preferred Acculturation Orientations of International Students. *International Journal of Intercultural Relations*. 39, 183-187.

Tran, Ly Thi 2013. *International Student Adaptation to Academic Writing in Higher Education*. Newcastle upon Tyne, UK: Cambridge Scholars.

Valdez, Gabriela 2015. US Higher Education Classroom Experiences of Undergraduate Chinese International Students. *Journal of International Students*. 5/2, 188-200.

Wang, Anhui / Liyanage, Indika / Walker, Anthony 2019. Scrutinising Critical Thinking (CT) in Chinese Higher Education: Perceptions of Chinese Academics. In Liyanage, Indika / Walker, Anthony (eds) *Multilingual Education Yearbook 2019*. Cham, Switzerland: Springer, 189-208.

Wang, Chia-Chih D. / Mallinckrodt, Brent 2006. Acculturation, Attachment, and Psychosocial Adjustment of Chinese/Taiwanese International Students. *Journal of Counseling Psychology*. 53/4, 422-433.

Wang, Isobel Kai-Hui 2018. Long-term Chinese Students' Transitional Experiences in UK Higher Education: A Particular Focus on Their Academic Adjustment. *International Journal of Teaching and Learning in Higher Education*. 30/1, 12-25.

Wang, Ting / Shan, Xiaojing 2006. A Qualitative Study on Chinese Postgraduates Students Learning Experiences in Australia. *AARE 2006 International Education Research Conference, Adelaide*.

Ward, Colleen / Bochner, Stephen / Furnham, Adrian 2001. *The Psychology of Culture Shock* (2nd ed.). London: Routledge.

Wei, Meifen / Liao, Kelly Yu-Hsin / Heppner, Puncky Paul / Chao, Ruth Chu-Lien / Ku, Tsun-Yao 2012. Forbearance Coping, Identification with Heritage Culture, Acculturative Stress, and Psychological Distress among Chinese International Students. *Journal of Counseling Psychology*. 59/1, 97-106.

Xing, Deyu / Bolden, Benjamin / Hogenkamp, Sawyer 2019. The Sound of Silence: A Musically Enhanced Narrative Inquiry into the Academic Acculturation Stories of Chinese International Students with Low Spoken English Proficiency. *Journal of Curriculum and Pedagogy*. 17/1, 1-23.

Xue, Fei 2018. *Factors that Contribute to Acculturative Stress of Chinese International Students*. Dissertation, University of Windsor, Ontario, Canada.

Yan, Kun / Berliner, David C. 2011. Chinese International Students in the United States: Demographic Trends, Motivations, Acculturation Features and Adjustment Challenges. *Asia Pacific Education Review*. 12/2, 173-184.

Yang, Tingzhong / Jiang, Shuhan / Yu, Lingwei / Cottrell, Randall R. / Si, Qi 2018. Life Stress, Uncertainty Stress and Self-reported Illness: A Representative Nationwide Study of Chinese Students. *Journal of Public Health*. 26/2, 205-209.

Yauch, Charlene A. / Steudel, Harold J. 2003. Complementary Use of Qualitative and Quantitative Cultural Assessment Methods. *Organizational Research Methods*. 6/4, 465-481.

Yeung, Lorrita 2019. Dialectics Versus Polemics in Chinese Rhetoric: A Study of Indirection in Chinese and Chinese ESL Argumentative Writing as Compared with English Argumentative Writing. *Chinese as a Second Language Research*. 8/1, 29-55.

Yu, Baohua / Wright, Ewan 2017. Academic Adaptation Amid Internationalisation: The Challenges for Local, Mainland Chinese, and International Students at Hong Kong's Universities. *Tertiary Education and Management*. 23/4, 347-360.

Yuan, Wenli 2011. Academic and Cultural Experiences of Chinese Students at an American University: A Qualitative Study. *Intercultural Communication Studies*. 20/1, 141-157.

Zhang, Christabel Ming 2002. *Valuing Cultural Diversity: The Academic Adjustment Experiences of Undergraduate Chinese International Business Students at Victoria University*. Dissertation, Victoria University, Victoria, Australia.

Zhang, Hong 2013. *Academic Adaptation and Cross-cultural Learning Experiences of Chinese Students at American Universities: A Narrative Inquiry*. Thesis, Northeastern University, Boston, Massachusetts.

Zhang, Ying 2013. Expatriate Development for Cross-cultural Adjustment: Effects of Cultural Distance and Cultural Intelligence. *Human Resource Development Review*. 12/2, 177-199.

Zheng, X. / Berry, J. W. 1991. Psychological Adaptation of Chinese Sojourners in Canada. *International Journal of Psychology*. 26/4,

451-470.

Zhou, Yalun / Wei, Michael 2020. *The Lived Experience of Chinese International Students in the US: An Academic Journey*. Singapore: Springer Nature.

Appendix A: Background questionnaire

1. Name
2. Age
3. Gender
4. Major
5. Degree
6. Your IELTS/TOEFL score
7. Which region of China are you from?
8. What is the highest degree you obtained before coming to the Australian university?
9. Please state whether you have previous studying experience outside of mainland China. And if so, please state place(s) and duration of study.
10. How long have you been studying at the Australian university? (excluding pre-enrolment courses)

Appendix B: Demographic data of participants

Pseudo-nym	**Age**	**Gen-der**	**Major**	**Degree**	**Region of origin**	**Stage of study**
Cathy	25	F	Education (TESOL)	Master	Northeast China	Second semester
Daisy	27	F	Education (General)	Master	Shanghai	Second semester
Hana	30	F	Education (Leadership & Manage-ment)	Master	Beijing	Second semester
Heidi	24	F	Education (Leadership & Manage-ment)	Master	Northern China	Second semester
May	23	F	Education (Psychology)	Master	Hunan	Second semester
Victoria	26	F	Education (Psychology)	Master	Jilin	Second semester

Appendix C: Interview schedule

Part A: Academic differences

1. Do you perceive any differences between studying in China and studying at the Australian university? What are they? How do you feel about them?
2. How do you feel about the teaching style, classroom participation mode and assessment tasks at the Australian university?
3. Have you experienced any academic challenges while studying at the Australian university? What are they? What are the feelings associated with these difficulties? Did you have similar challenges when you studied in China?
4. What do you think of your English language proficiency? Do you think it has any impact on your academic achievement?
5. Are you satisfied with your studying experience at the Australian university? Are you satisfied with your academic performance?

Part B: Responses to academic differences

6. Have you responded to any of the academic differences mentioned in Part A? Why or why not? What strategies have you used in overcoming academic challenges/difficulties if any? Do you think they are effective?
7. Have you used any support (friends, lectures, learning center, academic staff) in helping you with academic tasks?
8. What suggestions would you like to give to the teachers and the university to better support Chinese international students?
9. What suggestions would you like to give to other Chinese international students with regard to the academic adjustment process?

Part C: Self-report academic experience

10. Is there anything you would like to share concerning your academic experience at the Australian university?

Appendix D: Phases of data analysis

Phase	Description of the process
1.Preparing raw data files	Listening, transcribing, translating, formatting the raw data files and backing up each data file.
2.Member checking and modifying	Sending interview transcripts and English translations to the interviewees to check their accuracy, getting feedback and modifying accordingly.
3.Generating the initial codes	Identifying potential themes and underlining key words.
4.Grouping of codes and creating themes	Grouping similar codes to generate themes.
5.Making cross-case comparisons and generating core themes	Comparing themes among the interview data sets and generating core themes.
6.Reviewing, verifying and defining the themes	Checking themes against the initial data, verifying their representativeness and naming each of the themes.

Notes on Contributors

APISAK SUKYING completed his PhD from the University of Sydney in 2017. He is a lecturer in English at Mahasarakham University, Thailand, where he teaches on the Master of Education (ELT) Program. His research interests include second language vocabulary acquisition and development, language testing and assessment, academic writing and writing development, and English for Academic Purposes. He is currently investigating the semantic and linguistic roles of affix knowledge in vocabulary development in Thai English as a Foreign Language (EFL) university learners. The study reported in this volume is based on his doctoral research.

DAVID HIRSH is Associate Professor in TESOL at the University of Sydney where he teaches on the Master of Education (TESOL) program. His research interests include second language vocabulary, second language writing, and language revitalization. His research has appeared in *Frontiers in Psychology, Journal of Research in International Education, Reading in a Foreign Language* and *Revue Francaise de Linguistique Appliquee.* He supervises doctoral students in the areas of vocabulary studies and higher education.

MAKOTO TAKENOYA is a part-time lecturer in English Education at Musashino University, Japan. He has been working as an English teacher at a public junior high school in Tokyo and private senior high schools in Saitama, Japan. He completed his Master of Education (TESOL) degree from the University of Sydney. His research interests include English pronunciation, phonetics, EFL teaching, and second language acquisition.

MARIANA SÁEZ is a teacher of English as a foreign language, currently teaching in Chile. She has experience working with students from preschool, elementary, high school and adults and language centres. She completed her Master's degree in Education (TESOL) at the University of Sydney in 2021. Her research interest is learning strategies for the acquisition of English as a foreign language.

QIAN YANG is a PhD student in Education at Sydney School of Education and Social Work, The University of Sydney. Her PhD project explores how international postgraduate coursework students navigate academic writing expectations in Australian universities. She graduated with a Master's degree in Education from The University of Sydney, researching on the academic adaptation experiences of Chinese international students in Australia. Her areas of interest include international students' experiences, academic literacy, and tacit knowledge in education.

RAHMA FITRIANA is currently a lecturer in the Faculty of Languages and Arts at Yogyakarta State University, Indonesia. She received her Master of Education (TESOL) from the School of Education and Social Work, the University of Sydney. Her research interests revolve around classroom discourse, second language acquisition, bilingualism and bilingual education. The author has also been involving in several research and development projects for ESP modules used in the higher education, including English for Agriculture, English for Geography, and English for History.

WENJUN BU is a high school English teacher from China. She graduated with the Master of Education (TESOL) from the Sydney School of Education and Social Work at the University of Sydney. Her Master's dissertation focused on Chinese international students' considerations of oral participation and quietness in Australian tutorials. She has a research interest in participation behavior and beliefs of international students.

XUAN WANG is currently Assistant Professor at the School of Foreign Studies, Northwestern Polytechnical University, China. She completed her PhD from the University of Sydney in 2017 and her research interest is second language vocabulary development and language teaching. Her results of research have been presented in the 2018 conference of the American Association for Applied Linguistics (AAAL) in Chicago. She is now heading two research projects granted by Chinese provincial-level institutions.

YAN LI is a PhD candidate in the Sydney School of Education and Social Work, The University of Sydney. She has had teaching experience at the secondary and tertiary level in China. Her research interests include the acquisition and instruction of vocabulary in second languages and mobile-assisted language learning.

Linguistic Insights

Studies in Language and Communication

This series aims to promote specialist language studies in the fields of linguistic theory and applied linguistics, by publishing volumes that focus on specific aspects of language use in one or several languages and provide valuable insights into language and communication research. A cross-disciplinary approach is favoured and most European languages are accepted.

The series includes two types of books:

- Monographs – featuring in-depth studies on special aspects of language theory, language analysis or language teaching.
- Collected papers – assembling papers from workshops, conferences or symposia.

Each volume of the series is subjected to a double peer-reviewing process.

Vol. 1 Maurizio Gotti & Marina Dossena (eds)
Modality in Specialized Texts. Selected Papers of the 1st CERLIS Conference.
421 pages. 2001. ISBN 3-906767-10-8 · US-ISBN 0-8204-5340-4

Vol. 2 Giuseppina Cortese & Philip Riley (eds)
Domain-specific English. Textual Practices across Communities and Classrooms.
420 pages. 2002. ISBN 3-906768-98-8 · US-ISBN 0-8204-5884-8

Vol. 3 Maurizio Gotti, Dorothee Heller & Marina Dossena (eds)
Conflict and Negotiation in Specialized Texts. Selected Papers of the 2nd CERLIS Conference.
470 pages. 2002. ISBN 3-906769-12-7 · US-ISBN 0-8204-5887-2

Vol. 4 Maurizio Gotti, Marina Dossena, Richard Dury, Roberta Facchinetti & Maria Lima
Variation in Central Modals. A Repertoire of Forms and Types of Usage in Middle English and Early Modern English.
364 pages. 2002. ISBN 3-906769-84-4 · US-ISBN 0-8204-5898-8

Editorial address:

Prof. Maurizio Gotti Università di Bergamo, Dipartimento di Lingue, Letterature e Culture Straniere Piazza Rosate 2, 24129 Bergamo, Italy
Fax: +39 035 2052789, E-Mail: m.gotti@unibg.it

Vol. 5 Stefania Nuccorini (ed.)
Phrases and Phraseology. Data and Descriptions.
187 pages. 2002. ISBN 3-906770-08-7 · US-ISBN 0-8204-5933-X

Vol. 6 Vijay Bhatia, Christopher N. Candlin & Maurizio Gotti (eds)
Legal Discourse in Multilingual and Multicultural Contexts.
Arbitration Texts in Europe.
385 pages. 2003. ISBN 3-906770-85-0 · US-ISBN 0-8204-6254-3

Vol. 7 Marina Dossena & Charles Jones (eds)
Insights into Late Modern English. 2nd edition.
378 pages. 2003, 2007.
ISBN 978-3-03911-257-9 · US-ISBN 978-0-8204-8927-8

Vol. 8 Maurizio Gotti
Specialized Discourse. Linguistic Features and Changing Conventions.
351 pages. 2003, 2005.
ISBN 3-03910-606-6 · US-ISBN 0-8204-7000-7

Vol. 9 Alan Partington, John Morley & Louann Haarman (eds)
Corpora and Discourse.
420 pages. 2004. ISBN 3-03910-026-2 · US-ISBN 0-8204-6262-4

Vol. 10 Martina Möllering
The Acquisition of German Modal Particles. A Corpus-Based Approach.
290 pages. 2004. ISBN 3-03910-043-2 · US-ISBN 0-8204-6273-X

Vol. 11 David Hart (ed.)
English Modality in Context. Diachronic Perspectives.
261 pages. 2003. ISBN 3-03910-046-7 · US-ISBN 0-8204-6852-5

Vol. 12 Wendy Swanson
Modes of Co-reference as an Indicator of Genre.
430 pages. 2003. ISBN 3-03910-052-1 · US-ISBN 0-8204-6855-X

Vol. 13 Gina Poncini
Discursive Strategies in Multicultural Business Meetings.
2nd edition. 338 pages. 2004, 2007.
ISBN 978-3-03911-296-8 · US-ISBN 978-0-8204-8937-7

Vol. 14 Christopher N. Candlin & Maurizio Gotti (eds)
Intercultural Aspects of Specialized Communication.
2nd edition. 369 pages. 2004, 2007.
ISBN 978-3-03911-258-6 · US-ISBN 978-0-8204-8926-1

Vol. 15 Gabriella Del Lungo Camiciotti & Elena Tognini Bonelli (eds)
Academic Discourse. New Insights into Evaluation.
234 pages. 2004. ISBN 3-03910-353-9 · US-ISBN 0-8204-7016-3

Vol. 16 Marina Dossena & Roger Lass (eds)
Methods and Data in English Historical Dialectology.
405 pages. 2004. ISBN 3-03910-362-8 · US-ISBN 0-8204-7018-X

Vol. 17 Judy Noguchi
The Science Review Article. An Opportune Genre in
the Construction of Science.
274 pages. 2006. ISBN 3-03910-426-8 · US-ISBN 0-8204-7034-1

Vol. 18 Giuseppina Cortese & Anna Duszak (eds)
Identity, Community, Discourse. English in Intercultural Settings.
495 pages. 2005. ISBN 3-03910-632-5 · US-ISBN 0-8204-7163-1

Vol. 19 Anna Trosborg & Poul Erik Flyvholm Jørgensen (eds)
Business Discourse. Texts and Contexts.
250 pages. 2005. ISBN 3-03910-606-6 · US-ISBN 0-8204-7000-7

Vol. 20 Christopher Williams
Tradition and Change in Legal English. Verbal Constructions in Prescriptive Texts.
2nd revised edition. 216 pages. 2005, 2007. ISBN 978-3-03911-444-3.

Vol. 21 Katarzyna Dziubalska-Kolaczyk & Joanna Przedlacka (eds)
English Pronunciation Models: A Changing Scene.
2nd edition. 476 pages. 2005, 2008. ISBN 978-3-03911-682-9.

Vol. 22 Christián Abello-Contesse, Rubén Chacón-Beltrán, M. Dolores López-Jiménez & M. Mar Torreblanca-López (eds)
Age in L2 Acquisition and Teaching.
214 pages. 2006. ISBN 3-03910-668-6 · US-ISBN 0-8204-7174-7

Vol. 23 Vijay K. Bhatia, Maurizio Gotti, Jan Engberg & Dorothee Heller (eds)
Vagueness in Normative Texts.
474 pages. 2005. ISBN 3-03910-653-8 · US-ISBN 0-8204-7169-0

Vol. 24 Paul Gillaerts & Maurizio Gotti (eds)
Genre Variation in Business Letters. 2nd printing.
407 pages. 2008. ISBN 978-3-03911-681-2.

Vol. 25 Ana María Hornero, María José Luzón & Silvia Murillo (eds)
Corpus Linguistics. Applications for the Study of English.
2nd printing. 526 pages. 2006, 2008. ISBN 978-3-03911-726-0

Vol. 26 J. Lachlan Mackenzie & María de los Ángeles Gómez-González (eds)
Studies in Functional Discourse Grammar.
259 pages. 2005. ISBN 3-03910-696-1 · US-ISBN 0-8204-7558-0

Vol. 27 Debbie G. E. Ho
Classroom Talk. Exploring the Sociocultural Structure of Formal ESL Learning.
2nd edition. 254 pages. 2006, 2007. ISBN 978-3-03911-434-4

Vol. 28 Javier Pérez-Guerra, Dolores González-Álvarez, Jorge L. Bueno-Alonso & Esperanza Rama-Martínez (eds)
'Of Varying Language and Opposing Creed'. New Insights into Late Modern English.
455 pages. 2007. ISBN 978-3-03910-788-9

Vol. 29 Francesca Bargiela-Chiappini & Maurizio Gotti (eds)
Asian Business Discourse(s).
350 pages. 2005. ISBN 3-03910-804-2 · US-ISBN 0-8204-7574-2

Vol. 30 Nicholas Brownlees (ed.)
News Discourse in Early Modern Britain. Selected Papers of CHINED 2004.
300 pages. 2006. ISBN 3-03910-805-0 · US-ISBN 0-8204-8025-8

Vol. 31 Roberta Facchinetti & Matti Rissanen (eds)
Corpus-based Studies of Diachronic English.
300 pages. 2006. ISBN 3-03910-851-4 · US-ISBN 0-8204-8040-1

Vol. 32 Marina Dossena & Susan M. Fitzmaurice (eds)
Business and Official Correspondence. Historical Investigations.
209 pages. 2006. ISBN 3-03910-880-8 · US-ISBN 0-8204-8352-4

Vol. 33 Giuliana Garzone & Srikant Sarangi (eds)
Discourse, Ideology and Specialized Communication.
494 pages. 2007. ISBN 978-3-03910-888-6

Vol. 34 Giuliana Garzone & Cornelia Ilie (eds)
The Use of English in Institutional and Business Settings.
An Intercultural Perspective.
372 pages. 2007. ISBN 978-3-03910-889-3

Vol. 35 Vijay K. Bhatia & Maurizio Gotti (eds)
Explorations in Specialized Genres.
316 pages. 2006. ISBN 3-03910-995-2 · US-ISBN 0-8204-8372-9

Vol. 36 Heribert Picht (ed.)
Modern Approaches to Terminological Theories and Applications.
432 pages. 2006. ISBN 3-03911-156-6 · US-ISBN 0-8204-8380-X

Vol. 37 Anne Wagner & Sophie Cacciaguidi-Fahy (eds)
Legal Language and the Search for Clarity / Le langage juridique et la quête de clarté. Practice and Tools / Pratiques et instruments.
487 pages. 2006. ISBN 3-03911-169-8 · US-ISBN 0-8204-8388-5

Vol. 38 Juan Carlos Palmer-Silveira, Miguel F. Ruiz-Garrido & Inmaculada Fortanet-Gómez (eds)
Intercultural and International Business Communication.
Theory, Research and Teaching.
2nd edition. 343 pages. 2006, 2008. ISBN 978-3-03911-680-5

Vol. 39 Christiane Dalton-Puffer, Dieter Kastovsky, Nikolaus Ritt & Herbert Schendl (eds)
Syntax, Style and Grammatical Norms. English from 1500–2000.
250 pages. 2006. ISBN 3-03911-181-7 · US-ISBN 0-8204-8394-X

Vol. 40 Marina Dossena & Irma Taavitsainen (eds)
Diachronic Perspectives on Domain-Specific English.
280 pages. 2006. ISBN 3-03910-176-0 · US-ISBN 0-8204-8391-5

Vol. 41 John Flowerdew & Maurizio Gotti (eds)
Studies in Specialized Discourse.
293 pages. 2006. ISBN 3-03911-178-7

Vol. 42 Ken Hyland & Marina Bondi (eds)
Academic Discourse Across Disciplines.
320 pages. 2006. ISBN 3-03911-183-3 · US-ISBN 0-8204-8396-6

Vol. 43 Paul Gillaerts & Philip Shaw (eds)
The Map and the Landscape. Norms and Practices in Genre.
256 pages. 2006. ISBN 3-03911-182-5 · US-ISBN 0-8204-8395-4

Vol. 44 Maurizio Gotti & Davide Giannoni (eds)
New Trends in Specialized Discourse Analysis.
301 pages. 2006. ISBN 3-03911-184-1 · US-ISBN 0-8204-8381-8

Vol. 45 Maurizio Gotti & Françoise Salager-Meyer (eds)
Advances in Medical Discourse Analysis. Oral and Written Contexts.
492 pages. 2006. ISBN 3-03911-185-X · US-ISBN 0-8204-8382-6

Vol. 46 Maurizio Gotti & Susan Šarcević (eds)
Insights into Specialized Translation.
396 pages. 2006. ISBN 3-03911-186-8 · US-ISBN 0-8204-8383-4

Vol. 47 Khurshid Ahmad & Margaret Rogers (eds)
Evidence-based LSP. Translation, Text and Terminology.
584 pages. 2007. ISBN 978-3-03911-187-9

Vol. 48 Hao Sun & Dániel Z. Kádár (eds)
It's the Dragon's Turn. Chinese Institutional Discourses.
262 pages. 2008. ISBN 978-3-03911-175-6

Vol. 49 Cristina Suárez-Gómez
Relativization in Early English (950-1250). the Position of Relative Clauses.
149 pages. 2006. ISBN 3-03911-203-1 · US-ISBN 0-8204-8904-2

Vol. 50 Maria Vittoria Calvi & Luisa Chierichetti (eds)
Nuevas tendencias en el discurso de especialidad.
319 pages. 2006. ISBN 978-3-03911-261-6

Vol. 51 Mari Carmen Campoy & María José Luzón (eds)
Spoken Corpora in Applied Linguistics.
274 pages. 2008. ISBN 978-3-03911-275-3

Vol. 52 Konrad Ehlich & Dorothee Heller (Hrsg.)
Die Wissenschaft und ihre Sprachen.
323 pages. 2006. ISBN 978-3-03911-272-2

Vol. 53 Jingyu Zhang
The Semantic Salience Hierarchy Model. The L2 Acquisition of Psych Predicates
273 pages. 2007. ISBN 978-3-03911-300-2

Vol. 54 Norman Fairclough, Giuseppina Cortese & Patrizia Ardizzone (eds)
Discourse and Contemporary Social Change.
555 pages. 2007. ISBN 978-3-03911-276-0

Vol. 55 Jan Engberg, Marianne Grove Ditlevsen, Peter Kastberg & Martin Stegu (eds)
New Directions in LSP Teaching.
331 pages. 2007. ISBN 978-3-03911-433-7

Vol. 56 Dorothee Heller & Konrad Ehlich (Hrsg.)
Studien zur Rechtskommunikation.
322 pages. 2007. ISBN 978-3-03911-436-8

Vol. 57 Teruhiro Ishiguro & Kang-kwong Luke (eds)
Grammar in Cross-Linguistic Perspective.
The Syntax, Semantics, and Pragmatics of Japanese and Chinese.
304 pages. 2012. ISBN 978-3-03911-445-0

Vol. 58 Carmen Frehner
Email – SMS – MMS
294 pages. 2008. ISBN 978-3-03911-451-1

Vol. 59 Isabel Balteiro
The Directionality of Conversion in English. A Dia-Synchronic Study.
276 pages. 2007. ISBN 978-3-03911-241-8

Vol. 60 Maria Milagros Del Saz Rubio
English Discourse Markers of Reformulation.
237 pages. 2007. ISBN 978-3-03911-196-1

Vol. 61 Sally Burgess & Pedro Martín-Martín (eds)
English as an Additional Language in Research Publication and Communication.
259 pages. 2008. ISBN 978-3-03911-462-7

Vol. 62 Sandrine Onillon
Pratiques et représentations de l'écrit.
458 pages. 2008. ISBN 978-3-03911-464-1

Vol. 63 Hugo Bowles & Paul Seedhouse (eds)
Conversation Analysis and Language for Specific Purposes.
2nd edition. 337 pages. 2007, 2009. ISBN 978-3-0343-0045-2

Vol. 64 Vijay K. Bhatia, Christopher N. Candlin & Paola Evangelisti Allori (eds)
Language, Culture and the Law.
The Formulation of Legal Concepts across Systems and Cultures.
342 pages. 2008. ISBN 978-3-03911-470-2

Vol. 65 Jonathan Culpeper & Dániel Z. Kádár (eds)
Historical (Im)politeness.
300 pages. 2010. ISBN 978-3-03911-496-2

Vol. 66 Linda Lombardo (ed.)
Using Corpora to Learn about Language and Discourse.
237 pages. 2009. ISBN 978-3-03911-522-8

Vol. 67 Natsumi Wakamoto
Extroversion/Introversion in Foreign Language Learning.
Interactions with Learner Strategy Use.
159 pages. 2009. ISBN 978-3-03911-596-9

Vol. 68 Eva Alcón-Soler (ed.)
Learning How to Request in an Instructed Language Learning Context.
260 pages. 2008. ISBN 978-3-03911-601-0

Vol. 69 Domenico Pezzini
The Translation of Religious Texts in the Middle Ages.
428 pages. 2008. ISBN 978-3-03911-600-3

Vol. 70 Tomoko Tode
Effects of Frequency in Classroom Second Language Learning.
Quasi-experiment and stimulated-recall analysis.
195 pages. 2008. ISBN 978-3-03911-602-7

Vol. 71 Egor Tsedryk
Fusion symétrique et alternances ditransitives.
211 pages. 2009. ISBN 978-3-03911-609-6

Vol. 72 Cynthia J. Kellett Bidoli & Elana Ochse (eds)
English in International Deaf Communication.
444 pages. 2008. ISBN 978-3-03911-610-2

Vol. 73 Joan C. Beal, Carmela Nocera & Massimo Sturiale (eds)
Perspectives on Prescriptivism.
269 pages. 2008. ISBN 978-3-03911-632-4

Vol. 74 Carol Taylor Torsello, Katherine Ackerley & Erik Castello (eds)
Corpora for University Language Teachers.
308 pages. 2008. ISBN 978-3-03911-639-3

Vol. 75 María Luisa Pérez Cañado (ed.)
English Language Teaching in the European Credit Transfer System. Facing the Challenge.
251 pages. 2009. ISBN 978-3-03911-654-6

Vol. 76 Marina Dossena & Ingrid Tieken-Boon van Ostade (eds)
Studies in Late Modern English Correspondence. Methodology and Data.
291 pages. 2008. ISBN 978-3-03911-658-4

Vol. 77 Ingrid Tieken-Boon van Ostade & Wim van der Wurff (eds)
Current Issues in Late Modern English.
436 pages. 2009. ISBN 978-3-03911-660-7

Vol. 78 Marta Navarro Coy (ed.)
Practical Approaches to Foreign Language Teaching and Learning.
297 pages. 2009. ISBN 978-3-03911-661-4

Vol. 79 Qing Ma
Second Language Vocabulary Acquisition.
333 pages. 2009. ISBN 978-3-03911-666-9

Vol. 80 Martin Solly, Michelangelo Conoscenti & Sandra Campagna (eds)
Verbal/Visual Narrative Texts in Higher Education.
384 pages. 2008. ISBN 978-3-03911-672-0

Vol. 81 Meiko Matsumoto
From Simple Verbs to Periphrastic Expressions: The Historical Development of Composite Predicates, Phrasal Verbs, and Related Constructions in English.
235 pages. 2008. ISBN 978-3-03911-675-1

Vol. 82 Melinda Dooly
Doing Diversity. Teachers' Construction of Their Classroom Reality.
180 pages. 2009. ISBN 978-3-03911-687-4

Vol. 83 Victoria Guillén-Nieto, Carmen Marimón-Llorca & Chelo Vargas-Sierra (eds)
Intercultural Business Communication and Simulation and Gaming Methodology.
392 pages. 2009. ISBN 978-3-03911-688-1

Vol. 84 Maria Grazia Guido
English as a Lingua Franca in Cross-cultural Immigration Domains.
285 pages. 2008. ISBN 978-3-03911-689-8

Vol. 85 Erik Castello
Text Complexity and Reading Comprehension Tests.
352 pages. 2008. ISBN 978-3-03911-717-8

Vol. 86 Maria-Lluisa Gea-Valor, Isabel García-Izquierdo & Maria-José Esteve (eds)
Linguistic and Translation Studies in Scientific Communication.
317 pages. 2010. ISBN 978-3-0343-0069-8

Vol. 87 Carmen Navarro, Rosa Mª Rodríguez Abella, Francesca Dalle Pezze & Renzo Miotti (eds)
La comunicación especializada.
355 pages. 2008. ISBN 978-3-03911-733-8

Vol. 88 Kiriko Sato
The Development from Case-Forms to Prepositional Constructions in Old English Prose.
231 pages. 2009. ISBN 978-3-03911-763-5

Vol. 89 Dorothee Heller (Hrsg.)
Formulierungsmuster in deutscher und italienischer Fachkommunikation. Intra- und interlinguale Perspektiven.
315 pages. 2008. ISBN 978-3-03911-778-9

Vol. 90 Henning Bergenholtz, Sandro Nielsen & Sven Tarp (eds)
Lexicography at a Crossroads. Dictionaries and Encyclopedias Today, Lexicographical Tools Tomorrow.
372 pages. 2009. ISBN 978-3-03911-799-4

Vol. 91 Manouchehr Moshtagh Khorasani
The Development of Controversies. From the Early Modern Period to Online Discussion Forums.
317 pages. 2009. ISBN 978-3-3911-711-6

Vol. 92 María Luisa Carrió-Pastor (ed.)
Content and Language Integrated Learning. Cultural Diversity.
178 pages. 2009. ISBN 978-3-3911-818-2

Vol. 93 Roger Berry
Terminology in English Language Teaching. Nature and Use.
262 pages. 2010. ISBN 978-3-0343-0013-1

Vol. 94 Roberto Cagliero & Jennifer Jenkins (eds)
Discourses, Communities, and Global Englishes
240 pages. 2010. ISBN 978-3-0343-0012-4

Vol. 95 Facchinetti Roberta, Crystal David, Seidlhofer Barbara (eds)
From International to Local English – And Back Again.
268 pages. 2010. ISBN 978-3-0343-0011-7

Vol. 96 Cesare Gagliardi & Alan Maley (eds)
EIL, ELF, Global English. Teaching and Learning Issues
376 pages. 2010. ISBN 978-3-0343-0010-0

Vol. 97 Sylvie Hancil (ed.)
The Role of Prosody in Affective Speech.
403 pages. 2009. ISBN 978-3-03911-696-6

Vol. 98 Marina Dossena & Roger Lass (eds)
Studies in English and European Historical Dialectology.
257 pages. 2009. ISBN 978-3-0343-0024-7

Vol. 99 Christine Béal
Les interactions quotidiennes en français et en anglais. De l'approche comparative à l'analyse des situations interculturelles.
424 pages. 2010. ISBN 978-3-0343-0027-8

Vol. 100 Maurizio Gotti (ed.)
Commonality and Individuality in Academic Discourse.
398 pages. 2009. ISBN 978-3-0343-0023-0

Vol. 101 Javier E. Díaz Vera & Rosario Caballero (eds)
Textual Healing. Studies in Medieval English Medical, Scientific and Technical Texts.
213 pages. 2009. ISBN 978-3-03911-822-9

Vol. 102 Nuria Edo Marzá
The Specialised Lexicographical Approach. A Step further in Dictionary-making.
316 pages. 2009. ISBN 978-3-0343-0043-8

Vol. 103 Carlos Prado-Alonso, Lidia Gómez-García, Iria Pastor-Gómez &
David Tizón-Couto (eds)
New Trends and Methodologies in Applied English Language Research.
Diachronic, Diatopic and Contrastive Studies.
348 pages. 2009. ISBN 978-3-0343-0046-9

Vol. 104 Françoise Salager-Meyer & Beverly A. Lewin
Crossed Words. Criticism in Scholarly Writing?
371 pages. 2011. ISBN 978-3-0343-0049-0.

Vol. 105 Javier Ruano-García
Early Modern Northern English Lexis. A Literary Corpus-Based Study.
611 pages. 2010. ISBN 978-3-0343-0058-2

Vol. 106 Rafael Monroy-Casas
Systems for the Phonetic Transcription of English. Theory and Texts.
280 pages. 2011. ISBN 978-3-0343-0059-9

Vol. 107 Nicola T. Owtram
The Pragmatics of Academic Writing.
A Relevance Approach to the Analysis of Research Article Introductions.
311 pages. 2009. ISBN 978-3-0343-0060-5

Vol. 108 Yolanda Ruiz de Zarobe, Juan Manuel Sierra &
Francisco Gallardo del Puerto (eds)
Content and Foreign Language Integrated Learning.
Contributions to Multilingualism in European Contexts
343 pages. 2011. ISBN 978-3-0343-0074-2

Vol. 109 Ángeles Linde López & Rosalía Crespo Jiménez (eds)
Professional English in the European context. The EHEA challenge.
374 pages. 2010. ISBN 978-3-0343-0088-9

Vol. 110 Rosalía Rodríguez-Vázquez
The Rhythm of Speech, Verse and Vocal Music. A New Theory.
394 pages. 2010. ISBN 978-3-0343-0309-5

Vol. 111 Anastasios Tsangalidis & Roberta Facchinetti (eds)
Studies on English Modality. In Honour of Frank Palmer.
392 pages. 2009. ISBN 978-3-0343-0310-1

Vol. 112 Jing Huang
Autonomy, Agency and Identity in Foreign Language Learning and Teaching.
400 pages. 2013. ISBN 978-3-0343-0370-5

Vol. 113 Mihhail Lotman & Maria-Kristiina Lotman (eds)
Frontiers in Comparative Prosody. In memoriam: Mikhail Gasparov.
426 pages. 2011. ISBN 978-3-0343-0373-6

Vol. 114 Merja Kytö, John Scahill & Harumi Tanabe (eds)
Language Change and Variation from Old English to Late Modern English.
A Festschrift for Minoji Akimoto
422 pages. 2010. ISBN 978-3-0343-0372-9

Vol. 115 Giuliana Garzone & Paola Catenaccio (eds)
Identities across Media and Modes. Discursive Perspectives.
379 pages. 2009. ISBN 978-3-0343-0386-6

Vol. 116 Elena Landone
Los marcadores del discurso y cortesía verbal en español.
390 pages. 2010. ISBN 978-3-0343-0413-9

Vol. 117 Maurizio Gotti & Christopher Williams (eds)
Legal Discourse across Languages and Cultures.
339 pages. 2010. ISBN 978-3-0343-0425-2

Vol. 118 David Hirsh
Academic Vocabulary in Context.
217 pages. 2010. ISBN 978-3-0343-0426-9

Vol. 119 Yvonne Dröschel
Lingua Franca English. The Role of Simplification and Transfer.
358 pages. 2011. ISBN 978-3-0343-0432-0

Vol. 120 Tengku Sepora Tengku Mahadi, Helia Vaezian & Mahmoud Akbari
Corpora in Translation. A Practical Guide.
135 pages. 2010. ISBN 978-3-0343-0434-4

Vol. 121 Davide Simone Giannoni & Celina Frade (eds)
Researching Language and the Law. Textual Features and Translation Issues.
278 pages. 2010. ISBN 978-3-0343-0443-6

Vol. 122 Daniel Madrid & Stephen Hughes (eds)
Studies in Bilingual Education.
472 pages. 2011. ISBN 978-3-0343-0474-0

Vol. 123 Vijay K. Bhatia, Christopher N. Candlin & Maurizio Gotti (eds)
The Discourses of Dispute Resolution.
290 pages. 2010. ISBN 978-3-0343-0476-4

Vol. 124 Davide Simone Giannoni
Mapping Academic Values in the Disciplines. A Corpus-Based Approach.
288 pages. 2010. ISBN 978-3-0343-0488-7

Vol. 125 Giuliana Garzone & James Archibald (eds)
Discourse, Identities and Roles in Specialized Communication.
419 pages. 2010. ISBN 978-3-0343-0494-8

Vol. 126 Iria Pastor-Gómez
The Status and Development of N+N Sequences in
Contemporary English Noun Phrases.
216 pages. 2011. ISBN 978-3-0343-0534-1

Vol. 127 Carlos Prado-Alonso
Full-verb Inversion in Written and Spoken English.
261 pages. 2011. ISBN 978-3-0343-0535-8

Vol. 128 Tony Harris & María Moreno Jaén (eds)
Corpus Linguistics in Language Teaching.
214 pages. 2010. ISBN 978-3-0343-0524-2

Vol. 129 Tetsuji Oda & Hiroyuki Eto (eds)
Multiple Perspectives on English Philology and History of Linguistics.
A Festschrift for Shoichi Watanabe on his 80th Birthday.
378 pages. 2010. ISBN 978-3-0343-0480-1

Vol. 130 Luisa Chierichetti & Giovanni Garofalo (eds)
Lengua y Derecho. líneas de investigación interdisciplinaria.
283 pages. 2010. 978-3-0343-0463-4

Vol. 131 Paola Evangelisti Allori & Giuliana Garzone (eds)
Discourse, Identities and Genres in Corporate Communication.
Sponsorship, Advertising and Organizational Communication.
324 pages. 2011. 978-3-0343-0591-4

Vol. 132 Leyre Ruiz de Zarobe & Yolanda Ruiz de Zarobe (eds)
Speech Acts and Politeness across Languages and Cultures.
402 pages. 2012. 978-3-0343-0611-9

Vol. 133 Thomas Christiansen
Cohesion. A Discourse Perspective.
387 pages. 2011. 978-3-0343-0619-5

Vol. 134 Giuliana Garzone & Maurizio Gotti
Discourse, Communication and the Enterprise. Genres and Trends.
451 pages. 2011. ISBN 978-3-0343-0620-1

Vol. 135 Zsuzsa Hoffmann
Ways of the World's Words.
Language Contact in the Age of Globalization.
334 pages 2011. ISBN 978-3-0343-0673-7

Vol. 136 Cecilia Varcasia (ed.)
Becoming Multilingual.
Language Learning and Language Policy between Attitudes and Identities.
213 pages. 2011. ISBN 978-3-0343-0687-5

Vol. 137 Susy Macqueen
The Emergence of Patterns in Second Language Writing.
A Sociocognitive Exploration of Lexical Trails.
325 pages. 2012. ISBN 978-3-0343-1010-9

Vol. 138 Maria Vittoria Calvi & Giovanna Mapelli (eds)
La lengua del turismo. Géneros discursivos y terminología.
365 pages. 2011. ISBN 978-3-0343-1011-6

Vol. 139 Ken Lau
Learning to Become a Professional in a Textually-Mediated World.
A Text-Oriented Study of Placement Practices.
261 pages. 2012. ISBN 978-3-0343-1016-1

Vol. 140 Sandra Campagna, Giuliana Garzone, Cornelia Ilie & Elizabeth Rowley-Jolivet (eds)
Evolving Genres in Web-mediated Communication.
337 pages. 2012. ISBN 978-3-0343-1013-0

Vol. 141 Edith Esch & Martin Solly (eds)
The Sociolinguistics of Language Education in International Contexts.
263 pages. 2012. ISBN 978-3-0343-1009-3

Vol. 142 Forthcoming.

Vol. 143 David Tizón-Couto
Left Dislocation in English. A Functional-Discoursal Approach.
416 pages. 2012. ISBN 978-3-0343-1037-6

Vol. 144 Margrethe Petersen & Jan Engberg (eds)
Current Trends in LSP Research. Aims and Methods.
323 pages. 2011. ISBN 978-3-0343-1054-3

Vol. 145 David Tizón-Couto, Beatriz Tizón-Couto, Iria Pastor-Gómez & Paula Rodríguez-Puente (eds)
New Trends and Methodologies in Applied English Language Research II.
Studies in Language Variation, Meaning and Learning.
283 pages. 2012. ISBN 978-3-0343-1061-1

Vol. 146 Rita Salvi & Hiromasa Tanaka (eds)
Intercultural Interactions in Business and Management.
306 pages. 2011. ISBN 978-3-0343-1039-0

Vol. 147 Francesco Straniero Sergio & Caterina Falbo (eds)
Breaking Ground in Corpus-based Interpreting Studies.
254 pages. 2012. ISBN 978-3-0343-1071-0

Vol. 148 Forthcoming.

Vol. 149 Vijay K. Bhatia & Paola Evangelisti Allori (eds)
Discourse and Identity in the Professions. Legal, Corporate and Institutional Citizenship.
352 pages. 2011. ISBN 978-3-0343-1079-6

Vol. 150 Maurizio Gotti (ed.)
Academic Identity Traits. A Corpus-Based Investigation.
363 pages. 2012. ISBN 978-3-0343-1141-0

Vol. 151 Priscilla Heynderickx, Sylvain Dieltjens, Geert Jacobs, Paul Gillaerts &
Elizabeth de Groot (eds)
The Language Factor in International Business.
New Perspectives on Research, Teaching and Practice.
320 pages. 2012. ISBN 978-3-0343-1090-1

Vol. 152 Paul Gillaerts, Elizabeth de Groot, Sylvain Dieltjens, Priscilla Heynderickx &
Geert Jacobs (eds)
Researching Discourse in Business Genres. Cases and Corpora.
215 pages. 2012. ISBN 978-3-0343-1092-5

Vol. 153 Yongyan Zheng
Dynamic Vocabulary Development in a Foreign Language.
262 pages. 2012. ISBN 978-3-0343-1106-9

Vol. 154 Carmen Argondizzo (ed.)
Creativity and Innovation in Language Education.
357 pages. 2012. ISBN 978-3-0343-1080-2

Vol. 155 David Hirsh (ed.)
Current Perspectives in Second Language Vocabulary Research.
180 pages. 2012. ISBN 978-3-0343-1108-3

Vol. 156 Seiji Shinkawa
Unhistorical Gender Assignment in Lahamon's *Brut*. A Case Study of a Late Stage
in the Development of Grammatical Gender toward its Ultimate Loss.
186 pages. 2012. ISBN 978-3-0343-1124-3

Vol. 157 Yeonkwon Jung
Basics of Organizational Writing: A Critical Reading Approach.
151 pages. 2014. ISBN 978-3-0343-1137-3.

Vol. 158 Bárbara Eizaga Rebollar (ed.)
Studies in Linguistics and Cognition.
301 pages. 2012. ISBN 978-3-0343-1138-0

Vol. 159 Giuliana Garzone, Paola Catenaccio, Chiara Degano (eds)
Genre Change in the Contemporary World. Short-term Diachronic Perspectives.
329 pages. 2012. ISBN 978-3-0343-1214-1

Vol. 160 Carol Berkenkotter, Vijay K. Bhatia & Maurizio Gotti (eds)
Insights into Academic Genres.
468 pages. 2012. ISBN 978-3-0343-1211-0

Vol. 161 Beatriz Tizón-Couto
Clausal Complements in Native and Learner Spoken English. A corpus-based study with Lindsei and Vicolse. 357 pages. 2013. ISBN 978-3-0343-1184-7

Vol. 162 Patrizia Anesa
Jury Trials and the Popularization of Legal Language. A Discourse Analytical Approach.
247 pages. 2012. ISBN 978-3-0343-1231-8

Vol. 163 David Hirsh
Endangered Languages, Knowledge Systems and Belief Systems.
153 pages. 2013. ISBN 978-3-0343-1232-5

Vol. 164 Eugenia Sainz (ed.)
De la estructura de la frase al tejido del discurso. Estudios contrastivos español/italiano.
305 pages. 2014. ISBN 978-3-0343-1253-0

Vol. 165 Julia Bamford, Franca Poppi & Davide Mazzi (eds)
Space, Place and the Discursive Construction of Identity.
367 pages. 2014. ISBN 978-3-0343-1249-3

Vol. 166 Rita Salvi & Janet Bowker (eds)
Space, Time and the Construction of Identity.
Discursive Indexicality in Cultural, Institutional and Professional Fields.
324 pages. 2013. ISBN 978-3-0343-1254-7

Vol. 167 Shunji Yamazaki & Robert Sigley (eds)
Approaching Language Variation through Corpora. A Festschrift in Honour of Toshio Saito.
421 pages. 2013. ISBN 978-3-0343-1264-6

Vol. 168 Franca Poppi
Global Interactions in English as a Lingua Franca. How written communication is changing under the influence of electronic media and new contexts of use.
249 pages. 2012. ISBN 978-3-0343-1276-9

Vol. 169 Miguel A. Aijón Oliva & María José Serrano
Style in syntax. Investigating variation in Spanish pronoun subjects.
239 pages. 2013. ISBN 978-3-0343-1244-8

Vol. 170 Inés Olza, Óscar Loureda & Manuel Casado-Velarde (eds)
Language Use in the Public Sphere. Methodological Perspectives and Empirical Applications
564 pages. 2014. ISBN 978-3-0343-1286-8

Vol. 171 Aleksandra Matulewska
Legilinguistic Translatology. A Parametric Approach to Legal Translation.
279 pages. 2013. ISBN 978-3-0343-1287-5

Vol. 172 Maurizio Gotti & Carmen Sancho Guinda (eds)
Narratives in Academic and Professional Genres.
513 pages. 2013. ISBN 978-3-0343-1371-1

Vol. 173 Madalina Chitez
Learner corpus profiles. The case of Romanian Learner English.
244 pages. 2014. ISBN 978-3-0343-1410-7

Vol. 174 Chihiro Inoue
Task Equivalence in Speaking Tests.
251 pages. 2013. ISBN 978-3-0343-1417-6

Vol. 175 Gabriel Quiroz & Pedro Patiño (eds.)
LSP in Colombia: advances and challenges.
339 pages. 2014. ISBN 978-3-0343-1434-3

Vol. 176 Catherine Resche
Economic Terms and Beyond: Capitalising on the Wealth of Notions.
How Researchers in Specialised Varieties of English Can Benefit from Focusing on Terms.
332 pages. 2013. ISBN 978-3-0343-1435-0

Vol. 177 Wei Wang
Media representation of migrant workers in China. Identities and stances
198 pages. 2018. 978-3-0343-1436-7

Vol. 178 Cécile Desoutter & Caroline Mellet (dir.)
Le discours rapporté: approches linguistiques et perspectives didactiques.
270 pages. 2013. ISBN 978-3-0343-1292-9

Vol. 179 Ana Díaz-Negrillo & Francisco Javier Díaz-Pérez (eds)
Specialisation and Variation in Language Corpora.
341 pages. 2014. ISBN 978-3-0343-1316-2

Vol. 180 Pilar Alonso
A Multi-dimensional Approach to Discourse Coherence. From Standardness to Creativity.
247 pages. 2014. ISBN 978-3-0343-1325-4

Vol. 181 Alejandro Alcaraz-Sintes & Salvador Valera-Hernández (eds)
Diachrony and Synchrony in English Corpus Linguistics.
393 pages. 2014. ISBN 978-3-0343-1326-1

Vol. 182 Runhan Zhang
Investigating Linguistic Knowledge of a Second Language.
207 pages. 2015. ISBN 978-3-0343-1330-8

Vol. 183 Hajar Abdul Rahim & Shakila Abdul Manan (eds.)
English in Malaysia. Postcolonial and Beyond.
267 pages. 2014. ISBN 978-3-0343-1341-4

Vol. 184 Virginie Fasel Lauzon
Comprendre et apprendre dans l'interaction. Les séquences d'explication en classe
de français langue seconde.
292 pages. 2014. ISBN 978-3-0343-1451-0

Vol. 185 Forthcoming.

Vol. 186 Wei Ren
L2 Pragmatic Development in Study Abroad Contexts
256 pages. 2015. ISBN 978-3-0343-1358-2

Vol. 187 Marina Bondi & Rosa Lorés Sanz (eds)
Abstracts in Academic Discourse. Variation and Change.
361 pages. 2014. ISBN 978-3-0343-1483-1

Vol. 188 Giuditta Caliendo
Rethinking Community. Discourse, Identity and Citizenship in the European Union.
240 pages. 2017. ISBN 978-3-0343-1561-6

Vol. 189 Paola Evangelisti Allori (ed.)
Identities in and across Cultures.
315 pages. 2014. ISBN 978-3-0343-1458-9

Vol. 190 Erik Castello, Katherine Ackerley & Francesca Coccetta (eds).
Studies in Learner Corpus Linguistics. Research and Applications for Foreign Language Teaching and Assessment.
358 pages. 2015. ISBN 978-3-0343-1506-7

Vol. 191 Ruth Breeze, Maurizio Gotti & Carmen Sancho Guinda (eds)
Interpersonality in Legal Genres.
389 pages. 2014. ISBN 978-3-0343-1524-1

Vol. 192 Paola Evangelisti Allori, John Bateman & Vijay K. Bhatia (eds)
Evolution in Genre. Emergence, Variation, Multimodality.
364 pages. 2014. ISBN 978-3-0343-1533-3

Vol. 193 Jiyeon Kook
Agency in Arzt-Patient-Gesprächen. Zur interaktionistischen Konzeptualisierung von Agency
271 pages. 2015. ISBN 978-3-0343-1666-8

Vol. 194 Susana Nicolás Román & Juan José Torres Núñez (eds)
Drama and CLIL. A new challenge for the teaching approaches in bilingual education.
170 pages. 2015. ISBN 978-3-0343-1629-3

Vol. 195 Alessandra Molino & Serenella Zanotti (eds)
Observing Norm, Observing Usage. Lexis in Dictionaries and in the Media.
430 pages. 2015. ISBN 978-3-0343-1584-5

Vol. 196 Begoña Soneira
A Lexical Description of English for Architecture. A Corpus-based Approach.
267 pages. 2015. ISBN 978-3-0343-1602-6

Vol. 197 M Luisa Roca-Varela
False Friends in Learner Corpora. A corpus-based study of English false friends in the written and spoken production of Spanish learners.
348 pages. 2015. ISBN 978-3-0343-1620-0

Vol. 198 Rahma Al-Mahrooqi & Christopher Denman
Bridging the Gap between Education and Employment. English Language Instruction in EFL Contexts.
416 pages. 2015. ISBN 978-3-0343-1681-1

Vol. 199 Rita Salvi & Janet Bowker (eds)
The Dissemination of Contemporary Knowledge in English. Genres, discourse strategies and professional practices.
171 pages. 2015. ISBN 978-3-0343-1679-8

Vol. 200 Maurizio Gotti & Davide S. Giannoni (eds)
Corpus Analysis for Descriptive and Pedagogical Purposes. ESP Perspectives.
432 pages. 2014. ISBN 978-3-0343-1516-6

Vol. 201 Ida Ruffolo
The Perception of Nature in Travel Promotion Texts. A Corpus-based Discourse Analysis.
148 pages. 2015. ISBN 978-3-0343-1521-0

Vol. 202 Ives Trevian
English suffixes. Stress-assignment properties, productivity, selection and combinatorial processes.
471 pages. 2015. ISBN 978-3-0343-1576-0

Vol. 203 Maurizio Gotti, Stefania Maci & Michele Sala (eds)
Insights into Medical Communication.
422 pages. 2015. ISBN 978-3-0343-1694-1

Vol. 204 Carmen Argondizzo (ed.)
European Projects in University Language Centres. Creativity, Dynamics, Best Practice.
371 pages. 2015. ISBN 978-3-0343-1696-5

Vol. 205 Aura Luz Duffé Montalván (ed.)
Estudios sobre el léxico. Puntos y contrapuntos.
502 pages. 2016. ISBN 978-3-0343-2011-5

Vol. 206 Maria Pavesi, Maicol Formentelli & Elisa Ghia (eds)
The Languages of Dubbing. Mainstream Audiovisual Translation in Italy.
275 pages. 2014. ISBN 978-3-0343-1646-0

Vol. 207 Ruth Breeze & Inés Olza (eds)
Evaluation in media discourse. European perspectives.
268 pages. 2017. ISBN 978-3-0343-2014-6

Vol. 208 Vijay K. Bhatia & Maurizio Gotti (eds)
Arbitration Discourse in Asia.
331 pages. 2015. ISBN 978-3-0343-2032-0

Vol. 209 Sofía Bemposta-Rivas, Carla Bouzada-Jabois, Yolanda Fernández-Pena, Tamara Bouso, Yolanda J. Calvo-Benzies, Iván Tamaredo (eds)
New trends and methodologies in applied English language research III. Synchronic and diachronic studies on discourse, lexis and grammar processing.
280 pages. 2017. ISBN 978-3-0343-2039-9

Vol. 210 Francisco Alonso Almeida, Laura Cruz García & Víctor González Ruiz (eds)
Corpus-based studies on language varieties.
285 pages. 2016. ISBN 978-3-0343-2044-3

Vol. 211 Juan Pedro Rica Peromingo
Aspectos lingüísticos y técnicos de la traducción audiovisual (TAV).
177 pages. 2016. ISBN 978-3-0343-2055-9

Vol. 212 Maria Vender
Disentangling Dyslexia. VenderPhonological and Processing Deficit in Developmental Dyslexia.
338 pages. 2017. ISBN 978-3-0343-2064-1

Vol. 213 Zhilong Xie
Bilingual Advantages. Contributions of Different Bilingual Experiences to Cognitive Control Differences Among Young-adult Bilinguals.
221 pages. 2016. ISBN 978-3-0343-2081-8

Vol. 214 Larissa D'Angelo
Academic posters. A textual and visual metadiscourse analysis.
367 pages. 2016. ISBN 978-3-0343-2083-2

Vol. 215 Evelyne Berger
Prendre la parole en L2. Regard sur la compétence d'interaction en classe de langue.
246 pages. 2016. ISBN 978-3-0343-2084-9

Vol. 216 David Lasagabaster and Aintzane Doiz (eds)
CLIL experiences in secondary and tertiary education: In search of good practices.
262 pages. 2016. ISBN 978-3-0343-2104-4

Vol. 217 Elena Kkese
Identifying Plosives in L2 English: The Case of L1 Cypriot Greek Speakers.
317 pages. 2016. ISBN 978-3-0343-2060-3

Vol. 218 Sandra Campagna, Elana Ochse, Virginia Pulcini & Martin Solly (eds)
Languaging in and across Communities: New Voices, New Identities. Studies in Honour of Giuseppina Cortese.
507 pages. 2016. ISBN 978-3-0343-2073-3

Vol. 219 Adriana Orlandi & Laura Giacomini (ed.)
Defining collocation for lexicographic purposes. From linguistic theory to lexicographic practice.
328 pages. 2016. ISBN 978-3-0343-2054-2

Vol. 220 Pietro Luigi Iaia
Analysing English as a Lingua Franca in Video Games. Linguistic Features, Experiential and Functional Dimensions of Online and Scripted Interactions.
139 pages. 2016. ISBN 978-3-0343-2138-9

Vol. 221 Dimitrinka G. Níkleva (ed.)
La formación de los docentes de español para inmigrantes en distintos contextos educativos.
390 pages. 2017. ISBN 978-3-0343-2135-8

Vol. 222 Katherine Ackerley, Marta Guarda & Francesca Helm (eds)
Sharing Perspectives on English-Medium Instruction.
308 pages. 2017. ISBN 978-3-0343-2537-0

Vol. 223 Juana I. Marín-Arrese, Julia Lavid-López, Marta Carretero, Elena Domínguez Romero, Mª Victoria Martín de la Rosa & María Pérez Blanco (eds)
Evidentiality and Modality in European Languages. Discourse-pragmatic perspectives.
427 pages. 2017. ISBN 978-3-0343-2437-3

Vol. 224 Gilles Col
Construction du sens : un modèle instructionnel pour la sémantique.
292 pages. 2017. ISBN 978-3-0343-2572-1

Vol. 225 Ana Chiquito & Gabriel Quiroz (eds)
Pobreza, Lenguaje y Medios en América Latina.
362 pages. 2017. ISBN 978-3-0343-2142-6

Vol. 226 Xu Zhang
English Quasi-Numeral Classifiers. A Corpus-Based Cognitive-Typological Study.
360 pages. 2017. ISBN 978-3-0343-2818-0

Vol. 227 María Ángeles Orts, Ruth Breeze & Maurizio Gotti (eds)
Power, Persuasion and Manipulation in Specialised Genres. Providing Keys to the Rhetoric of Professional Communities.
368 pages. 2017. ISBN 978-3-0343-3010-7

Vol. 228 Maurizio Gotti, Stefania Maci & Michele Sala (eds)
Ways of Seeing, Ways of Being: Representing the Voices of Tourism.
453 pages. 2017. ISBN 978-3-0343-3031-2

Vol. 229 Dino Selvaggi
Plurilingual Code-Switching between Standard and Local Varieties.
A Socio-Psycholinguistic Approach
371 pages. 2018. ISBN 978-3-0343-2663-6

Vol. 230 Anca-Cristina Sterie
Interprofessional interactions at the hospital. Nurses' requests and reports of problems in calls with physicians.
371 pages. 2017. ISBN 978-3-0343-2734-3

Vol. 231 Xiaodong Zhang
Understanding Chinese EFL Teachers' Beliefs and Practices in the Textbook-Based Classroom.
189 pages. 2017. ISBN 978-3-0343-3053-4

Vol. 232 Manuela Caterina Moroni & Federica Ricci Garotti (Hrsg.)
Brücken schlagen zwischen Sprachwissenschaft und DaF-Didaktik.
345 pages. 2017. ISBN 978-3-0343-2667-4

Vol. 233 Dimitrinka Georgieva Níkleva
Necesidades y tendencias en la formación del profesorado de español como lengua extranjera
401 pages. 2017. ISBN 978-3-0343-2946-0

Vol. 234 Juan Santana-Lario & Salvador Valera (Hrsg.)
Competing patterns in English affixation.
272 pages. 2017. ISBN 978-3-0343-2701-5

Vol. 235 Francisco Salgado-Robles
Desarrollo de la competencia sociolingüística por aprendices de español en un contexto de inmersión en el extranjero
241 pages. 2018. ISBN 978-3-0343-2323-9

Vol. 236 Maria Chiara Janner
Sguardi linguistici sulla marca. Analisi morfosintattica dei nomi commerciali in italiano
345 pages. 2017. ISBN 978-3-0343-2667-4

Vol. 237 Bárbara Herrero Muñoz-Cobo & Otman El Azami Zalachi
La primavera del árabe marroquí.
192 pages. 2017. ISBN 978-3-0343-3104-3

Vol. 238 Consuelo Pascual Escagedo
El papel del oyente en la construcción de la conversación espontánea de estudiantes italianos en su interlengua y en su lengua materna
295 pages. 2017. ISBN 978-3-0343-3186-9

Vol. 239 Stefania M. Maci
The MS Digby 133 *Mary Magdalene*. Beyond scribal practices: language, discourse, values and attitudes.
336 pages. 2017. ISBN 978-3-0343-3256-9

Vol. 240 Eliecer Crespo-Fernández
Taboo in Discourse. Studies on Attenuation and Offence in Communication.
326 pages. 2018. ISBN 978-3-0343-3018-3

Vol. 241 Jana Altmanova, Maria Centrella, Katherine E. Russo (eds)
Terminology & Discourse / Terminologie et discours.
424 pages. 2018. ISBN 978-3-0343-2417-5

Vol. 242 Xavier Blanco et Inès Sfar (dir.)
Lexicologie(s) : approches croisées en sémantique lexicale.
442 pages. 2018. ISBN 978-3-0343-3056-5

Vol. 243 Yunfeng Ge
Resolution of Conflict of Interest in Chinese Civil Court Hearings.
A Perspective of Discourse Information Theory.
302 pages. 2018. ISBN 978-3-0343-3313-9

Vol. 244 Carla Vergaro
Illocutionary Shell Nouns in English
322 pages. 2018. ISBN 978-3-0343-3069-5

Vol. 245 Paolo Frassi
L'adjectif en français et sa définition lexicographique.
270 pages. 2018. ISBN 978-3-0343-3394-8

Vol. 246 Suwilai Premsrirat and David Hirsh (eds)
Language Revitalization. Insights from Thailand
328 pages. 2018. ISBN 978-3-0343-3497-6

Vol. 247 Wei Wang
Researching Learning and Learners in Genre-based Academic Writing Instruction
282 pages. 2018. ISBN 978-3-0343-3297-2

Vol. 248 Isusi Alabarte, Alberto & Lahuerta Martínez, Ana Cristina (eds)
La comprensión lectora de lengua extranjera
Estudio de los factores de familiaridad, interés, género y métodos de evaluación
336 pages. 2018. ISBN 978-3-0343-3493-8

Vol. 249 Mercedes Eurrutia Cavero
Approche didactique du langage techno-scientifique
Terminologie et discours
374 pages. 2018. ISBN 978-3-0343-3512-6

Vol. 250 Aurora Ruiz Mezcua (ed.)
Approaches to Telephone Interpretation
Research, Innovation, Teaching and Transference
268 pages. 2018. ISBN 978-3-0343-3330-6

Vol. 251 Morini Massimiliano
A Day in the News
A Stylistic Analysis of Newsspeak
188 pages. 2018. ISBN 978-3-0343-3507-2

Vol. 252 Ignacio Guillén-Galve & Ignacio Vázquez-Orta (eds.)
English as a Lingua Franca and Intercultural Communication
Implications and Applications in the Field of English Language Teaching
414 pages. 2018. ISBN 978-3-0343-2763-3

Vol. 253 Bianca Del Villano
Using the Devil with Courtesy
Shakespeare and the Language of (Im)Politeness
216 pages. 2018. ISBN 978-3-0343-2315-4

Vol. 254 David Hirsh (ed.)
Explorations in Second Language Vocabulary Research
252 pages. 2018. ISBN 978-3-0343-2940-8

Vol. 255 Tania Baumann (ed.)
Reiseführer - Sprach- und Kulturmittlung im Tourismus / Le guide turistiche - mediazione linguistica e culturale in ambito turistico
270 pages. 2018. ISBN 978-3-0343-3402-0

Vol. 256 Ariadna Sánchez-Hernández & Ana Herraiz-Martínez (eds)
Learning second language pragmatics beyond traditional contexts
376 pages. 2018. ISBN 978-3-0343-3437-2

Vol. 257 Albert Bastardas-Boada, Emili Boix-Fuster, Rosa Maria Torrens (eds)
Family Multilingualism in Medium-Sized Linguistic Communities
336 pages. 2019. ISBN 978-3-0343-2536-3

Vol. 258 Yuyang Cai
Examining the Interaction among Components of English for Specific Purposes Ability in Reading. The Triple-Decker Model
296 pages. 2020. 978-3-0343-2913-2

Vol. 259 Catia Nannoni
Participe présent et gérondif dans la presse française contemporaine
176 pages. 2019. ISBN 978-3-0343-3631-4

Vol. 260 Nieves Rodríguez Pérez & Bárbara Heinsch (eds.)
Contextos multilingües. Mediadores interculturales, formación del profesorado de lenguas extranjeras
289 pages. 2019. ISBN 978-3-0343-3768-7

Vol. 261 Giuliana Elena Garzone, Mara Logaldo, Francesca Santulli (eds.)
Investigating Conflict Discourses in the Periodical Press
244 pages. 2020. ISBN 978-3-0343-3668-0

Vol. 262 Laura Nadal
Lingüística experimental y contraargumentación
233 pages. 2019. ISBN 978-3-0343-3791-5

Vol. 263 Claudia Claridge & Merja Kytö (eds.)
Punctuation in Context – Past and Present Perspectives
288 pages. 2019. ISBN 978-3-0343-3790-8

Vol. 264 Maurizio Gotti, Stefania Maci, Michele Sala (eds.)
Scholarly Pathways
530 pages. 2020. ISBN 978-3-0343-3860-8

Vol. 265 Ruth Breeze, Ana M. Fernández Vallejo (eds.)
Politics and populism across modes and media
350 pages. 2020. ISBN 978-3-0343-3707-6

Vol. 266 Jean Marguerite Jimenez
Understanding the Effects of Immediate Electronic Corrective Feedback on Second Language Development
252 pages. 2020. ISBN 978-3-0343-3815-8

Vol. 267 Sergio Rodríguez-Tapia, Adela González-Fernández (eds)
Lenguas y turismo: estudios en torno al discurso, la didáctica y la divulgación
380 pages. 2020. ISBN 978-3-0343-3881-3

Vol. 268 Ana Bocanegra-Valle (ed.)
Applied Linguistics and Knowledge Transfer. Employability, Internationalisation and Social Challenges
344 pages. 2020. ISBN 978-3-0343-3714-4

Vol. 269 Beatrice Garzelli
La traducción audiovisual español-italiano.Películas y cortos entre humor y habla soez
202 pages. 2020. ISBN 978-3-0343-4013-7

Vol. 270 Iván Tamaredo
Complexity, Efficiency, and Language Contact. Pronoun Omission in World Englishes
292 pages. 2020. ISBN 978-3-0343-3902-5

Vol. 271 Silvia Domenica Zollo,
Origine et histoire du vocabulaire des arts de la table. Analyse lexicale et exploitation de corpus textuels
239 pages. 2020. ISBN 978-3-0343-3890-5

Vol. 272 Paola Paissa, Michelangelo Conoscenti, Ruggero Druetta, Martin Solly (eds.)
Metaphor and Conflict / Métaphore et conflit
385 pages. 2021. 978-3-0343-4068-7

Vol. 273 María Martínez-Atienza de Dios,
Entre el léxico y la sintaxis: las fases de los eventos
178 pages. 2021. 978-3-0343-4173-8

Vol. 274 Noelia Castro-Chao,
Argument Structure in Flux. The Development of Impersonal Constructions in Middle and Early Modern English, with Special Reference to Verbs of Desire.
300 pages. 2021. 978-3-0343-4189-9

Vol. 275 Gabriella Carobbio, Cécile Desoutter, Aurora Fragonara (eds.)
Macht, Ratio und Emotion: Diskurse im digitalen Zeitalter / Pouvoir, raison et émotion: les discours à l'ère du numérique
246 pages. 2020. 978-3-0343-4184-4

Vol. 276 Miguel Fuster-Márquez, José Santaemilia, Carmen Gregori-Signes, Paula Rodríguez-Abruñeiras (eds.)
Exploring discourse and ideology through corpora
293 pages. 2021. 978-3-0343-3969-8

Vol. 277 Tamara Bouso
Changes in Argument Structure
The Transitivizing Reaction Object Construction
392. 2021. 978-3-0343-4095-3

Vol. 278 Maria Luisa Maggioni, Amanda Murphy (eds.)
Back to the Future. English from Past to Present
250 pages. 2021. 978-3-0343-4273-5

Vol. 279 Luisa Chierichetti
Diálogos de serie. Una aproximación a la construcción discursiva de personajes basada en corpus
246 pages. 2021. 978-3-0343-4274-2

Vol. 280 Cristina Lastres-López
From subordination to insubordination. A functional-pragmatic approach to if/si-constructions in English, French and Spanish spoken discourse
258 pages. 2021. 978-3-0343-4220-9

Vol. 281 Eleonora Federici, Stefania Maci (eds.)
Gender issues. Translating and mediating languages, cultures and societies
500 pages. 2021. 978-3-0343-4022-9

Vol. 282 José Mateo, Francisco Yus (eds.)
Metaphor in Economics and specialised Discourse
354 pages. 2021. 978-3-0343-4048-9

Vol. 283 Nicholas Brownlees (ed.)
The Role of Context in the Production and Reception of Historical News Discourse
376 pages. 2021. 978-3-0343-4181-3

Vol. 284 Catalina Fuentes Rodriguez, María Ester Brenes Peña, Víctor Pérez Béjar (eds.)
Sintaxis discursiva: construcciones y operadores en español
396 pages. 2021. 978-3-0343-4306-0

Vol. 285 Dominic Stewart
Frequency in the dictionary. A corpus-assisted contrastive analysis of English and Italian
176 pages. 2021. 978-3-0343-4368-8

Vol. 286 Carla Bouzada-Jabois
Nonfinite supplements in the recent history of English
320 pages. 2021. 978-3-0343-4226-1

Vol. 287 Sofía Bemposta Rivas
Verb-governed infinitival complementation in the recent history of English
320 pages. 2021. 978-3-0343-4227-8

Vol. 288 Mirella Agorni
Translating Italy for the Nineteenth Century. Translators and an Imagined Nation in the Early Romantic Period 1816–1830s
180 pages. 2021. 978-3-0343-3612-3

Vol. 289 David Hirsh (ed.)
Research Perspectives in Language and Education
276 pages. 2022. 978-3-0343-4219-3

www.ingramcontent.com/pod-product-compliance
Ingram Content Group UK Ltd.
Pitfield, Milton Keynes, MK11 3LW, UK
UKHW041830100926
8556IPUK00002B/107

9 783034 342193